Praise for *Money, Magic, and How to Dismantle a Financial Bomb*

'Orrell argues that modelling markets with the mathematical toolbox of quantum mechanics could lead to a better understanding of them ... Such ideas may still sound abstract. But they will soon be physically embodied on trading floors ... One way or another, finance will catch up.'
  Economist

'[An] impressive, intelligent and imaginative bomb of a book ... [it] entertains, educates and delights ... A highly recommended read for all connoisseurs of curiosity and hope. And an absolute must-read for would-be economists.'
  Chris A. Weitz, Gaiageld.com

'This is a super addition to the literature on the quantum approach towards money, its cyber-version, and how it will change our lives. David Orrell has pulled together different thinking and approaches to guide us through the maze of magic money.'
  Andrew Sheng, former central banker and financial regulator, and
  distinguished fellow at the Asia Global Institute, University of Hong Kong

'David is our go-to source for anything and everything about quantum finance and economics. He's at the forefront of the subject and, what's more, he can explain it well.'
  Paul Wilmott, Editor-in-Chief, *Wilmott* magazine

Praise for *Quantum Economics*

'Beautifully written, inherently ethical, and often hilarious, this book is a must-read for anyone wanting to understand the weird, and getting weirder, world of modern finance.'
  Margaret Wertheim, author of *Pythagoras' Trousers* and *The Pearly Gates of Cyberspace*

'As money becomes more digital and diffuse, it also becomes more quantum. In this timely and illuminating book, David Orrell brings us to the frontier of where economics, physics and psychology intersect. You'll never look at money the same again!'
  Dr Parag Khanna, author of *Connectography: Mapping the Future of Global Civilization*

'On the cusp of an earlier revolution, Karl Marx said all that is solid melts into air and all that is holy is profaned. Constructing a less mechanistic and even more revolutionary science of quantum economics, David Orrell proves it so. Orrell does not dabble in metaphor or metaphysics: he intellectually, persuasively and corrosively transmutates money into a quantum phenomenon. In the process, classical economics is profaned to good effect and a quantum future glimmers as a real possibility.'
    James Der Derian, Chair of International Security Studies,
    University of Sydney

Praise for *Economyths*

'A fascinating, funny and wonderfully readable take down of mainstream economics. Read it.'
    Kate Raworth, author of *Doughnut Economics*

'Consistently interesting and enjoyable reading ... A wide audience including many non-economists could benefit from reading it.'
    International Journal of Social Economics

'Lists 10 crucial assumptions (the economy is simple, fair, stable, etc.) and argues both entertainingly and convincingly that each one is totally at odds with reality. Orrell also suggests that adopting the science of complex systems would radically improve economic policymaking.'
    William White, former Deputy Governor of the Bank of Canada
    (Bloomberg Best Books of 2013)

'This is without doubt the best book I've read this year, and probably one of the most important books I've ever read ... Orrell exposes the rotten heart of economics ... [S]hould be required reading for every politician and banker. No, make that every voter in the land. This ought to be a real game changer of a book. Read it.'
    Brian Clegg, PopularScience.co.uk

MONEY, MAGIC,

and How to

DISMANTLE
A FINANCIAL

BOMB

MONEY, MAGIC,

and How to

DISMANTLE
A FINANCIAL

BOMB

Quantum Economics
for the Real World

David Orrell

ICON

Published in the UK and USA in 2022
by Icon Books Ltd, Omnibus Business Centre,
39–41 North Road, London N7 9DP
email: info@iconbooks.com
www.iconbooks.com

Sold in the UK, Europe and Asia
by Faber & Faber Ltd, Bloomsbury House,
74–77 Great Russell Street,
London WC1B 3DA or their agents

Distributed in the UK, Europe and Asia
by Grantham Book Services, Trent Road, Grantham NG31 7XQ

Distributed in the USA
by Publishers Group West,
1700 Fourth Street, Berkeley, CA 94710

Distributed in Australia and New Zealand
by Allen & Unwin Pty Ltd,
PO Box 8500, 83 Alexander Street,
Crows Nest, NSW 2065

Distributed in South Africa
by Jonathan Ball, Office B4, The District,
41 Sir Lowry Road, Woodstock 7925

Distributed in India by Penguin Books India,
7th Floor, Infinity Tower – C, DLF Cyber City, Gurgaon 122002, Haryana

Distributed in Canada by Publishers Group Canada,
76 Stafford Street, Unit 300, Toronto, Ontario M6J 2S1

ISBN: 978-178578-828-4

Typeset in Sabon MT by Marie Doherty

Printed and bound in Great Britain
by Clays Ltd, Elcograf S.p.A.

For my mother

CONTENTS

INTRODUCTION

Money has long been associated with a kind of magic, and finance with alchemy. After all, how can something like a piece of paper with numbers on it be treated as if it were made of gold?

Money has other apparently magical properties. It can be created out of the void – and vanish without so much as a puff of smoke. It can flash through space. It can grow without limit. And it can blow up without warning.

Money is like nothing else in the world – except, that is, the basic operations of the universe.

Drawing on the findings of the emerging area of quantum economics, this book will take the reader on a journey through money, magic, and quantum reality – and show how we can dismantle the money bomb that threatens social cohesion, financial stability, and the planet.

GOING NUCLEAR

The figure below shows two phenomena which at first glance may seem to have little to do with one another. The image on the top, from 1945, is of the first detonation of a nuclear device, known as the Trinity test.[1]

The image on the bottom is of an empty house down my street in Toronto. The photograph was taken by my daughter as part of a high school geography project. It was during the COVID-19 pandemic, so the schools were closed and courses were online. Students were asked to take a picture of something of interest in their neighbourhood to write a short comment

1

on, and she chose this house. The house had then been empty for well over a year, and at the time of writing it is empty still. The sign on the front door is a notice of demolition, but it has yet to be knocked down.

When we first arrived in the neighbourhood, to rent a place up the road, the house – a detached property on a standard lot – was occupied by an elderly man. I chatted with him a few times; I knew he used to be a chemical engineer, and was a climate change sceptic (he told me he'd written a newspaper letter on the subject). One day the house was vacated, and I heard later that he had died. The house was apparently bought and sold more than once, but remained empty. It was last sold for $2,240,000 (Canadian dollars) or about $1.8 million US. For comparison, that is about 64 times the median income for an individual in Toronto, or 32 times the median income of a household with two workers.[2] Anyone on the provincial minimum wage for Ontario obviously need not apply, since the cost would represent about a century of full-time labour, or a few centuries if money were set aside for things like living expenses.[3] And at 180 times the global median household income, the price of the house, should they come across it on the internet, might seem unworldly to most of the world's population – especially for the bottom 10 per cent or so of people living in areas of extreme poverty and earning a couple of dollars a day, where entire villages could basically toil forever and not get close.

So what is the connection between these pictures? One is that, at least to the uninitiated, or the unjaded, they both seem to involve a kind of magic. How can less than a kilogram of nuclear material create a giant mushroom cloud? And how can that house be worth so much money?

Another is that they both involve a kind of energy, which as we will see has an intimate connection with money. There are a number of ways to calculate the relationship between a financial asset such as a house and energy, but perhaps the simplest is to base it on the cost of a barrel of oil, which serves as a kind of proxy for energy in the economy. If we assume a typical price of about US$60 per barrel, which as seen later is an appropriate long-term average, the money from the house sale could buy 30,000 barrels – which is a lot of oil.[4] Imagine a train with 40 tank cars and you have an idea.[5] A different approach is to view the economy as a thermodynamic system, and ask how much physical energy is needed to sustain it, which as seen later gives a very similar result.

The Trinity test bomb, meanwhile, released a fearsome 92 terajoules of energy – which works out to about 20 tank cars full of oil. In a very real sense, the empty house therefore contains (or represents a claim on) more energy than the Trinity blast, and the same could be said for the average detached property in Toronto, or for homes in many cities across the world.[6] What kind of sorcery is this?

As we'll see, though, the most direct connection between the nuclear device and the house is that they both rely on similar technologies, which appear magical but are better described as quantum. And while the house doesn't look like it is going to blow up any time soon, it does form part of a different, and much larger, kind of bomb, whose fissile material includes everything from payday loans to obscure financial derivatives.

This bomb isn't a Trinity test – it is the equivalent of all the nuclear devices in the world, many times over. And mishandling it could result in the financial version of a nuclear winter.

HOW MUCH

Of course, it may seem strange to compare money's ancient form of wizardry with advanced quantum technology. But despite its age, money still manages to retain the capacity for surprise. The wheel was probably invented around the same kind of time, but we aren't constantly taken aback by its remarkable properties. Money is different. It has a special brand of magic that never ceases to amaze or thrill. If it had a show at Las Vegas, it would run forever. (Actually, it does have a show at Las Vegas – it's called the casino.)

As with a magic trick, the way money works seems shrouded in mystery (assuming we pause long enough from trying to earn the stuff to even consider the question). On the one hand, we are accustomed to thinking about money as no more than a banal counting device, as just numbers on a spreadsheet or coins in our pockets, subject to the boring laws of addition and subtraction, profit and loss. It doesn't help, as one personal finance coach put it, that 'money is a taboo. Most people don't talk about it. And because they don't talk about it, they don't learn about it.'[7] (As will be discussed later, this money taboo extends quite generally.) But if we think a little deeper, the actual nature of money is an enigma. How is it that pieces of paper with numbers written on them – or, more usually today, just the numbers themselves, stored electronically in an account – can take on a quasi-religious significance, and become the central driving and organisational force of society? Even economists and financial experts seem dazzled and confused, as witnessed by their inability to predict the forces they help to unleash.

It is no surprise that money and the financial sector are associated with magic and alchemy. A documentary film on quantitative analysts is called *Quants: The Alchemists of Wall Street*; a leading book on central bankers is called *The Alchemists*; a member of the European Central Bank said that 'we are magic people. Each time we take something and give to the markets – a rabbit out of the hat.'[8] Richard Dzina from the New York Federal Reserve described the act of money creation, by pressing a button, as 'a magical process'.[9] In his 1967 book *The Magic of Money*, Hjalmar Schacht, who served as president of the Reichsbank under the Weimar Republic, wrote that 'money really is quite an uncanny thing ... Because I was able to master it, I earned myself the title of magician or wizard.'[10] Even the US dollar bill has an all-seeing eye on it which resembles the sort of imagery used by fairground mind-readers.

This book will show that the reason money's properties seem so strange, though, is because we are viewing them through the mental equivalent of a classical operating system.

Just as quantum computers replace classical logic with a quantum version, so we need to upgrade our mental operating system in order to understand money. And just as any technology, or sorcery, can be put to creative or destructive uses, so the money system has the capacity for good or evil.

As commentators often note, the world economy is facing the interconnected problems of social inequality, financial instability, and the threat of impending environmental disaster. All of these have a common thread, which is the tension between the virtual economy of money and Wall Street and retirement accounts, and the real economy of things and people and the planet; between a mortgage, and a roof over your head. This book will argue that this tension is inherent to the quantifying and dualistic nature of money, as captured by the word *quantum*, from the Latin for 'how much' – as in, how much is this going to cost?

Inequality is to some extent a 'natural' phenomenon[11] and has many causes, but a main driver of extreme inequality is that, as observed by the French economist Thomas Piketty, over history, the rate of return on financial investments has been greater than the rate of economic growth. Since rich people tend to have much of their income tied to virtual investments, which can also be preserved in families through inheritance, while the rest have their income tied to things like pay packets, the result is a positive feedback loop in which the rich magically get richer. In some years, my neighbour the engineer probably made multiples of his salary through the appreciation of his property, and younger generations may find their future standard of living depends as much on what they inherit as on what they earn.[12] A related cause, though, is that money is not so much a store of utility, as it is portrayed by mainstream economists, as a source of power; and power isn't by nature egalitarian. The rise of automation and robotics will only accentuate this trend.

Financial instability is caused in large part by a similar dynamic, which is that, in boom times at least, the rate of credit growth exceeds the rate of economic growth. A millennial or Gen Zer who wanted to buy a similar Toronto house today would probably have to take on an epic amount of debt in order to afford it, even with a grant from the bank of mum and dad.* At least they wouldn't be alone: according to the Institute of International Finance, global debt, which comprises borrowings from households, companies, and governments, was around $275 trillion in 2020, up by about a third in five years.[13] As economists such as Hyman Minsky have long argued, credit is inherently unstable, because it builds up when the economy is doing well (or during a pandemic, as it turns out) and then in a crisis everyone wants to call in their loans at the same time.[14]

The situation is exacerbated today by highly complex financial derivatives, which represent bets on the prices of financial assets, and whose dynamics are poorly understood even by the banker wizards who sell them.[15] The notional value of these derivatives is around a quadrillion (i.e. a million billion) dollars, which truly is a magical number, since it is larger than the world economy.[16] Central banks keep the debt system aloft by repressing interest rates so that loans are cheaper, which, as former central banker William White notes, only leads to 'ever greater instability in the financial system'.[17] And as political economist Susan Strange wrote in her 1986 book *Casino Capitalism*, it is this 'chronic instability of the world's financial system' which leads in turn to the 'ever-increasing disparity and

---

* In 2021 a Reddit group paid for a billboard in Toronto which read, 'Can't Afford a Home? Have You Tried Finding Richer Parents?'

inequality in the social distribution of risk and of opportunities for gain'.[18] While anyone can play the game of betting on markets, only the large and powerful firms get rescued when things go wrong, as they regularly do.[19]

The most urgent problem with our financial system is caused by another growth imbalance, which is that the real economy, as reflected by inputs such as material and energy use and outputs such as pollution, is colliding with natural limits. While debt may be virtual, it acts as both a carrot and a stick to propel physical economic activity. Credit allows businesses and governments and individuals to press ahead with their plans; but at the same time loans charge interest, meaning that the economy has to grow continuously, and consume more energy and resources, just to meet its own obligations, which is a problem on a finite planet. As ecological economist Nate Hagens notes, 'The energy/credit/growth dynamic is the least understood but most important phenomenon driving the current global economic and ecological situation.'[20] Having an empty house on a busy street might seem to reduce damaging emissions, rather than add to them, but as will be discussed later, the real estate-financial complex as a whole is a major contributor to the climate crisis. Decarbonised it is not.

PANDEMIC

The COVID-19 pandemic lent new focus to these interconnected problems. Some headlines from 2020:

'U.S. now has 22 million unemployed, wiping out a decade of job gains'

(*Washington Post*, 16 April)

'U.S. stocks have their best month since 1987'

(*New York Times*, 30 April)

'Climate crisis: Coronavirus pandemic has caused
17% drop in global carbon emissions'

> (*Independent*, 19 May)

'"Essential" workers are just forced laborers'

> (*Washington Post*, 21 May)

'Tsunami of pandemic debt mounting in millions of
British households'

> (*Independent*, 9 June)

'Wealth of US billionaires rises by nearly a third
during pandemic'

> (*Guardian*, 17 September)

'Pandemic fuels unprecedented global "debt tsunami"'

> (*Financial Times*, 18 November)

'Default fuels fears of African "debt tsunami" as
Covid impact bites'

> (*Guardian*, 25 November)

In Canada, realtors quickly lobbied to see themselves designated as essential workers on the basis that 'shelter is one of life's basic necessities' (even if it's unaffordable).[21] However, one thing that the pandemic exposed was the connection between financial health and the physical sort, as shown by the disparity of outcomes between wealthy people secluded in large houses, and the real essential workers who often lived in crowded homes and relied on public transport. Not to mention the growing numbers who, in a city with a homelessness crisis, just needed a roof over their heads. One of the more visible signs of the crisis in Toronto was the encampments that sprang up around the city, as people felt safer living in tents than in crowded shelters. No wonder the United Nations has called similar housing bubbles a human rights issue.[22]

The crisis highlighted like never before the disconnect between the virtual economy and the real economy, as stock markets and real estate alike reached new heights in the middle of record-breaking unemployment. It also made a mockery of the idea that markets set prices to reflect intrinsic value, when the reason they were soaring was largely because of massive central bank intervention, including buying bonds to crash the interest rates charged on loans such as mortgages, in what amounted to a huge inequality-boosting subsidy to capital markets (at last count the Bank of Canada owned 40 per cent of outstanding government bonds).

The pandemic exposed the fragile nature of our debt-based economy, where around a half of Canadian workers drew on government support, and one in six mortgage holders arranged for deferrals on payments.[23] In the UK, the charity StepChange warned in June of a 'debt tsunami' (a phrase that became popular with headline writers, as seen in the examples above) that would take years to be resolved. And finally, the crisis gave people around the world a taste of what it takes to slow emissions and burn less oil – and showed that we are willing to shut down some parts of the economy when our personal safety is at risk.

Together, these three growth dynamics of inequality, debt, and environmental damage combine to form a financial version of a nuclear bomb, which policy makers around the world have long been afraid to dismantle, even though they also fear an eventual explosion. And making up its atomic core is our money system, which in a kind of alchemy fuses the real and the virtual to create a stream of ever-expanding but ultimately self-annihilating credit and debt.

MONETARY MAGIC

Arthur C. Clarke wrote that 'Any sufficiently advanced technology is indistinguishable from magic', and this book will argue that the money system can be described as a quantum social technology, whose quantum properties both create the illusion of magic and give money its power. As some examples of its magical prowess, money can jump instantaneously from one place to another (magicologists call this a transportation trick, though with money it is as easy as tapping your card at the store). It can change from metal to paper to numbers in an account (the transformation trick). It can be created out of nothing by banks (the production trick) or disappear into the void (the vanish trick). It can lift the price of a house to the sky (the levitation trick) or bring the economy to an apparent equilibrium (the restoration trick). As we will see, all of these tricks are the result not of sorcery, but of the quantum properties of money. And only by bringing this remarkable substance back into economics can we address the problems of inequality, instability, and environmental damage.

Mainstream economics has traditionally given short shrift to money, because it does not fit into the mental model held by economists of how the economy works. This concentrates on 'real' goods, such as manufactured items or commodities, or on services, which are produced by real human labour. As Paul Samuelson wrote in his classic textbook *Economics*, 'if we strip exchange down to its barest essentials and peel off the obscuring layer of money, we find that trade between individuals and nations largely boils down to barter.'[24] There are allowances for legal effects such as patents, but these can be considered as the mental counterparts of physical objects – ideas that can be owned and sold, like the rights to a property. And because economists think in terms of averages and aggregates, if one person loans money to another then the net effect is zero. As the Nobel-laureate economist Paul Krugman scream-tweeted to his 4.6 million followers: 'DEBT IS MONEY WE OWE TO OURSELVES'.[25] (By the same logic, theft isn't a problem either.) This book will argue, though, that the economy is driven by forces, entanglements, and power relationships which elude a classical analysis; and that we need a new approach to economics if we are to better allocate our energy and resources.

Physics progressed from the equilibrium view of Aristotle in ancient times, to the dynamical view of Newton in the seventeenth century, to the quantum view in the twentieth century. In quantum physics, at least according to standard interpretations, matter has both particle-like and wave-like properties. For example, the position of a quantum particle is described by a probabilistic 'wave function' which only 'collapses' down to a specific value at the time of measurement. Entities can also become mysteriously entangled so that a measurement on one reveals something about another. Instead of self-contained objects obeying mechanistic laws, matter turns out to be more like a shifting, holistic, and indeterminate form of information, where measurements are questions and the response depends on context and timing.

Economics, as we'll see, has in contrast long been arrested in the stage of Aristotelian equilibrium. Economists found it impossible to arrive at meaningful analogues for concepts such as force or mass, for the simple reason that money does not behave like a classical object. However, the aim of this book is not to link economics directly to quantum physics, but rather to something that is both simpler and deeper – namely what might be described as our mental operating system, which shapes how we see and experience the world. To do this we will need to draw on quantum mathematics.

When the word 'quantum' is used in everyday language, it immediately conjures images of a strange and spooky world in which objects can translocate from one place to another and a cat can be alive and dead at the same time. As discussed later, the air of mystery is partly by design; however, it is unfortunate because it gets in the way of understanding the quantum approach for what it is, namely a set of mathematical tools that can be applied to different situations, from the subatomic world to the behaviour of people.

Of course, a common criticism of economics is that it puts too much emphasis on elaborate mathematics – but as an applied mathematician and writer, I believe that words and symbols can work together. The neoclassical economist Alfred Marshall described his system in a letter to a younger colleague: '(1) Use mathematics as a shorthand language, rather than an engine of inquiry. (2) Keep to them till you have done. (3) Translate into English. (4) Then illustrate by examples that are important in real life. (5) Burn the mathematics. (6) If you can't succeed in 4, burn 3. This last I do often.'[26] I have taken a somewhat different tack.

My 2018 book *Quantum Economics: The New Science of Money* proposed, in as clear language as I was capable, how economics could be quantised. It built on the insights of researchers in areas such as quantum cognition and quantum finance, and combined them with a quantum theory of value, which argued that money has dual real/virtual properties. Its technical companion *Quantum Economics and Finance: An Applied Mathematics Introduction* translated these ideas into mathematical equations, and also extended them in new directions, towards things like the pricing of financial options, the intricacies of supply and demand, and the energy encoded by money.

Although I am not an academic, I published many of the

results in specialised scientific journals, in areas ranging from quantum mathematics to international relations to economics to quantitative finance; and was exposed to the works of a wide range of scholars who are working in and between these disciplines. This book will re-translate these new findings back into English (the non-academic sort) and show how they can be applied to our present situation. Many books promise the reader a new take on economics or the economy, but here the insights are derived less from a particular ideological viewpoint than from a fundamentally different form of logic and probability.

So what are these quantum ideas that I will be proposing? Here is a sample:

- Money has the properties of both a virtual number and a real, owned thing
- Money jumps, instead of moving in a continuous flow
- People don't obey classical logic, or even adjusted versions of classical logic of the sort used in behavioural economics
- The financial system entangles people in a web of debt
- Economic behaviour is affected by things like subjective feelings and altruism
- The economy is a dynamical system, i.e. it moves around
- Transactions are inherently probabilistic, rather than deterministic
- Money creation out of the void is one of the most important phenomena in economics, but also one of the least understood
- Eternal growth cannot be supported
- Ethics are important.

If these proposals all seem painfully obvious and pedestrian compared to the stories peddled by mainstream economists, such as the marvellous *Invisible Hand of Capitalism* which drives prices to equilibrium, or the equally amazing *Efficient Market Hypothesis* which says that prices magically incorporate all available information, then don't worry – that is the point. As we will see, they are all incompatible with some of the basic tenets of mainstream economics (and for that matter a lot of non-mainstream economics), at least in the absence of epicycles. And together, they point the way to a new economics, which has no need for such ungainly appendages, and which has room for the truly magical and creative properties of money.

MINDBOMB

The field known as quantum natural language processing is based on the idea that language can be treated as a quantum system, in which words are bound together through grammar and meaning to form what researchers from the firm Cambridge Quantum Computing call an 'entangled whole'.[27] This book, too, can be viewed as a series of quanta: chapters on topics that are separate, but entangled at the same time. Chapter 1 describes the alchemical process of money creation. Chapter 2 investigates the two-sided nature of money, and its connection with Greek philosophy, while Chapter 3 shows how quantum computers are rewriting the basics of logic, and economics. Chapter 4 explores why topics related to money – including subjectivity, gender, and all things quantum – are downplayed, ignored, and even treated as taboo by mainstream economists, and why this has impeded our understanding of the economy. Chapter 5 describes the atomic power of finance, and explains why money is the economy's uranium. Chapter 6 shows how the quantum approach upends the most famous – but strangely unverifiable – result from economics, namely the 'law' of supply and demand. Chapter 7 reveals how economists performed an amazing sleight of hand when they introduced their theory of utility. Chapter 8 introduces the quantum view of human psychology, while Chapter 9 explores the mysterious phenomenon of entanglement. Chapter 10 compares economic models with the marvellous mechanical automata that have long been beloved of magicians. Chapter 11 reveals the paranormal quantum model for pricing financial options. Chapter 12 explores in greater detail the relationship between money and energy. Finally, Chapter 13 gives a three-step plan for how to safely dismantle a financial bomb, and as a free bonus reveals the secret of money.

On the way we will explore: the connection between money and ancient gods; how our modern monetary system was designed by a group of seventeenth-century alchemists; the relationship between heavy metal music, Pythagorean harmony, and quantum social science; the thread which links Newton's theory of gravity, the quantum theory of entanglement, and a loan contract; how money has a colour, but it's not green; how a medieval tally can be modelled on a quantum computer; what economic decisions have to do with the dual-slit experiment in quantum physics; how to price financial options using particles of light; how quantum approaches provide alternatives to some of the most famous results from economics and finance; why the rise of quantum computing is eyed with both excitement and fear by Wall Street; and how finance, like physics, involves quantum processes that have the capacity for either creation or destruction.

As a theory and mathematical model of human behaviour, mainstream or neoclassical economics has probably been the most influential (and certainly the best funded) in history; however, it is based on the misconception that humans – and the economy as a whole – behave according to classical logic. The quantum approach is a better description of the economy, is more useful at making predictions, and also changes what we see, and don't see. Quantum cognition can model and predict the outcomes of psychological experiments, or the behaviour of mortgage-holders during a crisis, but also provides a different vision for humanity. The quantum version of supply and demand can be used to build sophisticated models of economic transactions, but also draws our attention to the non-equilibrium and sometimes unfair nature of their dynamics. The quantum model of money gives an expression for the social force and effort needed to create money, but just as importantly it shows how money, far from being an inert chip, is a form of information with a profound link to energy. Quantum models of financial markets lead naturally to new methods for pricing things like financial options, but they also make us acknowledge that the entangling tissues of contracts which underly the financial system are based as much on unquantifiable subjective forces as they are on objective calculations. Above all, the quantum approach draws our attention to topics such as money and power which have been sidelined in mainstream economics.

In 1944, as Allied physicists were nearing their goal of a nuclear bomb, the Bretton Woods conference extended a version of the gold standard into the post-war period, with the US dollar acting as a reserve currency pegged to gold. As the banking expert Andrew Sheng noted for a Bretton Woods Committee report commemorating its 75th anniversary, a new approach to finance is called for today. 'To put it simply, we can no longer use the reductionist neoclassical economic paradigm, because the invisible hand of the market cannot deal with climate change, nor the inequities of war and disruptive technology ... The neoclassical blindness arose because its framework was founded on the classical mathematics and physics of Descartes and Newton ... A quantum paradigm of finance and the economy is slowly emerging, and its non-linear, complex nature may help the design of a future global economy and financial architecture ... Financial assets and virtual liabilities have quantum characteristics of entanglement with each other that are not yet fully understood ... All of these developments suggest that using a new "quantum" imagination, the Bretton Woods framework can be reengineered.'[28]

This book will give a hint of how such a quantum framework might look. In 2010 I wrote a book called *Economyths: Ten Ways Economics Gets It Wrong* which was in part my reaction to the financial crisis. It ended with an exhortation – reproduced by *Adbusters* magazine during Occupy Wall Street, an event which the magazine had initiated – for economics students to overturn neoclassical orthodoxy and do something new.[29]

It was an example of what we might call a mindbomb – but this particular bomb had little effect on economics, which as we'll see has remained rather unchanged. So, some years on, please consider this latest quantum entertainment to be my own humble, and I hope diverting, attempt at something new. We start in the next chapter with our first magic trick, which in alchemical circles used to go by the name of transmutation.

Front cover of the UK edition of *Adbusters*, November/ December 2011 issue.

CHAPTER 1

TRANSMUTATION

*For a long time now an increasing number of
people have been asking questions about the
world counting-house, getting down at last to such
fundamental questions as 'What is money?' and
'Why are Banks?' It is disconcerting but stimulating
to find that no lucid answer is forthcoming.*
H.G. WELLS, THE NEW WORLD ORDER, 1940

*For Mike's sake, Soddy, don't call it transmutation.
They'll have our heads off as alchemists.*
ERNEST RUTHERFORD, 1901

The ancient goal of alchemists was to transform one substance
into another – especially if the end product was gold. The money
system performs a similar alchemical trick by transforming labour
and material into numbers in an account – or an empty house into
two million dollars. To appreciate the quantum nature of money,
a first step is to understand the magical nature of transmutation,
which underpins interactions of both the nuclear and financial sort.
This chapter shows how our current financial system was actually
first designed by alchemists, and reveals some of the secrets behind
its sorcery.

While problems such as financial inequality and instability
seem particularly pressing now, concerns about the financial
system are not exactly new. One person to warn of the unstable

real/virtual nature of the financial system – and link it with an out-of-control nuclear device, though in a different way – was the English chemist-turned-economist Frederick Soddy a century ago.

Following his Nobel Prize-winning work on the basic properties of radiation, which he carried out at McGill University with Ernest Rutherford, Soddy became something of a proselytizer for the wonders of atomic energy. In his 1909 book *The Interpretation of Radium*, he wrote that this energy source held the promise to 'transform a desert continent, thaw the frozen poles, and make the whole world one smiling Garden of Eden'. Fans of Soddy's book included the author H.G. Wells, who acknowledged it in the dedication of his novel *The World Set Free*. However, Wells took Soddy's technological utopianism to a different and harsher level. His story begins with a war in which aeroplanes dropping 'atomic bombs' destroy hundreds of cities. From the aftermath of the destruction emerges a new world run by a socialist global government.

Wells saw the outbreak of the First World War as confirming his prediction, and described the conflict in hopeful terms as 'the war that will end war'. Soddy agreed with Wells about the potential of atomic weapons, but was less sure about the healing properties of nuclear conflict. In a 1915 speech, he noted of radioactive materials that 'a pound weight could be made to do the work of 150 tons of dynamite. Ah! there's the rub. Imagine … what the present war would be like if such an explosive had actually been discovered.'[1] And in another speech the same year he concluded that 'the social effect of recent advances in physical science promises to be annihilating, unless, before it is too late, there arises an equal and compensating advance, of which there is at present no sign, in the moral and spiritual forces of society.'

Soddy realised that the economic system in particular, with its split between what he called real and virtual wealth, held within it the seeds of a collapse, which could ultimately trigger the nuclear war which he feared. To prevent such an event, he had five main policy proposals. These were to abandon the gold standard; let international exchange rates float; use federal budgets as a way to counterbalance cyclical trends; establish bureaus to compile statistics for things like prices; and finally, stop private banks from creating money out of nothing.

At the time, hardly anyone took Soddy or his suggestions seriously. The Nobel-laureate physicist Robert Millikan, for example, described Soddy's idea of a nuclear weapon as a 'hobgoblin'. A 1926 review of one of his economic treatises by *The Times Literary Supplement* remarked that 'it was sad to see a respected chemist ruin his reputation by writing on a subject about which he was quite ignorant'.[2] An exception was the economist Frank Knight, who agreed in another review that handing the job of money creation to private banks leads to 'important evils ... notably the frightful instability of the whole economic system and its periodical collapse in crises'.[3]

Soddy's predictions were borne out by the arrival three years later of the Great Depression, which led in short order to the rise of the Nazis, the outbreak of war, and the first use of nuclear weapons. But after his death in 1956, an obituary in *Science* wrote that he was widely perceived as a 'crank' on monetary affairs whose 'fanatical devotion to schemes of this sort, derided by the orthodox economists ... was surprising to many who knew him first as a pioneer in chemical science'.[4]

As we'll see, mainstream economists remain equally derisive towards outsider criticism, especially when it comes from 'monetary cranks', to use Paul Krugman's phrase (defined as people who don't understand economists' 'intellectual strategy' towards money, which seems quite broad and inclusive).[5] However, while Soddy's ideas were considered crazy at the time, today most of them are standard practice: the gold standard is history, exchange rates float, federal budgets are used to counterbalance cyclical trends, and bureaus exist to compile statistics for things like prices. The only idea not to have been adopted was the prohibition against money creation by private banks.

This lack of interest would not have surprised Soddy; as he observed in 1934, 'orthodox economics has never yet been anything but the class economics of the owners of debts' and those who own debts may not want to abandon that privilege, or draw attention to it.[6] And as Irving Fisher wrote, 'It has been maintained – and the assertion is scarcely an exaggeration – that the theorems of Euclid would be bitterly controverted if financial or political interests were involved.'[7] However, it does point to an interesting anomaly, which is that while money is at the heart of the economy, it has long been missing from mainstream economics. This goes back at least to the time of Adam Smith, who as discussed later treated money as a 'veil' over the real economy; and finance is still treated as a technical arena that doesn't quite connect with the rest of the field. One of the reasons why the financial crisis of 2007/8 wasn't predicted, for example, was explained by Vítor Constâncio of the European Central Bank ten years later in a 2017 speech: 'In the prevalent macro models, the financial sector was absent, considered to have a remote effect on the real economic activity.' In particular, the models 'ignored the fact that banks create money by extending credit *ex nihilo*' (out of nothing).[8]

Since the crisis, there have been efforts to add so-called 'financial frictions' to mainstream economic models, which account for effects such as varying abilities to obtain credit.[9]

(Or as Servaas Storm from the Institute for New Economic Thinking put it in 2021, 'practitioners are frantically trying to incorporate money in their otherwise money-less models.')[10] However, the use of the word 'friction' seems a little strange, given that other writers have described money as a 'lubricant' for economic activity, and events such as mass defaults represent sudden cascading behaviour. As we'll see, such 'frictions' are the economics version of epicycles: the patches that ancient astronomers made to their geocentric model of the cosmos, in order to make it conform more closely with observations.

But, while the threat of nuclear war hasn't gone away – and no other human invention compares to the horror of nuclear weapons – what if the quantum alchemy we should be worrying about most is not the atomic bomb, but the financial sort?

QUANTUM ALCHEMY

Soddy's insights into both physics and finance may have been primed and influenced by his longstanding interest in the field of alchemy. While at McGill he delivered a series of lectures on 'The History of Chemistry from Earliest Time' which included two on alchemy. In these, he described the alchemists' 'quackery' and 'feverish desire' for wealth as something that had nothing to do with 'the normal development of chemistry' but was instead 'the result of a mental aberration'.[11] However, he soon changed his mind. Even before his discovery of radiation, the old idea of the atom as an immutable, indivisible, fundamental unit of matter was breaking down with the recent discovery of the electron by Rutherford's mentor J.J. Thomson. This seemed to open up the possibility of one element transforming into another – i.e. transmutation. It also meant that Soddy's history of chemistry, which was based on the classical picture, was looking a little out of date.

In an unpublished paper titled 'Alchemy and Chemistry' he revisited the topic. His earlier history had dated alchemy to the fourth century, but in his new paper he described its birth as being in 'an antiquity so remote that its origins appear in the records of mythology rather than in those of history'. And he argued that 'The constitution of matter is the province of chemistry, and little indeed can be known of this constitution until transmutation is accomplished. This is today as it has always been the real goal of the chemist before this is a science that will satisfy the mind.'

In other words, the ultimate goal of chemistry was the same as that of alchemy – transmutation. When he and Rutherford discovered that the radiation they were studying was produced by the transmutation of thorium, he 'was overwhelmed with something greater than joy ... a kind of exaltation, intermingled with a certain feeling of pride that I had been chosen from all chemists of all ages to discover natural transmutation'.

Rutherford was more guarded. 'For Mike's sake, Soddy, don't call it transmutation,' he said.* 'They'll have our heads off as alchemists.'[12] And Soddy's excitement itself transformed into a sense of horror as the implications sank in.

THE INTELLIGENCER

The Western tradition of alchemy, with its emphasis on transmutation and wealth, has its roots in the notion, endorsed by Aristotle, that all things in the universe are composed of four elements: earth ▽, water ▽, air △, and fire △. The stars and planets – basically everything beyond the Moon – were made of the fifth element, ether (also known as the quintessence,

---

* 'Mike' being a euphemism for God.

denoted QE*). According to Aristotle, each element belonged in a separate sphere – with earth in the centre, surrounded by water, then air, then fire – to which it would tend to return. But elements could also transmute; so, for example, heating water turns it into air (steam actually but you know what they meant). Or, more hopefully, lead could turn into gold.

During the Middle Ages, the discovery of ancient Greek texts led to a renewed interest in alchemy. Alchemists – who became known as 'puffers' because of the time they spent blowing air into their fires in order to achieve the necessary temperatures for transmutation to occur – did a (literally) roaring trade selling their research and development services to European governments, and their laboratories were regular features in cities such as Paris, Prague, and London. However, as the quest for things like an elixir of life, or a philosopher's stone which could transmute a base metal into gold, proved more elusive than anticipated, some alchemists turned their attention to another way of producing infinite wealth: banking. Chief among these financial magicians were the Hartlibians.[13]

The Hartlibians were a group of social reformers, natural philosophers, and utopians centred around the 'intelligencer' (i.e. an intellectual figure) Samuel Hartlib. Their broad range of intellectual interests included both alchemy and finance. Economic development at the time was hampered by a lack of access to money. Commerce was largely carried out on the basis of credit, but the terms had to be negotiated on a case-by-case basis, which slowed trade. The Hartlibians believed that credit could be used as a kind of financial philosopher's stone to transform the economy.

---

* Not to be confused with quantitative easing, which is the central banking version.

One member of the group, William Potter, wrote a pamphlet called 'The Key of Wealth, or, A New Way for Improving of Trade'. (In alchemical discourse, 'the key' referred to the knowledge of how to transmute matter.) Henry Robinson, another Hartlibian, described his own scheme as 'capable of multiplying the stock of the Nation, for as much as concernes trading in Infinitum: In breife, it is the Elixir or Philosopher's Stone'.

The alchemical key in this case was the idea that the 'base metal' of things like land or goods or future earnings could be converted into the 'gold' of money through the magic of credit. For example, suppose someone had a valuable plot of land which they wanted to keep, but they needed to raise money in order to pursue a business venture. The usual method was to borrow money from someone, in exchange for a claim against the land. If the business venture failed, then the creditor would have their claim, but would have to wait a long time to be repaid. However, if the creditor instead received paper notes, and these notes could be exchanged, then they would be as good as money. The creditor could then spend them immediately (i.e. pass the debt on to someone else), and the money supply would expand accordingly.

This new money was effectively as good as gold, but was backed by a legal claim on an asset rather than by precious metal. As William Potter wrote, the resulting credit currency would unlock society's 'store-house of Riches', making credit 'the true Seed of Riches'. He estimated that the scheme could double England's capital every two years, so after twenty years £1,000 would grow to a million pounds.

Some critics worried that creating such a source of infinite credit would lead to runaway inflation, just as discovering an actual philosopher's stone would mean that, after a while, 'gold and silver will grow cheap, like dung', as the alchemist George

Starkey, writing under the pseudonym of Eirenaeus Philalethes, observed. As we have since discovered, though, what counts is not the quantity of money, but its velocity of circulation – and money parked in inert assets like houses doesn't circulate. Asset prices can therefore expand without leading to either price or wage inflation, at least in the short term. Of course, just as debt money can be created by making more loans, so it is extinguished when those loans are called in, which is why new loans have to be constantly generated in order to keep the show on the road.

IS THIS REALITY?

A number of land banks along these lines were attempted, but didn't manage to attract enough broad interest to survive. However, a similar Hartlibian scheme was carried out in France by the expatriate Scots mathematician John Law, who with the backing of the sovereign opened a small bank, the *Banque Royale*, which went on to become for a short time the largest in the world. A difference was that the notes were effectively backed not by land directly, but by investments in Law's Mississippi Company, which had trading rights over a huge expanse of what is now the United States.

One reason for Law's success, while it lasted, was his stage-craft. For example, he didn't just hand potential investors in the Mississippi Company a prospectus – he turned the whole thing into a show. Emigrants on their way to America – their ranks supplemented by prisoners and prostitutes – were given a leaving parade. Rumours were propagated about the enormous supplies of gold, silver and diamonds that awaited them in Louisiana. Tales of the immense riches won by speculators were spread. As the journalist and author John Flynn wrote in his biography of Law, 'It is not to be wondered that for a few brief months Paris hailed the magician who had produced all these rabbits from his hat.'[14] Still, not everyone was convinced. As Voltaire wrote: 'Is this reality? Is this a chimera? Has half the nation found the philosopher's stone in the paper mills?'

A similar company known as the South Sea Company was launched around the same time in England. In return for an offer to help fund the English national debt, the company was granted a permanent monopoly on trade with Mexico and South America, that included the right to carry African slaves to Spanish ports in the New World. The company's public relations efforts were assisted by wordsmiths including Daniel Defoe and Jonathan Swift, who were paid to write articles promoting the scheme. Part of their job was to give the public a positive view of the brutal Atlantic slave trade. This was done by emphasising the exotic nature of the locations, and what one anonymous author (possibly Defoe) called the 'inexhaustible Fountain' of gold and silver available in the New World.

Again, not everyone was convinced, as shown by a song called the 'South Sea Ballad', which was apparently sung for months around the streets of London:

> 'Tis said that Alchemists of old,
> Could turn a brazen kettle,
> Or leaden cistern into gold,
> That noble tempting metal.
> But if it here may be allow'd,
> To bring in great with small things,
> Our cunning South Sea, like a god,
> Turns nothing into all things.

It concluded by noting that 'all the riches that we boast; Consist in scraps of paper'.

Neither of these schemes ended particularly well. You may have heard of the Alaska Gold Rush, or the Colorado Gold Rush, or the California Gold Rush, or even the Yukon Gold Rush, but you probably haven't heard of the Mississippi Gold Rush. The reason is because *there wasn't any gold*. The failure of Law's *Banque Royale* meant that for the next couple of hundred years, financial institutions in France preferred to describe themselves as anything other than a bank. The South Sea bubble, meanwhile, introduced the word 'bubble' into the financial lexicon (this use was probably first due to Defoe, though Swift helped popularise it).

One problem with the Hartlibian analysis was that it missed the most important part of the equation, which is power. Law, for example, had the backing of the French crown, but his boundless ambitions to take over every aspect of the money system, including tax collection, alienated the financial community. The Bank of England solved this problem by a power-sharing arrangement. In exchange for a £1.2 million loan, King William III granted the bank a number of things including, apart from regular interest payments, the right to issue banknotes backed by the debt. The crown and its creditors were thus entangled like the two sides of a coin; neither could exist without the other, but together they were money.

The modern era of fiat currencies – named after the Latin for 'let it be done', since they are backed by the state rather than by metal – began with the 1971 'Nixon Shock' in which President Nixon delinked the US dollar from the price of gold. This time Nixon made sure to have the bankers on board – and the new money was secured by something even more powerful than the divine right of kings: nuclear weapons.

However the Hartlibian idea of a land bank is alive and well. In fact, it is the basis of much of our modern financial system. And today the alchemists all work in finance, where they puff up prices.

THE FREE LUNCH

A common principle in economics is that, to quote the title of one of Milton Friedman's books, 'There's No Such Thing as a Free Lunch'. Or as the neoclassical economist William Stanley Jevons put it, 'there is no law better established in physics than that man can neither create nor annihilate matter.'[15]

Of course, Jevons was writing in the late nineteenth century, so was unaware of later developments in quantum physics, in which the appearance and disappearance of subatomic particles is handled mathematically by the use of so-called creation and annihilation operators, and matter can be transformed into energy in nuclear devices. It also doesn't apply to money, which is regularly ushered in and out of existence by the actions of banks.

In fact, in most modern economies, the vast majority of money (in the UK, for example, about 97 per cent) is created not by central banks, but by private banks lending money for things like mortgages on houses. As Jon Nicolaisen, Deputy Governor of the Bank of Norway, explained in a 2017 speech: 'When you borrow from a bank, the bank credits your bank account. The deposit – the money – is created by the bank the moment it issues the loan. The bank does not transfer the money from someone else's bank account or from a vault full of money. The money lent to you by the bank has been created by the bank itself – out of nothing.'[16]

As discussed later, money creation has long been something of a no-go topic in polite economics circles. Indeed the nature of money creation was not even openly or widely acknowledged until 2014, when the Bank of England admitted in a paper that 'The reality of how money is created today differs from the description found in some economics textbooks' (by which they meant all mainstream textbooks of the sort the average student was likely to encounter).[17] The conventional views were either that banks redistribute funds from savers to borrowers, or that they lend money under a so-called fractional reserve system in which loans are limited by the bank's requirement to hold a certain cash reserve.

As the Bank of England pointed out, though, the reality is that bank lending is limited only by regulatory or self-imposed requirements on reserves (money to pay back depositors), liquidity (stuff that can be easily sold to cover temporary shocks), and capital (net worth, to make sure the bank is solvent) – and since banks can borrow to make up any shortfalls, such constraints are better seen as a profitability consideration.

In his 2016 book *The End of Alchemy*, former governor of the Bank of England Mervyn King spelled out that banks 'are at the heart of the alchemy of our financial system. Banks are the main source of money creation. They create deposits as a byproduct of making loans to risky borrowers. Those deposits are used as money.' The Bundesbank followed up in 2017, adding that 'this refutes a popular misconception that banks act simply as intermediaries at the time of lending – i.e. that banks can only grant credit using funds placed with them previously as deposits by other customers'.[18] Sometimes even bankers are unaware that they create money. In 2018, during a Swiss referendum on banking, a Basel banker told the *Financial Times*: 'It was a surprise – we were simply not aware. A client rang ... and said "you create money, how can that be?" And I said, "no, we don't create money, we're an intermediary".'[19]

As former chairman of the UK's Financial Services Authority Adair Turner notes, the amount of private credit and money that banks can create is 'potentially infinite', just as the alchemists had predicted. And yet: 'To a quite striking extent, the role of banks in creating credit, money and purchasing power, was written out of the script of modern macro-economics.'[20] This is changing to a degree as heterodox areas such as MMT (Modern Monetary Theory, or Magic Money Tree to its critics), which focuses on the idea that the state can never default on debts in its own currency, grow in influence. But as the economist and former central banker Tony Yates explained on Twitter in 2020, 'Most people who teach macro do it by leading people through simple models without money' and only later add in things like 'inflation, exchange rates, business cycles'. Heterodox types such as the MMT crowd 'have confused the hell out of themselves by starting with what fascinated them most, the funny bits of paper whizzing around that you seem to be able to swap for stuff'.[21]

LAND BANK

As we'll see, the role of economists is like that of the magician's famulus, or assistant, which is to distract the audience from what is really going on, through misdirections such as accusing them of being distracted. To return to the question of the empty house on my street, one of the more concrete demonstrations of Hartlibian alchemy – and its 'funny bits of paper whizzing around' – is the Canadian real estate-financial complex. I will focus on this because I live in Toronto, but of course other countries have their own versions. In fact, the biggest asset class in the world is not stocks or bonds but real estate, which with an estimated value of about US$200 trillion is about three times the size of the market for publicly traded shares.[22]

Here is a list of the top five industries in Canada, along with their contribution to GDP in 2020:[23]

Real estate and rental and leasing	13.7%
Manufacturing	9.5%
Finance and insurance	7.6%
Mining, quarrying, and oil and gas extraction	7.5%
Construction	7.3%

Since large parts of the construction and financial industries involve real estate, it seems that around a fifth of the Canadian economy has a serious stake in residents (or non-residents) building homes and selling them to each other, which makes it the most important component outside of government (this doesn't include money laundering through real estate, which in Canada is big business and may contribute another per cent or so of GDP).[24] These firms are the modern version of Law's Mississippi Company, promising gold in the form of real estate. Their contributions to local economies in boom areas such as Toronto and Vancouver may be even higher. Perhaps this is what the Ontario government meant when they labelled real estate an essential service during the pandemic.

So what is it that sustains this frenzied activity? In part, the process is subsidised by the fourth-largest sector of the economy, namely 'mining, quarrying, and oil and gas extraction', which represents the ultimate free lunch since most of the value comes from natural resources rather than human labour. It is striking that the energy of the real estate-financial complex, as measured by GDP, is far larger than the actual energy sector. As with Law's parade of emigrants, a steady supply of new immigrants with fresh balance sheets is an important part of the show, though it dried up during the pandemic. But most important is a flow of new money. This new money is created every time a home is mortgaged.

The money creation procedure is just as the Hartlibians described. The money is in the form of a loan, secured against the property. This loan is enforced by the state, but the state does not receive interest payments. Instead, these go to the bank, in theory to compensate for the bank's risk. The new money created through the mortgage goes to the person selling the property, and much of this is typically reinvested in real estate – thus boosting the price of real estate, even as inflation in the real economy remains muted. The result is that the money supply tends to track housing prices as they ramp up exponentially.

This is shown by Figure 1.1, which compares the growth of a broad measure of money supply with the growth of house prices since 1999 (when the housing index began). The two curves, which are normalised so that both equal 1 at the start

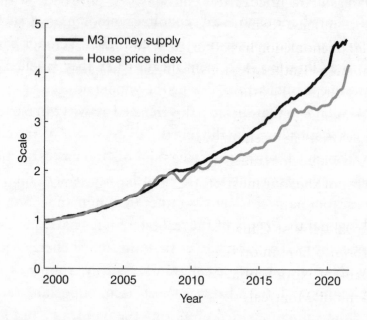

FIGURE 1.1   Plot showing relative house prices from the Teranet index and M3 money supply in Canada. Both curves are normalised so they equal 1 at the start of 2000.

of 2000, grew in a roughly exponential fashion until around 2008. The financial crisis caused a brief hiccup, but growth soon resumed, with house prices now slightly lagging behind the money supply. The near-vertical growth of the money supply in 2020 occurred as the government desperately tried to stop this fragile Hartlibian scheme from collapsing during the COVID-19 lockdown by injecting massive amounts of money into the financial system.

Of course, the money supply depends on factors other than the price of houses. The index also shows only the typical house price, rather than the total value of all the housing stock which should grow a little faster due to new construction. However, any Hartlibian who saw this plot would immediately recognise that the main reason there is more money is because of money creation through real estate transactions; and the main reason the price of real estate is going up is because there is more money. As market strategist Chris Watling notes, a similar phenomenon has occurred in most of the world's major economies: 'Rather than a shortage of housing supply, as is often postulated as the key reason for high house prices, it's the abundant and rapid growth in mortgage debt that has been the key driver in recent decades.'[25]

And where does much of this money end up? A hint is given by a list of the four most profitable companies in Canada:

Royal Bank of Canada
Toronto-Dominion Bank
Bank of Nova Scotia
Bank of Montreal

The common factor is that they all have the word 'bank' in the title.[26] It isn't just house prices which are inflating – it is also banker bonuses, along with the prices of shares in these firms that, like the houses themselves, are predominantly owned by the wealthy, thus exacerbating inequality.

THE LEVITATION TRICK

One of the most famous magic tricks is the levitation trick, in which a magician makes it look as if an object or person is floating in the air, defying the force of gravity. I don't think I'm giving away too much to say that the levitation is in fact an illusion, and something mechanical is needed to make it happen. But just as important is the magician's patter, his ability to distract the audience from what is going on by creating a different narrative. An example was the 'ethereal suspension' performed by the great nineteenth-century French magician Jean-Eugène Robert-Houdin, where he claimed that the incredible properties of the newly popularised substance ether could make his son float in the air.

The compound known to alchemists as 'sweet vitriol' had been renamed as ether by the eighteenth-century German scientist W.G. Frobenius, who had first found a way to manufacture it. He chose the name not, of course, because he genuinely believed that he had discovered the quintessence, but rather because of its levitating effects on the human psyche. Popularisers included 'Doctor' James Graham, a 'pedlar of health through sex-therapy and mudbaths', who would publicly inhale an ounce or two several times a day 'with manifest placidity and enjoyment'. As well as being used for recreational purposes, ether also found use as a medical treatment, as an anaesthetic for surgery or childbirth, and as a prop for a magic show. During Robert-Houdin's trick, an assistant would sprinkle a little ether around the theatre so that audience members could catch a whiff of the mysterious new substance.

Today, banks perform a similar levitation trick with house prices, while their economist sidekicks mist the air with carefully phrased misinformation, and evocations of notions such as the invisible hand, or supply and demand. One of Canada's leading academic economics blogs, for example, reported in 2017 that 'the drivers of housing prices in Ontario seem fairly straightforward to most of us. There has been an increase in Ontario's population since 1990 of nearly 36 per cent, which should serve to boost housing demand. More importantly, interest rates have dropped and remain at historic lows, which make financing homes much easier even with the price increases. If economic factors are driving demand up faster than supply, then one would expect prices to increase.'[27] Stephen Poloz, who was then governor of the Bank of Canada, agreed that the rise in house prices was due to 'fundamentals' and in particular the fact that population growth 'automatically generates more demand for housing at a time when there are constraints around supply'.[28]

Economists are essentially led to this conclusion by their law of supply and demand, which implies that price rises should normally result in decreased demand. The fact that demand remains high even as prices soar suggests that there must be pressure due to population growth. To be sure, cities such as Toronto are a magnet for skilled immigrants, and things like zoning restrictions limit supply; however, a population growth of 36 per cent between 1990 and 2017 works out to an annual rate of about 1.1 per cent, which is not exactly blistering, especially considering that in 2017 house prices in Toronto were increasing at about 25 times that rate. And while mortgage rates were very low, total consumer debt was also at an all-time high, which more than compensated.

Obviously something else was going on, but economists,

trained as they were in the classical logic of supply and demand and no free lunch, couldn't see it. They were like Victorian scientists trying to calculate the yield of an atomic bomb by figuring out how much of the recently invented dynamite it might contain. As discussed later, price rises do not necessarily depress demand – instead they can do the opposite, through effects such as the fear of missing out. Such emotions are fuelled by realtors, like one who wrote on Twitter: 'Many people miss the leverage factor in RE. Buy a condo for $500k with 10% down. 3 yrs later that condo has appreciated to $550k many look at it as a 10% return when it's actually a 100% return. Leverage is how true wealth is built. You need to get your money working.'[29]

Even a year after the COVID-19 pandemic brought on a recession and the highest unemployment rate in Canadian history, the amazing levitating housing market was still 'Defying gravity', as a *Globe and Mail* headline put it, and most Canadian economists remained remarkably sanguine about the risks.[30] For example, in a 2021 note to investors, Bank of Montreal's chief economist Douglas Porter puzzled over the question of why it was that, after adjusting for purchasing power and exchange rates, houses cost 46 per cent more in Canada than in the US.[31] Given that the prop of immigration had been kicked away – the population growth rate was the lowest since 1916 – Porter suggested that 'a much more fundamental answer may simply be that on balance Canadians have made a collective choice to allocate more resources to (and thus "consume" more) housing than other countries. And that's not necessarily a bad thing, just a consumption choice. It's debatable that the heavy investment in housing relative to other areas is a misalignment of resources – as some have suggested – if that truly represents the preference of Canadians. After all …

who is to judge if this type of consumption is better or worse than other forms of spending?'

In other words, prices were high because Canadians think real estate is very valuable. This explanation is again consistent with mainstream economics, which assumes as a truism that price is a measure of subjective utility; however, it seems odd that this affection for houses is not just large but also grows in time at an astounding clip (in 2020, at ten times the rate of inflation). Another banker called in April 2021 for more research into the question of home prices, but said there was no 'magic-wand policy that will deal with this situation', and in any case Canada is 'still pretty far from an excessive bubble, and even further from the bursting of it'.[32]

So, to summarise: the Canadian housing bubble, which is probably the most important economic phenomenon in the country, is viewed by economists from banks and academia as cool and normal.[33] The government and central bank (which is theoretically independent)[34] were also on board, with the latter helping to support the process with near-zero interest rates. Poloz's replacement as governor at the central bank, Tiff Macklem, said that 'we need the growth', by which he meant inequality-boosting debt-inducing price inflation, but warned of the gains that 'if people start to think those go on indefinitely, that becomes a concern' (the bank would definitely do something in that case!).[35] As prices rose at the fastest pace in three decades, Poloz chimed in to say that 'We cut interest rates to boost the economy ... If the side-effect is a hot housing market, that's one I'll take every day.'[36]

Governments for their part sometimes complain about house price inflation, and blame it on someone else – our local socialist MPP sent out a leaflet in 2021 announcing that 'We will take on the billionaires, foreign speculators, and bad faith developers who have made the market unaffordable for regular Ontarians', even though it was regular Ontarians, facilitated and enabled by banks, economists, politicians, and media cheerleaders, who were actually buying the houses and driving up prices – but the reality is that they generally act to support it because capital gains are perceived as a substitute for stagnating wages. The main housing policy proposal from the same MPP's party was to increase the maximum amortization period for insured mortgages from 25 to 30 years, which would just lift prices by making it possible to borrow more.[37] In the UK, the Conservative party's most reliable policy idea and election strategy since the time of Margaret Thatcher has similarly been to boost house prices through programmes such as 'Help to Buy', this being easier than helping to create actual prosperity. More cynically perhaps, debt is also always a good way to keep the population in line (as Noam Chomsky observed of student debt, 'When you trap people in a system of debt, they can't afford the time to think').[38] Above all, governments are terrified of a housing bust occurring on their watch. In 2021 Canada's housing secretary even described his need 'to protect the investments Canadians have made in their homes' – as he put it, 'hands up if you'd like to see 10 percent of the equity in your home suddenly disappear overnight' – apparently confusing an investment backstop with housing policy (at the time, that decline would have represented less than four months' worth of growth).[39]

But as with other such schemes which try to transmute the 'lead' of land and homes into the 'gold' of economic growth, the Canadian experiment in Hartlibian alchemy looks likely to end badly, because it is eventually destined to collide with real limits. Look at any metric – the ratio of house prices to rents, the ratio of house prices to income, the growth rate of house prices after inflation, the ratio of household debt to GDP, and so on – and Canada is consistently at or near the top of the pack in an international comparison, leaving traditional competitors such as the US and UK in the dust (Australia and New Zealand are among the main contenders, with China being the largest in terms of total financial scale).[40] And as economist Herbert Stein once pointed out, if something can't go on forever it will stop (though the corollary is that it may take longer than you think). The main question, though, is not if or when the scheme will collapse, but how much damage it has already done.

BLACK MAGIC

In one sense, the mechanics of this levitation trick are extremely simple, and don't seem all that magical. While this book will argue that the underlying processes are quantum in nature, that doesn't mean you need a degree in quantum mathematics to understand exponential growth, or spot a market bubble, any more than you need quantum wave equations to calculate the yield of a nuclear device. Exponential growth, for example, is a basic property of many natural systems – bacteria colonies grow exponentially in a petri dish, until they run out of nutrients. As 2020 taught us, viruses spread exponentially until it becomes harder for them to find vulnerable hosts.

Also, while a nuclear bomb is designed to destroy cities and their inhabitants, one could argue that the real estate-financial complex is doing the opposite, by making homes for people to live in, or helping them to upgrade their living conditions. The aspiration to own your own home is a core value and source of meaning for citizens of many countries, including Canada. Surely, if an ethereal housing market is any kind of magic, it is the fun kind that you buy tickets to see, rather than the darker sort where people get hurt?

However, as anyone who lived through an event like the US subprime mortgage crisis will know – some of whom are still underwater on their homes[41] – a housing bust is immensely damaging to an economy and leaves long-lasting scars. Canadians have among the highest debt loads in the world so are especially vulnerable to any downturn. House price inflation is also increasingly recognised as a key driver of inequality. According to Larry Hu, head of China economics at Macquarie Securities Ltd, 'Property is the single most important source of financial risks and wealth inequality in China', and the same is true in other countries, including Canada.[42] And the fact that the real estate-financial complex constitutes such a large fraction of the national economy represents a massive misallocation of resources. Because it is inherently unproductive, it acts as a brake on the economy by raising prices for workers, pricing new recruits out of the market, and diverting resources from more useful purposes. This is one reason why the *Economist* magazine described the emphasis on home ownership as 'the west's biggest policy mistake' in 2020.[43] Studies have shown the same for the financial sector as a whole, which, as a paper from the Bank for International Settlements notes, tends to 'suck in more than its share of talent, hampering the development of other sectors'.[44] An economy obtains its strength and resilience from things like innovation and creativity. The real estate-financial complex is the opposite of this – it makes money by passively exploiting legal boundaries and property rights (they even trademarked the word REALTOR®).

The real estate-financial complex is an example of what this book calls a financial bomb – and like many similar bombs around the world, it poses a danger to society. Just as Soddy saw alchemy as a bridge to science, a first step towards understanding the nature of such devices is to appreciate that money – the substance which makes up their nuclear core – has apparently magical properties. Which, because our worldview is rooted in classical logic, just means that it doesn't behave like a classical system.

In classical logic, there is no metaphorical free lunch, but the reality is that our economy is based on the principle of creating something from nothing, in what amounts to financial alchemy. And underlying the trick is a form of transmutation, in which real objects are turned into virtual numbers.

To understand the deeper secrets of how this trick works, we need to step back further, to a period when both science and money were in their infancy, and one of the most profound magic tricks of all time was first performed.

CHAPTER 2

THE PENETRATION TRICK

*Practically all the great European philosophers have been
bachelors ... Great men, simply by their ignorance of a
topic, can lay a remarkably strong taboo on the mention
of it even where it happens to be entirely relevant.*
MARY MIDGLEY, 'RINGS AND BOOKS', 1950s

———

A penetration trick is one in which the magician makes solid
objects pass through one another, as when a person walks through
a mirror or a wall. Harry Houdini had his Walking Through A
Brick Wall illusion a hundred years ago, and it has since become a
staple; David Copperfield walked through the Great Wall of China.
But money is up to this kind of thing all the time – as shown,
for example, by all those capital flows out of China. We think of
money as being somehow solid and durable, like a gold bar, but at
the same time it is elastic and fluid, capable of moving instantly
through space, or tunnelling through apparently impenetrable barriers. This chapter will show that these magical properties are no
obvious stunt or cheap illusion, but are due to the intrinsically
dualistic nature of money, which involves real matter being pen-
etrated by abstract numbers.

———

Modern economics, like Western science in general, has roots
that go back to the sixth century BC. According to a story from
the time, a gem engraver and his wife visited the Pythian oracle
in Delphi for some business advice. The oracle was called the

Pythia because originally the oracles were said to have been supplied by the earth goddess Gaia, aka Mother Earth, and sung out by a prophetess known as the Sybil. The site was protected by Gaia's daughter, a snake called Python, who lived in a nearby spring. However, the young god Apollo slayed Python and took over the oracle. From then on, he was known as the Pythian Apollo, and was considered the god of prediction.

The 'Delphic oracle', as it styled itself, was without doubt the most successful magic show in history, lasting for almost a thousand years. Imagine a marquee show at Vegas where, when the lead dies, he or she gets replaced by a lookalike. The way it worked was that a supplicant would show up at the temple and offer a gift, such as a sacrificial goat (though this varied). The supplicant was then admitted to the temple, where the Pythia, who was always a woman, sat on a three-legged stool known as the tripod. A priest would ask her the pre-screened question. The Pythia then went through an elaborate show of channelling the spirit of Apollo, and spout some incomprehensible gibberish. The priest decoded it into a coherent response, which he would read out in verse.

One of the Pythia's more famous visitors was King Croesus, who was immensely rich thanks to his discovery of a way to refine gold to make coins (as always, the best way to make money is to literally make it). His donation to the temple included 3,000 animals for sacrifice, a gold lion weighing ten talents (about 240 kg), and various other gold and silver offerings. Croesus was considering a military expedition against Cyrus the Great of Persia, and asked the oracle for advice. She told him that if he went ahead, 'a great empire would fall', which he took as a green light. However, he had neglected to ask which empire – it was his – which just goes to show that, even with a lot of money, it is hard to get reliable and transparent advice.

In the case of the gem engraver and his wife, as the legend goes, the Pythia informed the couple that the woman would give birth to a son who would surpass in beauty and wisdom all who had ever lived. This came as a shock since the wife didn't even know she was pregnant. When the child was born, the parents gave him the name Pythagoras, which means 'the oracle speaks'.

THE MAGIC SCHOOL

Born on the island of Samos in the Aegean Sea, Pythagoras travelled extensively as a young man. One of the places he visited was Miletus, a city near Lydia which was home to the mathematician/philosopher Thales, whom Bertrand Russell credited with basically founding Western philosophy. Miletus was also the first Greek city to produce its own coins, so Pythagoras was present at the birth of coin money. Pythagoras also dropped in on the sages of Syria, the high priests of Egypt, and the Magi of Babylon, where, according to his biographer Iamblichus, he 'was instructed in their sacred rites and learnt about a very mystical worship of the gods'.[1]

On his return to Samos, he set up a school teaching mathematics and philosophy. The school, known as the semicircle, was located in a cave. It wasn't a big hit because the approach, based on that of the Egyptian priests Pythagoras had met, was too hard and abstract. There were all sorts of restrictions; for example, you weren't supposed to eat beans, or wear clothes made from animal skins, or listen to the wrong sort of music. He moved on to a town called Croton in southern Italy, where he started a new school. This had some of the trappings of a religious cult, and some of a scientific academy, but is better described as a school for magic, in the deepest sense of that word.

Today we associate magic with tricks and entertainment, but ancient Greece was the real golden age for magic, where people valued the chance to get a prediction from an oracle, astrological advice from a mathematician, a spell from a magician, or intensive training at the hands of a master like Pythagoras. The word magic comes from the Greek *magos*, which referred to religious figures like shamans, who were believed to have access to the Otherworld. In the case of Pythagoras, his followers actually believed that he was a demi-god, fathered by the god Apollo. He was said to have a golden thigh which he would show to people to convince them of his semi-divinity.

One of the magic tricks in which Pythagoras is said to have been expert was the transportation trick. Iamblichus told of a priest/sage figure called Abaris who was returning to his home in the Caucasus after a fundraising mission for his Apollonian temple. Passing through Italy, he met Pythagoras and became convinced that this was none other than Apollo himself. He offered Pythagoras a sacred arrow, which he claimed had once belonged to Apollo. According to Abaris, the arrow had magical powers, which allowed its owner to fly across obstacles such as rivers or mountains.

Another speciality was the prediction trick.[2] Pythagoras taught various methods, such as the reading of entrails or listening to oracles, but the highest form of prediction was that of divination through numbers, which Pythagoras thought more closely connected with the gods than other methods. Like an early version of the entertainers Siegfried & Roy, he was also skilled at the art of mesmerism; according to Iamblichus, he could tame a bear or eagle just by 'stroking it gently with his hand', and could control wild animals using only the 'power of his voice' or 'influence of his touch'.

But the biggest trick, by far, was the penetration trick. Pythagoras's version differed substantially from the Walking Through A Brick Wall-style antics later practised by Houdini – and if you're wondering whether it has anything to do with sex, don't worry, it does. But to see how it works we first need to think a bit about number.

NUMBER IS ALL

The main core belief of the Pythagoreans was that reality is based on number – or rather, that it actually *was* number. According to the Pythagoreans, each number had a special significance. One represented Unity, which in their version of a creation myth was the original unblemished state of the universe. Two was the dyad, which represented the division into duality, and was associated with change and the feminine. Three, the triad, enabled all things, with a beginning, middle and end, or a past, present and future. It was the number associated with prophecy, e.g. the tripod at Delphi. Number four, the tetrad, represented completion, as in the four seasons that make up a year. The tetrad also later came to represent the four classical elements of fire, air, water, and earth. The greatest and most magical number was ten: as the sum of the first four numbers, this symbolised the universe. It was represented by the tetractys, a sacred triangular symbol consisting of ten dots in the 4-3-2-1 arrangement nowadays used for bowling pins. The Pythagoreans associated this symbol with the Delphic oracle.

The author Arthur Koestler wrote of Pythagoras that 'his influence on the ideas, and thereby on the destiny, of the human race was probably greater than that of any single man before or after him'.[3] This might seem an overstatement given that most people's only exposure to him is in elementary mathematics, through his theory about the hypotenuse of right-angled

49

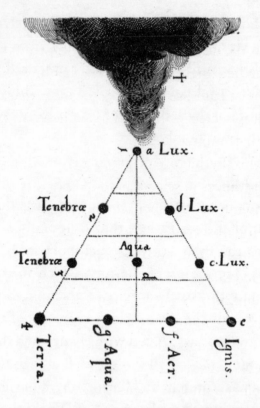

FIGURE 2.1 A seventeenth-century version of the Pythagorean tetractys by the physician and alchemist Robert Fludd, which also illustrates the Pythagorean creation myth.[4] The dark cloud represents the state of chaos before the universe was born. The creation of the universe was marked by the appearance of the monod, or unity, followed by the dyad, followed by the other numbers.

triangles. Like modern magicians, or bankers for that matter, the Pythagoreans insisted on strict loyalty and secrecy, so nothing was written down. As Iamblichus observed, the aim – as with any magic school – was 'to conceal, after an arcane mode, divine mysteries from the uninitiated'. Everything we know about Pythagoras therefore comes from secondary sources, such as Iamblichus or Aristotle. It seems that he wasn't very successful as a spiritual leader, certainly compared to his contemporary the Buddha. In fact, it is believed he died in exile after townspeople turned against his secretive group and burned down the school. However, his importance is due to his simple but amazingly powerful idea that 'number is all'. Or as the economist Paul Romer put it, the idea 'that math could tell you the deep secrets of the universe' (though he was talking about modern economists).[5]

Usually, this Pythagorean emphasis on number is connected with advances in science, and of course it did kick-start the development of Western science. But as the scholar W.K.C. Guthrie observed, it is likely that 'Pythagoras derived his enthusiasm for the study of number from its practical applications in commerce' – and the clearest manifestation of Pythagorean philosophy is to be found in the coins you carry in your pocket, or the numbers you store in your bank account.[6] The son of a gem engraver, who visited some of the earliest mints in Miletus, was writing at a time of unprecedented monetary development, and may according to some accounts have been involved in the design of his local coinage, was the first magician to show the world the magic of money; and to cast the spell from which we are yet to wake.

After all, what more powerful demonstration is there than money of the Pythagorean idea that number is all? The whole point of money is to reduce calculations of value to the same numeric playing field. Just as a musical note refers to the same tone on any instrument, so a unit of currency refers to a set value. Money therefore did the same thing for the world of exchange that Pythagorean mathematics did for the universe: reduce it to number.

Today we live in a world where everything has a price on it, as if it has been sprinkled with magical number powder, which when you think about it is quite a trick. How do you attach numbers to things? After all, numbers and things have very different properties. For example, you can lose or give or exchange a thing, but we can't really exchange numbers, because they are abstract ideas. If I pretend to give you a number 2, there is nothing to stop me from giving another number 2 to someone else. Or for you to come up with your own number 2. No one owns numbers, so no one can give them either. Similarly, things are perishable, but numbers last forever. A house can wear out, and the rain can get in, but the mortgage is weatherproof.

As will be seen below, by fusing the properties of real things and virtual numbers into a single package, money was performing a kind of penetration trick. If this sounds like the start of a joke, then maybe it is.

VIRTUAL REALITY

To understand this trick, it should first be pointed out that Greek philosophy was dualistic and also what we would describe as blatantly sexist. The Pythagoreans, for example, saw the universe as governed by opposing principles, which were divided into Good and Evil, and which included Male versus Female. Women were allowed into the group, but the female archetype was still associated with darkness and evil. Plato described women as originating from morally defective souls in *Timaeus*, and he and Aristotle excluded them from their schools.

The split between genders was tied up in Greek philosophy with the split between the real world and abstract ideas. The former was associated in Greek culture with the female principle, the latter with the male principle. According to science writer Margaret Wertheim, 'Mathematics was associated with the gods, and with transcendence from the material world; women, by their nature, were supposedly rooted in this latter, baser realm.'[7] There were no female philosophers to argue against this, because they weren't admitted to the club.

Plato took this division between the real and the virtual to its logical conclusion with his theory of forms. According to Plato, any real-world object, say a table, is an imperfect version of a form, in this case the Table form, which exists in some higher plane of reality, that can be accessed only through the intellect. However, coins straddle this divide, because the virtual symbol is physically pressed into the real material.

The word 'virtual' is from the Latin *virtus* for manliness, while 'material' is from the Latin *mater* for mother, and it isn't too much of a leap to link the creation of money objects with Aristotle's rather dated (it has been two millennia) theory of the creation of babies: 'The female always provides the material, the male provides that which fashions the material into shape; this, in our view, is the specific characteristic of each of the sexes: that is what it means to be male or female.'[8] In this view, procreation really is a penetration trick: like a magician pushing a coin through a latex screen so that it magically appears on the other side (the 'coin penetration trick'), or Apollo speaking through the oracle, the male seed is pushed through the female to appear again in the form of the child.

Seen this way, money is a kind of pocket version of Greek duality, in which virtual numbers penetrate physical matter, in an alchemical combination of the male ♂ and female ♀ principles. (It is ironic that we refer to gold coins as being a hard currency, when gold is an extremely soft metal which has traditionally been used as ornamentation for women's bodies.) The whole point of the money system is to put 'hard' numbers on 'soft' values. As in the mysterious quantum process of wave function collapse, the aim is to collapse a range of possible values down to a single number.[9] We will talk more about this process in later chapters, but the point for now is that money objects such as coins combine dual aspects which are inherently incompatible: that of a virtual number, and that of a real, owned thing. By trading these money objects, other objects become associated with a number as well, known as their price; however, money objects are unique in that they have a well-defined value. Most physical objects, for example, are subject to decay, but a ten-dollar note will always be worth ten dollars by definition (how much it will buy is another question).

It is the tension between money's two sides – the real and the virtual, the soft and the hard – that sparks money's creativity, and gives it its hypnotic power; but its aligning of value with number also points to another issue, which is the gendered nature of both money and economics.

QUANTUM IS A FEMINIST ISSUE

Money, as we will see, is surrounded by awkward topics, of which the discussion of gender is just one. Since we are here, though, it is obvious that science in general, and economics in particular, is still seen by many as, like ancient philosophy, a club for men – and this may have affected our understanding of money, by emphasising only one of its sides. So let's give this cauldron a careful stir to see what's bubbling.

Motivated by the link between ancient Greek philosophy and modern science, I have raised the topic of gender in some of my other books, but it doesn't raise a unanimously positive response. One physicist even worried that my argument was intended as a joke on the reader, which I can assure is not the case (though humour is a help).[10] Perhaps scientists see themselves as truth-seekers who are free of such cultural influences. However, the issue does seem especially relevant to the quantum approach, which mixes hard and soft by design.

For a start, the field of economics – like science in general – has long been dominated by men. The philosopher

Sandra Harding wrote in 1986 that 'Women have been more systematically excluded from doing serious science than from performing any other social activity except, perhaps, front-line warfare.'[11] With the result, as the feminist scholar Evelyn Fox-Keller put it in 1985, that modern science was developed 'not by humankind but by men'.[12] Quantum physics, for example, was constructed mostly by a small group of young men in their twenties. But economics seems to be something of an extreme case, and remains, as sociologist Elaine Coburn observed in 2016, 'remarkably "pre-feminist"'.[13] According to economics professor Veronika Dolar, 'there's a strong case to be made that economics is the worst academic field in which to be a woman.'[14] One recent study used data science to analyse the gender gap, and concluded that the discipline was best described as 'a crushing and unrewarding environment for female economists', which doesn't seem much of an advance over ancient Greece.[15] The problem has been increasingly acknowledged in recent years, prompted in a lagged way by the #MeToo movement. During a 2019 panel discussion on gender issues, Janet Yellen (now US treasury secretary) even said that addressing the issue of sex discrimination 'should be the highest priority' for economists.[16] But a related question is how this has affected economics.

One clue, perhaps, is given in a 2020 paper by Yellen's husband (and winner of the Nobel Memorial Prize) George Akerlof, which argues that economics 'gives rewards that favor the "hard" and disfavor the "soft"'.[17] He does not make the link himself – there is an entire section titled 'Reasons for Bias toward Hard' which manages to avoid the obvious one, namely association with a certain kind of masculinity. Indeed, his piece does not even mention words such as 'women', 'female', or 'gender'. Yet some have not been so reticent to draw a connection.

The philosopher Mary Midgley, for example, in 1985 compiled a list of opposites thought to distinguish science from things like magic and superstition. Reminiscent of the Pythagoreans' idea of opposing principles, the list included:

Hard	Soft
Reason	Feeling, Emotion
Objective	Subjective
Quantity	Quality
Male	Female
Clarity	Mystery

Midgley commented that the instruction to keep with the items in the first column 'has for the last century usually been issued to English-speaking scientists with their first test-tube and has often gone with them to the grave'.[18] In his book *The Gendered Atom*, the historian Theodore Roszak observed that 'physics came to be considered the "hardest" of the hard sciences' because it dealt with the 'fundamental stuff of the universe'. Atoms were seen as 'colorless, soulless, unlovely things. They lacked magic.'[19] And as feminist theologian and psychologist Catherine Keller noted, there was a strong correspondence between these 'separate, impenetrable' Newtonian atoms, and the male sense of self.[20]

The Greek-archetype masculinity of atoms was matched by the solidity of the equations used by physicists to model atoms, and by economists to model human behaviour. The economist Julie A. Nelson wrote in 1996 that 'analytical methods associated with detachment, mathematical reasoning, formality, and abstraction have cultural associations that are positive and masculine, in contrast with methods associated with connectedness, verbal reasoning, informality, and concrete detail, which are culturally considered feminine.'[21] The economist Deirdre McCloskey mocked the 'comical, anxious rigidity' with which male economists 'insist on square, fact, logic, science, numbers, cognition, rigor, truth, hardness, positiveness, and the object-ive'. She likened them to a motorcycle gang, 'strutting about the camp with clattering matrices and rigorously fixed points, sheathed in leather, repelling affection. They are not going to like being told that they should become more feminine.'[22] Or that they should hire more women.*

So, while the topic of gender in science and economics is controversial, it does seem fair to make the following empirical statements:

- Greek philosophy as advanced by e.g. Pythagoras, Plato and Aristotle reflected a gender divide, which associated that which is 'real' or material with the female principle and that which is 'virtual' or mental with the male principle.
- Coin money, which spread through Greece around the same time, is made when a virtual (Greek male archetype) symbol is pressed into real (Greek female archetype) material.
- Western science grew out of Greek philosophy, and emphasises 'hard' objectivity (male archetype) over 'soft' subjectivity (female archetype).
- The 'bias toward hard' is especially obvious in economics.
- The field of economics is famous for having a problem with gender bias and sexism.
- The field of economics downplays or ignores the complex properties of money.

---

* In an example of transmutation, McCloskey herself was first hired as a man called Donald, whose gender change related to her break with the 'main (i.e., male,) stream in economics'.

Possibly there is a connection! To be extremely clear, my point is not that the Greek archetypes are right and physics and economics are intrinsically male pursuits. It is that the Greek archetypes have been highly influential; one consequence is that we have a messed-up attitude towards money; economics needs to soften up; and quantum economics is a good way to do it, because it fundamentally challenges the reductionist view of people as the social equivalent of classical atoms and, as we'll see, provides a framework to treat 'hard' objectivity and 'soft' subjectivity as two sides of the same coin.

A defining feature of quantum mechanics, after all, is that it looks 'hard' – it has mechanics in the name! – but the picture that it paints of reality is soft and fuzzy. In many respects it isn't a hard science, it's a soft science. If it had been invented, and its evolution and interpretation been shaped, mostly by women, instead of those young men – if its 'founding fathers', as they are sometimes called, had been 'founding mothers' – we would be calling it the most feminist theory ever. Of course, rather than embrace their feminine side, physicists reacted by adopting a hardcore mathematical approach summed up later by physicist David Mermin in the direction to 'Shut up and calculate!'. In contrast, the social science version counted women and feminists among its first inventors. Danah Zohar, who trained as a physicist, described how her 1990 book *The Quantum Self* was inspired in part by her experience of pregnancy and early motherhood: 'There is something deeply feminine about seeing the self as part of a quantum process.'[23] Or as the social theorist (and trained physicist) Karen Barad put it in her 2007 quantum-queer-feminist (if that's a thing) book *Meeting the Universe Halfway: Quantum Physics and the Entanglement of Matter and Meaning*, 'Existence is not an individual affair. Individuals do not preexist their interactions;

rather, individuals emerge through and as part of their entangled intra-relating.'[24]

Like quantum matter, or what Zohar calls the quantum self, money combines soft subjectivity and hard objectivity, or matter and meaning, in a single package. It excites both shoppers and accountants, but in different ways. The tension between these two aspects is what gives money its intriguing brand of magic. The repression of money in economics, by treating it as little more than an accounting metric, might therefore be viewed as a way of repressing its subjective, touchy-feely, but also strangely stirring aspects in an attempt to make economics look more scientific and objective. It would explain the field's historical and still-lingering attachment to Victorian concepts such as rational economic man. And it also supplies the necessary smokescreen and distraction for money to perform some of its more amazing magic tricks.

Again, a similarly performative emphasis on hard objectivity is seen in other sciences. In 1913 the American psychologist John B. Watson wrote that 'Psychology, as the behaviorist views it, is a purely objective, experimental branch of natural science which needs introspection as little as do the sciences of chemistry and physics … It can dispense with consciousness in a psychological sense.'[25] Mary Midgley wrote that the word 'subjective' has become 'a simple term of abuse directed at any mention of thoughts or feelings, and the word "objective" a potent compliment for any approach which ignores them'.[26] In 2015, Alexander Wendt noted that 'in most of contemporary social science there seems to be a "taboo" on subjectivity', which seems strange given that social relations are surely based largely on subjective factors.[27] Economics, which is ultimately about subjective value, is therefore an extreme case of the same phenomenon. Specialities such as behavioural economics, which bring psychology back into the picture to a degree, can be seen as attempts to make economics seem a little more balanced by adding a few epicycles, while retaining the image of scientificity (see Chapter 7). One reason why the quantum approach is making headway in psychology, sociology, and economics is because it addresses the imbalance head on, and offers a mathematically consistent way not to reduce subjectivity to an exact calculation, but to bring it back into the picture and treat it on an equal footing.

In her 2021 book *Mother of Invention: How Good Ideas Get Ignored in an Economy Built for Men*, the writer Katrine Marçal argues that many useful innovations have failed to catch on because they are deemed 'too feminine' by marketers.[28] A classic example is the wheeled suitcase. The wheel was invented in ancient Mesopotamia around the same time as money; however, the possibility of attaching it to a case went against the whole idea of men showing off their strength by lugging heavy objects around, which is why wheeled suitcases weren't a thing until 1972. As Marçal wrote, 'Gender answers the riddle of why it took 5,000 years for us to put wheels on suitcases.' Perhaps quantum economics is the wheeled suitcase of science.

APOLLO'S MONEY

This book is not about reforming university economics departments, or making them more gender-neutral, which is a task best left to academics. Instead it is about developing a new type of economics which by its nature is likely to be more inclusive (if only because it is hard to be less inclusive than the current version). The gender aspect is important here because it helps to explain the institutional bias against exploring the dualistic real/virtual properties of money, which are at the heart of many economic phenomena, and is consistent with what economists themselves describe as a tendency to emphasise the hard over the soft. Money combines these two qualities in a single package, which as a social technology turns out to be highly productive, but also seems to make a lot of people uneasy – and any approach which favours one side over the other is going to struggle with it. For example, there is the 'surprising unwillingness to engage seriously with other disciplines (especially other social sciences that are seen as "soft")' which, according to economist Jayati Ghosh, 'has greatly impoverished economics'.[29] The hard/soft, objective/subjective dichotomy is at the heart of the quantum approach, and to make progress we need to unwind the Pythagorean associations which hang over the field of economics like an ancient hex. We return to this in Chapter 4.

Like Pythagoras's magical arrow, money has the ability to dart through both space and time. We can borrow money from the future, or transfer it anywhere in the world with the touch of a button. The reason is that money is the ultimate alchemical example of a penetration trick, in which a virtual number penetrates real objects. Which might explain why it is that, as the fourteenth-century abbot Gilles li Muisis put it:

Money and currency are very strange things.
They keep on going up and down and no one knows why;
If you want to win, you lose, however hard you try.

Or in other words, whatever you do with the stuff, you end up feeling screwed. One thing which seems to unite money and gender is that there are no absolute truths, because whatever you say about them, the opposite can also apply. In the next chapter, we show how this sentiment might be expressed in mathematical terms.

CHAPTER 3

TO BE, AND NOT TO BE

*Into the same river we both step and do
not step. We both are and are not.*
HERACLITUS, FRAGMENT 81[1]

*It is impossible for any one to believe the same thing
to be and not to be, as some think Heraclitus says.*
ARISTOTLE, *METAPHYSICS*

Western logic has traditionally been based on the idea that, just as the observed outcome of a coin toss is either heads or tails, so a statement is either true or false, but it can't be a bit of each at the same time. But while this might be true of coins that have already been tossed, it doesn't apply to potential outcomes, or to mental states. The psychic ability to be in two places at the same time, known as bilocation, used to be considered a demonic form of witchcraft. This chapter shows how the similarly magical principle of superposition underlies the difference between quantum and classical probability, and explores what it means for the way we think about both mind and money.

The dislike of duality and contradiction can be traced back again to the Pythagoreans. As we have seen, for them the number one was not just a number: it was a principle, the monad, which represented the singular original state of the cosmos. The dyad, two, was the principle of duality, which led to division and discord. This distrust of the number two fed into their numerology: the odd numbers were associated with the male, the limited, and the right hand, while the evens, which are multiples of two, were associated with the feminine, the unlimited, and the left hand. According to his biographer Iamblichus, Pythagoras asserted that 'the right hand is the principle of what is called the odd number, and is divine; but that the left hand is a symbol of the even number, and of that which is dissolved'.

In one sense at least, the Pythagoreans were right. Subatomic particles come in two types, fermions and bosons, which can be characterised by a quantum quantity known as spin, which describes a property analogous to rotation. The former, which include the basic components of the atom such as electrons and protons, have a spin which is an odd multiple of the lowest spin; the latter, which include force-carrying particles such as the photon, have an even-multiple spin. Fermions obey a rule known as the Pauli exclusion principle, which means that they don't share space with other particles; bosons in contrast are happy to co-exist. The odd-spinned fermions are singular, the even-spinned bosons are diffuse.

Interestingly, a similar odd/even divide appears also in the Chinese list of yin and yang attributes; however, unlike the Pythagoreans, Chinese philosophers saw odd and even as complementary qualities rather than as binary opposites. In other words, it is possible for something to be both odd and even, or singular and dissolved, at the same time. This difference turns out to be important, and in fact is what underpins the field of quantum mathematics.

THE NEW NORM

Now, we all know that quantum mechanics is a deep mystery that can only be understood by a small group of initiates. As the physicist Daniel Greenberger put it in a 1984 talk, 'Quantum mechanics is magic.' He later helpfully clarified that 'It is not black magic, but it is nonetheless magic!'[2] But the time has come to let you into a little secret which has not been widely reported – namely that the key ideas of quantum probability which underlie the theory are actually very simple, and not that magical or perplexing. In fact, they can be illustrated by tossing a coin.

In classical probability, a statement can be either true or false, but not both, just as Aristotle said. If you toss a coin, then the result must be either heads H or tails T. For a fair coin, the probability of either is 50 per cent, or 0.5 in decimal notation. If the coin is biased, then the probabilities might be 0.52 for H and 0.48 for T, but they must always add to 1, since there is a 100 per cent chance that one of the allowed outcomes must be true.

Suppose, though, that we want to picture not the physical process of a coin toss, nor the final observed outcome, but rather the probability of different outcomes, based on what we know about the coin. We could then denote the system, prior to measurement, by using a diagram like the one shown in Figure 3.1. Since there are two possible outcomes, the figure has two axes, which represent heads and tails. The diagonal line has length 1 and represents the probabilistic state of the coin.

The line has been drawn at an angle of 45 degrees to indicate that the coin is equally balanced between heads and tails. If the coin were biased to give heads, then the angle would be smaller, so that the line would lie closer to the horizontal axis. In general, the probability of getting heads is obtained by projecting the state down onto the horizontal axis, as shown by the dashed line, and taking the squared length of the projection H1. Similarly the squared length of the projection T1 is the probability of obtaining tails.

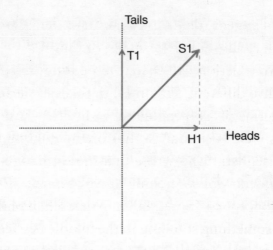

FIGURE 3.1 The propensity of a coin toss to give heads or tails can be represented as a 2D ray S1, which is a balanced superposition of the rays H1 and T1. H1 is obtained by taking the projection down onto the horizontal axis, as shown by the dashed line, while T1 is the projection onto the vertical axis.

This figure intuitively makes sense, but why do we have to take the squares? The reason is that we want the probabilities of obtaining heads or tails to add to 1 – which is equivalent to saying that one or the other has to happen – and by the Pythagorean theorem, the sum of the two squares does equal 1, as expected. In mathematics, the rule for determining the size of some quantity is called the norm. Classical probability uses the so-called 1-norm which is just the magnitude (if the probability is 0.5 then that is the norm). Quantum probability uses the 2-norm, which corresponds to the length of a line in a two-dimensional plane, hence the name.

In quantum physics, the position of a particle is described by a probabilistic wave function which collapses down to a particular number when measured. With a coin toss, the 'wave function' (which is here a single quantum state rather than a wave in time or space) is represented by the initial ambiguous state S1, and a measurement occurs when we observe the outcome, which can be either heads H1 or tails T1.

The wave function can therefore be interpreted as a propensity to give different outcomes, in this case heads or tails. It deals in terms of 'soft' potential rather than just the 'hard' result. This view is similar to that of the quantum physicist Werner Heisenberg, who wrote that the wave function represented 'a tendency for something. It was a quantitative version of the old concept of "potentia" in Aristotelian philosophy. It introduced something standing in the middle between the idea of an event and the actual event, a strange kind of physical reality just in the middle between possibility and reality.'[3]

Because the norm of a probability depends on the square, one could also imagine cases where the probabilities (in the sense of projections onto the axes) were negative. For example, in Figure 3.2 the probability of heads is negative (i.e. the projection H2 is pointing in the negative direction) but the norm of the probability, which is given by the length squared, is unchanged.

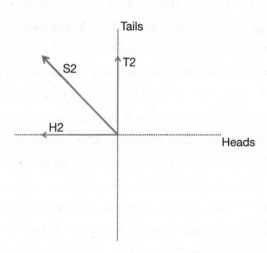

FIGURE 3.2 As for Figure 3.1, but flipped horizontally. The heads component H2 is now negative, but has the same magnitude as H1. The tails component T2 is unchanged from before.

In classical probability, negative probabilities don't make sense: if a forecaster announced a negative 30 per cent chance of rain tomorrow, we would think they were crazy. But a tendency to do something for one reason might be cancelled out by a tendency not to do it for another, and in a 2-norm there is nothing to prevent negative probabilities occurring in an intermediate step. It is only in the final step when we take the magnitude that negative probabilities are forced to become positive.

Finally, if we're going to allow negative numbers, then for mathematical consistency we also need to permit complex numbers, which involve the square root of -1, denoted i. The reason is that when we perform calculations, there are cases where we need to do things like calculate the square root of a probability.* If negative probabilities are permitted, the result can be a complex number; however, the 2-norm of a complex number is a positive number (or zero). Complex numbers therefore play an important role in quantum mechanics; the good news for math-phobes is that we don't need to discuss them further in this book, because they do their work behind the scenes.

To summarise, classical probability is the simplest kind of probability, which is based on the 1-norm and involves positive numbers. The next-simplest kind of probability, which seems a natural choice for describing propensity, uses the 2-norm, and includes complex numbers. This kind of probability is called quantum probability, for the historical reason that it turns out

---

* For example, if the probability of being struck by lightning in one year is one in a million, then the probability of not being struck in any one year is 0.999999. According to probability theory, the chance of going two years in a row is that number squared, which is slightly smaller. However to obtain the probability for six months, we take the square root instead which is slightly larger.

to be the right framework for quantum physics. It is also the basis for the quantum computing industry – and, as we'll see, for quantum economics.

SUPERPOSITION

Before getting on to these applications, though, we should note that one feature of quantum probability is that we can think about the solid line in the above figures as representing a super-position of two states, heads and tails, with the coin's final state only being determined at the time of measurement. Here, measurement again refers to checking whether the coin is heads or tails. So we could think about ways that we could manipulate this state mathematically prior to its being measured.

For example, we could rotate the state a little closer to the H axis, to improve the chances of the coin giving heads, as for a biased coin. Or we could flip it over, as in Figure 3.2, which would give the same final result. In fact, the only requirement is that the transformation must preserve the rule that probabilities will always add to 1, which will be the case if the length of the line is unchanged. (In math-speak, such a transformation is called unitary.)

As an example, suppose that we apply the so-called Hadamard transformation, which rotates the line by 45 degrees clockwise, then flips horizontally (see Figure 3.3). A coin in the superposed state of Figure 3.1 will then be transformed so that it aligns with the H axis, which means that when measured it will be heads for sure. This is like a coin that starts on heads and doesn't get tossed. The indeterminate system has become deterministic.

Another way to think about this is to recall that the initial propensity state is a superposition of two states, denoted H1 and T1 in Figure 3.1. (In standard quantum notation these rays

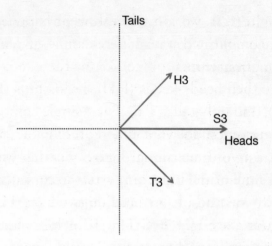

FIGURE 3.3 As for Figure 3.1, but after the Hadamard transformation is applied. The ray H3 can now be viewed as a superposition of horizontal and vertical parts (not shown), and the same for T3; however, the vertical parts now cancel out, leaving only a horizontal ray S3.

would be denoted $|H1\rangle$ and $|T1\rangle$ to distinguish them from numbers, but we will drop the weird brackets.) So let's see what the Hadamard transformation does to each of these in turn. The T1 ray is moved so that it has a positive heads and a negative tails component. However, the H1 ray is moved so that it has a positive heads and a positive tails. So what is happening is that the positive and negative tails parts are cancelling out, leaving only the positive heads parts. This phenomenon is known as interference, and it occurs because quantum probability allows negative probabilities. As computer scientist Scott Aaronson notes, 'cancellation between positive and negative amplitudes can be seen as the source of all "quantum weirdness" – the one thing that makes quantum mechanics different from classical probability theory'.[4] Like a coin or card in a magic trick, probability – in this case, the chance of getting tails – can be made to disappear. We return to this in Chapter 8, where we discuss interference effects of the mental and physical sort.

While we're at it, we can also ask what happens when we have a more complicated system, for example two coins instead of one. The possible final outcomes for the two coins, taken in order, are then heads-heads (HH), heads-tails (HT), tails-heads (TH), and tails-tails (TT). For a single coin, there were only two outcomes, so we could represent the superposed state using a two-dimensional figure, but representing the superposed state of the two-coin system is considerably more complicated – instead of just needing two axes, H and T, we now need four axes: HH, HT, TH, TT. This is hard to draw, because it requires four dimensions. In other words, the quantum model looks simple for a single coin toss, but add even a single extra coin and it quickly becomes difficult, because you have to account for all the possible outcomes. Three coins have eight possible outcomes, and 50 coins have 2^{50} outcomes which is a little over a quadrillion (a million billion). As discussed below, it is exactly this property which gives quantum computers their power.

Returning to the case with two coins, for some situations it may be possible to treat each coin separately, which would allow us to represent it in its own two-dimensional figure. But other cases exist. Suppose, for example, that the coins are somehow linked so that if one is heads, the other must be as well, and the same for tails. This means that the system is in a superposition of HH and TT. In such cases we say that the coins are entangled.

Classical probability has a similar concept known as correlation: we can say that the outcomes for the two coins are completely correlated because if one is heads, or tails, then so is the other. The difference is that in the quantum framework, the state of each coin prior to measurement is a superposition of heads and tails. Entanglement can therefore be viewed as a particular kind of superposed state, which leads to correlations in probabilities when the system is measured.

The rules of quantum probability – which again boil down to a choice of the 2-norm instead of the 1-norm – therefore lead naturally to the related phenomena of superposition, interference, and entanglement, which are characteristic of quantum systems.[5] The trick which makes this possible is that instead of modelling the coin itself, we are modelling the propensity of the coin toss to yield different outcomes, which is not quite the same thing. Quantum economics is what happens when we view the economy in this way, as a probabilistic system, and model it in terms of propensity.

A BIT OF EACH

One reason that quantum mechanics is considered strange and spooky is because of a thought experiment known as Schrödinger's cat.[6] This imagined a cat 'penned up in a steel chamber' along with a tiny amount of radioactive substance, a Geiger counter, and a mechanism to release a poisonous gas if a radioactive particle is detected. Because the release of a radioactive particle is a quantum event, 'The wave function of the entire system would express this by having in it the living and dead cat (pardon the expression) mixed or smeared out in equal parts'. The cat is alive and dead at the same time.

People have long quarrelled over what this experiment means, but for now the main point is that, until measured, a particle can exist in a superposition of different states. Which in classical terms does not compute. The main feature of classical computers, after all, is that they deal in bits, which can be either 0 or 1 but not both at the same time. Such computers run on an Aristotelian operating system. (As we'll see, so does mainstream economics.)

The difference between a quantum computer and a classical one is that it uses qubits instead of bits. And like Schrödinger's hypothetical cat, a qubit exists in a superposed state until the time it is measured. A candidate storage device for a qubit would be a single electron, whose spin (which as mentioned above is a quantum variable) can be measured as either up or down; but there are many other options, such as photons, or charged atoms held in place by an electromagnetic field.

So what does it mean to say that a qubit can be in a super-posed state? This might sound a little mysterious, but really – at the risk of anthropomorphising a computer component – it just means that the qubit is in a Hamlet-like state of to-be-or-not-to-be uncertainty, and is entertaining two different possibilities at the same time. The diagonal line in Figure 3.1 could also be interpreted as a possible propensity state of a qubit, if the horizontal H axis is replaced by 0 (or $|0\rangle$ in official notation), and the vertical T axis by 1 (or $|1\rangle$). When the qubit is measured, the probability of 0 is given by the square of the projection onto the horizontal axis, while the probability of 1 is given by the square of the projection onto the vertical axis.

Quantum computers are enormously difficult and expensive to construct, because qubits are very sensitive to any kind of external perturbation or noise, and are susceptible to what physicists call 'decoherence' due to interaction with the environment, which means that they lose their quantum nature and collapse to 0 or 1, just like a classical bit. Another problem is that a classical bit is inherently tolerant to errors because it is only supposed to have two values, so if it returns a 0.02 then that can be assumed to be a 0, and a 0.98 to be a 1. A qubit can take on any intermediate value, so doesn't have that feature.

So why are governments and companies around the world,

from tiny start-ups to the Googles and the IBMs, investing billions of dollars to build these bothersome devices? (The Chinese state alone has earmarked over $10 billion.) One reason, touched on above, is that their power scales up very quickly as more qubits are added. For example, one classical bit could represent one outcome (heads H or tails T) of a single coin toss. Four bits would therefore represent four particular outcomes in a row, such as HTHT. Four qubits however could represent all possible sequences (HHHH, HHHT, HHTH, etc.), of which there are sixteen, at the same time.

These states would exist in superposition, and only one would be measured at a time, so the system might have to be measured many times to get an accurate distribution. However, the quantum advantage becomes compelling as the number of qubits increases. As we saw in the earlier example, a game with 50 coin tosses would have over a quadrillion possible outcomes, but could be represented by only 50 qubits.

Because the qubits form an entangled system, operations such as changing the states of particular qubits, or adjusting the coupling between them, are equivalent to performing calculations with the overall wave function. The program can therefore take advantage of quantum phenomena such as superposition, interference and entanglement in order to make its calculations. The outcome of a particular simulation is determined by performing an observation, which collapses the state of each qubit down to a single value. Again, this represents only one of the possible outcomes, but by performing many simulations one can determine the probability of different outcomes.

Excitement in the area of quantum computing reached a new level in 2019 when Google announced that the company had achieved 'quantum supremacy' by using a 54-qubit quantum computer to solve a specially contrived problem that classical computers in practical terms cannot. However, twenty years earlier, when such machines were just a twinkle in a computer scientist's eye, scientists were already thinking of ways to play games on them.

THE MAGIC PENNY

Suppose you and I sit down to play a coin game where the rules are as follows:

1. You start by positioning the coin in the heads up state.
2. I can choose to flip the coin or not, without you seeing.
3. You can choose to flip the coin or not, without me seeing.
4. Finally I can choose to flip the coin or not, without you seeing.
5. If the coin ends heads up, then I win, otherwise you win.

As an example game, we start in move 1 with you preparing the coin facing heads up. In move 2, I decide to flip the coin, so I know that it is tails. In move 3, suppose that you make a random decision to not flip the coin, so it is still tails. In move 4, I guess correctly that you did not flip, so choose to flip myself. The coin is then heads up and I win.

This seems to be a rather boring game. Suppose, though, that we play a number of times, and every time I win. After a while you start to get suspicious, because the outcomes should be random, and on average I should only win half the time. The situation would resemble a trick performed by the magician Derren Brown, where he invites an audience member to come on stage, take a coin, conceal it behind their back in one hand, hold both hands out in front of them, and Brown has to guess which one the coin is in. He does this several times in a row, getting it right every time. So what is going on?

In Derren Brown's case, the answer, of course, is that it is magic. For the coin flip game, it is because the coin is a quantum coin, and I am cheating.

Instead of flipping or not flipping the coin, as I am supposed to, I am instead performing the Hadamard transformation, which this time rotates the quantum coin from heads into a superposition of heads and tails. After your move, I then apply the same transformation again, which always restores the coin to heads up. A classical analogy would be that I am putting the coin on its edge. Whether you then flip the coin or not makes no difference, because it will still be on edge. In my final move I then rotate the coin by 90 degrees to put the coin facing heads up.

This game was invented in 1999 by physicist David Meyer. Of course, it is just a simple parlour trick, but it does illustrate the fact that, as he wrote, 'Quantum strategies can be more successful than classical ones'.[7] Indeed, the Hadamard transformation is one of the main logic gates used in quantum algorithms currently being developed for use in areas such as finance, chemistry, database search and so on. An IBM report from 2019, for example, observed that: 'The data modeling capabilities of quantum computers are expected to prove superior in finding patterns, performing classifications, and making predictions that are not possible today because of the challenges of complex data structures.'[8] And as a side-effect, they also promise to change the way that we think about economics.

A QUANTUM OF CREDIT

As an example of an economic application, the diagram below shows a circuit that can be run on a quantum computer. The inputs on the left are two qubits, both initialised in the state 0. The bottom qubit is flipped completely by a so-called NOT gate, denoted B, so that it is in the state 1. The top qubit is acted on by another quantum gate, denoted *A*. This performs a unitary transformation which rotates the qubit into a superposed state where there is a very high, say 95 per cent, probability of observing 1 when the qubit is measured. We can think of it as a coin toss, where the coin is biased to give one result.

The two qubits are then acted on by a 'controlled not' or C-NOT gate. This has the effect of performing the NOT operation on the bottom qubit only when the top qubit is in the state 1. In classical computer programming, one of the most basic constructs is the if-then statement, which carries out a command only if some condition is satisfied. The C-NOT gate does something similar, because *if* the top qubit is 1, *then* the

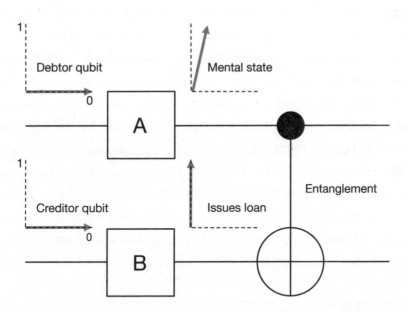

FIGURE 3.4 A two-qubit quantum circuit representing a loan. The first qubit (top line) represents the debtor, the lower qubit (bottom line) represents the creditor who issues the loan. The qubits start in the horizontal position (state 0) and are rotated by the gates *A* and *B* before being entangled. The arrows in the inset figures show the superposition state of the individual qubits prior to entanglement; as in Figure 3.1 they specify the probabilities of outcomes if these qubits were to be individually measured.

bottom qubit will be flipped back to 0; otherwise the bottom qubit will remain unchanged as 1. The difference is that, unlike in a classical computer, the top qubit is here in a superposition of 0 and 1, and so the C-NOT gate acts on each part separately. The net effect is that the two qubits are entangled, because they now form part of a coupled system.

To summarise, the circuit puts the qubits through four steps: initialise (to 0), rotate (superpose), entangle, and measure.

Imagine now that the top qubit is being used to model a person's state of mind with respect to a certain question. A measurement of 0 means 'no' while a measurement of 1 means 'yes'. This means that in the model, the gate A has the effect of changing the person's mind, or more precisely their propensity state. Instead of certainly saying no, they are now, with almost equal certainty, going to say yes.

My reason for choosing this simple circuit is that it can be used to represent a loan. The bottom qubit represents the creditor, with the NOT operation performed by gate B representing the creation of a loan. The top qubit is the debtor, with the rotation performed by gate A representing their mental state in response to the loan creation, i.e. whether they plan to default. After applying these gates, the probabilities of the debtor defaulting, and the creditor collecting, are as follows (note that at this point each gets its own table).

Debtor defaults	Probability
Yes	5
No	95

Creditor collects	Probability
Yes	0
No	100

Obviously there is a problem here because the probabilities do not match. To correct this, we apply the C-NOT gate, which represents the entangling loan contract that binds the two parties together. When the output is measured at the end, the debtor and creditor are now always in the opposite state, because if the debtor defaults then they get to keep the money but the creditor doesn't, and vice versa.

Debtor defaults	Creditor collects	Probability
Yes	Yes	0
No	Yes	95
Yes	No	5
No	No	0

We can also represent the circuit using the table below, which shows the percentage probability of the qubits being in a particular state before and after entanglement. Again there is a 95 per cent chance that the debtor will not default, so the loan is good, and a 5 per cent chance of default, so the loan is bad.

	State after gates A and B	After C-NOT gate (loan)
Top qubit is 0 (Debtor will default)	5	5
Top qubit is 1 (No plan to default)	95	95
Bottom qubit is 0 (Loan status good)	0	95
Bottom qubit is 1 (Loan status bad)	100	5

It is interesting to note the resemblance between the notation for quantum circuits and alchemical symbols. The sign for measurement $\nearrow$ resembles the alchemical symbol for iron ♂. The C-NOT symbol $\oplus$, when inverted, is similar to a female sign ♀ but with a cross in the circle, which is closer to Cinnabar of Antimony $\oplus$, or mercury sulfide. The symbol for Planck's constant, which we will discuss later, is the alchemical symbol for Saturn ♄, which was associated with lead. In the field of quantitative finance, the key parameters used by traders to value financial options are known as 'the Greeks' because they are represented by Greek letters, such as Δ (delta), Γ (gamma), Θ (theta), and so on.* Workers in quantum finance are returning to science's alchemical roots.

Of course, it might seem that there is no point in modelling something so simple using a quantum computer, but as we will see, it already raises some interesting points. One is that the quantum gate A has the effect of coercing the debtor from a state of certain default to a state of near-certain non-default. In a quantum computer, a quantum of energy is required in order to produce such a change in a qubit. Similarly, in the social world it may take a rather large amount of energy – for example, the threat of violence – to convince a person to repay a debt. The creditor must also be convinced that the debtor will repay, which requires information about creditworthiness. The same applies to property rights in general, which are defined by law and enforced by police. The quantum approach will allow us to formulate an expression for this energy and information.

Also, the fact that the debtor is in a superposed state means that we can think about the effects of context on this state. For

---

* Δ is the rate of change between the option price and that of the underlying asset; Γ is the rate of change between Δ and the underlying asset's price (so a second derivative, in math-speak); Θ is the option price rate of change in time.

example, what happens when other people are reneging on their debts, as in the phenomenon of mass default? In Chapter 8 we show how the decision-making process, with all its social entanglements, can be modelled using the same methods.

Finally, as we'll see, this simple quantum circuit captures the dynamics at the core of the financial bomb – and holds the key to its disarming. However, because anything that combines sex, power, magic, and the capacity for destruction will always excite strong reactions, before getting deeper into quantum economics we first need to confront some more taboos, hobgoblins, and other scary creatures which threaten and deter explorers of this territory.

CHAPTER 4

THE VANISH TRICK

Sunlight is said to be the best of disinfectants;
electric light the most efficient policeman.
LOUIS BRANDEIS, OTHER PEOPLE'S MONEY AND
HOW THE BANKERS USE IT, 1914

Above all things our royalty is to be reverenced, and if
you begin to poke about it you cannot reverence it ... Its
mystery is its life. We must not let in daylight upon magic.
WALTER BAGEHOT, THE ENGLISH CONSTITUTION, 1867

Just as the stories a people tell are revealing about a society, so are the ones they don't tell, and that are considered taboo. The fact that money has been sidelined by mainstream economics, and that the act of money creation is treated with the same squeamishness that a fundamentalist might apply to the creation of babies, tells you an awful lot about that field. Before getting on to the subject of how we can fix this, this chapter looks at the barriers and restrictions surrounding the topic of money, with which people like Frederick Soddy long grappled, and which deterred investigation to the point where it and related topics effectively disappeared from economics, in a version of what magicians call the vanish trick.

The political scientist Alexander Wendt cemented his academic reputation in 1999, with the publication of his *Social Theory of International Politics*. It was for this work that he was later (in 2013) named as 'the most influential scholar in international relations over the past 20 years'. And yet soon after writing it, he realised that it was based on a misconception about human nature.

As he wrote in a 2006 'auto-critique' of his book, the social sciences – including his own previous work – were grounded in a classical worldview, or what he calls a false consciousness, which incorporates fundamental basic assumptions: '1) that the elementary units of reality are physical objects (materialism); 2) that larger objects can be reduced to smaller ones (reductionism); 3) that objects behave in law-like ways (determinism); 4) that causation is mechanical and local (mechanism); and 5) that objects exist independent of the subjects who observe them (objectivism?)'.[1]

While this classical worldview has profoundly shaped the models used in social science to understand human behaviour, 'it is usually left unremarked that the models in question – corporate actors as billiard balls, utility as energy, rational actors as computational machines, and so on – are all taken from classical physics, not quantum. Thus, their perceived failure in social science could be one merely of the wrong kind of physics, not of physics per se ... Whether quantum models might do better therefore remains an open question.'

Wendt's interest in quantum theory was sparked when, while browsing a Chicago bookshop, he came across a book called *The Quantum Society* by Danah Zohar and Ian Marshall, which argued that the brain and society are quantum social phenomena. As he told an interviewer, 'the more I followed up on their citations and read about the ideas, the more I became convinced that the argument was true. So I decided that I wanted to write a book for a more academic audience where this would get taken more seriously.'[2] The result, after ten years of work, was his book *Quantum Mind and Social Science: Unifying Physical and Social Ontology*, which, as he admits, has won a lot of attention, including special issues of academic journals devoted to discussing its merits, but so far not any prizes.

To be sure, Wendt is not a typical academic. Most academics attain tenure by playing it safe, and by the time they do get tenure, any impulse to rock the boat has long since atrophied. One common criticism of the quantum approach, usually voiced by tenured academics, is that it is an easy way to get publicity or sell books.[3] Sure, it works for me (joke); but they might reflect on whether their own intellectual outlook has been shaped to any degree by the desire for security, conformity, and a pension, especially if it involves neoclassical economics (really, would anyone *invent* neoclassical economics now, given that we no longer live in the Victorian era?).

When Wendt was invited to give a TEDx talk in 2019, he didn't talk about quantum social science, let alone his first book. The title of his presentation was 'Wanted: A Science of UFOs'. It was based on a paper he had co-authored a decade earlier which he described as 'the only academic article I know of that takes UFOs seriously'.[4] Wendt's point was not that we are being visited by alien spacecraft (he describes his stance as one of 'militant agnosticism'[5]) but that despite numerous credible reports of things that are best described as UFOs, there has never been a systematic, scientific attempt to actually look for them and settle the question – which seemed to say something interesting about science, especially given that the task shouldn't be so hard using modern technology. As he told an interviewer, 'scientists won't touch it with a 10-foot pole. And that's the taboo.'[6] TEDx confirmed this by flagging his talk as falling outside their content guidelines.

His critics no doubt took it all as evidence that he had lost his quantum mind, though not, perhaps, the US Department of Defense, who a year later founded the Unidentified Aerial Phenomena Task Force (backed also by the Senate Select Committee on Intelligence)[7] to investigate the reports of phenomena discussed in Wendt's talk, which show or describe UFOs appearing from nowhere, jumping across space, appearing to change shape, vanishing into thin air, and generally behaving rather like our financial system. In 2021, Barack Obama could muse, without being taken for a crank, that 'there's footage and records of objects in the skies, that we don't know exactly what they are. We can't explain how they moved, their trajectory. They did not have an easily explainable pattern. And so, you know, I think that people still take seriously trying to investigate and figure out what that is.'[8] The *New York Times*, meanwhile, reported that 'the government could not definitively rule out theories that the phenomena observed by military pilots might be alien spacecraft'.[9] Taboos, it seems, can suddenly vanish into thin air too.

Wendt's approach to science, and his desire to retain the beginner's mind, is inspired in part by his love of music – in particular, metal. As he writes on his website: 'orthodoxy is confined to seeking consonance in its music, a perfect meshing of sounds (theories) that will be euphorically received by the people standing in line (the mainstream audience for our work). In music the mind apparently gravitates naturally toward harmony, which is why it's easy to hear metal as mere noise. But in the end, metal is still *music*, and a kind of music that is cognitively challenging precisely because it is dissonant. So making metal is a kind of alchemy, a process of transforming noise into music, or nothing into something. Academics – especially scientists – can probably never hope to pull off that trick. But the experience of metal is an inspiration for me, knowing that somewhere it can be done.'[10]

TURN UP THE VOLUME

It is interesting to compare Wendt's alchemical approach to the questions of harmony, creativity and metal with that of the Pythagoreans, whose philosophy was forged – literally – in their study of the relationship between number and music, and the discovery that musical harmony obeys mathematical laws.

The story goes that Pythagoras was passing a blacksmith's forge and noticed that the tone produced by metal hammers depended on the weight of the hammer. Some hammers, when struck together, produced a pleasing harmony, while other combinations sounded discordant. Investigating further, he discovered that those which sound good together have weights in a simple ratio, such as 1:2. He then applied the same idea to the strings of musical instruments, arguing that two strings, one twice as long as the other, will again differ by an octave. Furthermore, the notes which harmonise together are related by simple mathematical ratios, such as 1:1 (the open string), 1:2 (an octave), 2:3 (a musical fifth), and 3:4 (a fourth). These ratios are encoded in the rows of the Pythagorean tetractys – and, today, in the position of the frets on an electric guitar.

While it is a nice story, the details must be false, since the tone produced by a hammer is not a linear function of its weight. (Newton, who was a great Pythagorean, thought that Pythagoras knew the true relationship but kept it secret, as if following the magician's oath.) However, the correspondence between music and mathematics was certainly essential to the Pythagorean worldview, because the fact that music – considered the most expressive of art forms – could be reduced to simple ratios reinforced their belief that number was the basis for all reality.

According to his biographer Iamblichus, Pythagoras also used music as a kind of therapeutic calming device against 'every aberration of the soul'. On one occasion, walking home from a late-night astronomy session (probably not looking for UFOs), he came across an irate young man. The fellow had been listening to inflammatory music, and had decided to set fire to the house of his girlfriend, who was with another lover. Pythagoras ordered a piper to play some soothing music, and the man immediately calmed down: his fury 'being immediately repressed, he returned home in an orderly manner'. In this fashion, 'Pythagoras through music produced the most beneficial correction of human manners and lives.' He probably would have had a dim view of metal.

Given that Western science grew out of the Pythagorean number-based philosophy, with its calming emphasis on harmony and balance, it is no surprise that science is often viewed by critics as an attempt to impose order on unruly nature. As Aldous Huxley wrote in a 1929 essay, 'It is fear of the labyrinthine flux and complexity of phenomena that has driven men to philosophy, to science, to theology – fear of the complex reality driving them to invent a simpler, more manageable, and, therefore, consoling fiction … With a sigh of relief and a thankful feeling that here at last is their true home, they settle down in their snug metaphysical villa and go to sleep.'[11] He was echoed a year later by Ludwig Wittgenstein, who wrote that: 'Man has to awaken to wonder … Science is a way of sending him to sleep again.'[12]

The tranquillising power of science broke down, however; first with the dissonant findings of quantum science, and then with the development of the nuclear bomb. When the physicist

James Chadwick realised in 1941 that it would happen, 'I had then to start taking sleeping pills. It was the only remedy.'[13] He became a lifelong addict. It was the only way to shut out the noise.

NEGATIVE MAGIC

The word 'taboo', from the Tongan word for prohibited or forbidden, was introduced into English by Captain Cook in his 1784 book *A Voyage to the Pacific Ocean*. It is associated with both the holy and the unclean. It is also associated with the concepts of safety and security, since by making something taboo, the aim is to protect ourselves from what it represents. However, treating a topic as taboo can itself be dangerous, since it removes the possibility for dialogue and exploration.

In his 1890 book *The Golden Bough*, the Scottish anthropologist James George Frazer argued that taboos were a throwback to the Age of Magic. Human belief progressed through three stages: primitive magic was followed by religion, which in turn was followed by science. Each of these stages had its own set of rules and principles, and for magic these were the Law of Similarity and the Law of Contagion. The Law of Similarity was the magic of homeopathy, or of voodoo dolls. The Law of Contagion was based on the idea that the properties of one substance can be transferred to another through contact. Together they could be described as Sympathetic Magic, which was the idea that 'things act on each other at a distance through a secret sympathy, the impulse being transmitted from one to the other by means of what we may conceive as a kind of invisible ether'. In this picture, taboos are a kind of negative magic: 'The aim of positive magic or sorcery is to produce a desired event; the aim of negative magic or taboo is to avoid an undesirable one. But both consequences, the desirable and the undesirable, are supposed to be brought about in accordance with the laws of similarity and contact.'

Today, a topic that seems to be associated with the taboo, and the unclean, is that of the nature of money. For example, as already mentioned, the topic of bank credit creation, which so worried Soddy, has traditionally received little attention in economics. In fact, as economist Richard Werner remarks, the subject 'has been a virtual taboo for the thousands of researchers of the world's central banks during the past half century'.[14] According to economist Norbert Häring, 'Cursory observation suggests that credit creation or money creation are taboo words in the leading journals.' In particular, there is a 'complete absence in all major textbooks of any mention of the pecuniary benefit', which again 'points to a taboo imposed by the interest of a very powerful group'.[15]

According to the late monetary theorist Bernard Lietaer, who studied at MIT with Paul Krugman, 'Krugman told me personally that it was totally crazy to talk about the money issue ... The reason is you will not be invited in the right places and you can kiss goodbye the Nobel or anything else that is worthwhile getting. You're killing yourself academically if you touch the money system.'[16] This might explain why an online video 'masterclass' from Krugman begins by clarifying that 'Economics is, it's about people ... It's not about money.'[17]

As has also been mentioned, this reluctance to discuss money is changing to a degree, as central banks line up to explain how they, or rather private banks, whisk the stuff out of the void; however, money still seems to have been 'written out of the script of modern macro-economics', as Adair Turner notes. Nor does it play much of a role in other social sciences. One might think, for example, that money would be an important topic in the field of international relations. Since money was invented, the right to issue and control a currency has been a basic component of sovereignty. When one state has to use another state's money, that tells you something rather important about their relationship. And one couldn't discuss current power relations between China and the United States without talking about their financial entanglements with each other and with other nations. The financial analyst and author Michael Hudson goes so far as to say that 'The definition of statehood – and hence, international law – should be to put one's national solvency and self-determination above foreign financial attacks.'[18]

Yet with some exceptions, most international relations experts don't seem overly interested in the subject. In 1970, the scholar Susan Strange wrote a paper called 'International Relations and International Economics: A Case of Mutual Neglect' and things haven't changed much (and both fields neglect money).[19] (For their part, economists 'bar the door to outsiders ... we are welcome to try and learn from them, but they cannot see that they have much to learn from us'.[20]) When I was invited to submit a paper to an international relations journal, the first round of reviewers seemed bemused by what one called its 'detour' into the topic of money.[21] In fact, my feeling was that many social scientists distinguished themselves from economists exactly by not being interested in money – unaware, perhaps, that economists don't really cover it either. One reason, perhaps, for the lack of interest is that most social scientists lean left politically, and may see money as a right-wing obsession. As economists Jonathan Nitzan and Shimshon Bichler point out, 'With some obvious exceptions, present-day leftists prefer to avoid "the economy", and many are rather proud about it.'[22]

Money, it seems, is the unidentified flying object of the social sciences. This seems strange, given that the economy, and much of human activity in general, is based on the stuff. So what is the source of this unease? Perhaps we are worried that money was a superior technology granted to us by aliens as a way to speed or shape our development, like the monolith in Arthur C. Clarke's *2001: A Space Odyssey*?

In order to answer this question more seriously, this book will need to discuss a number of connected topics that have been largely avoided by the economics profession, including money creation, gender, subjectivity, and the word 'quantum'. Do you still want to continue? If the answer is yes, then please note:

HIC SUNT DRACONES (HERE BE DRAGONS)

To start with quantum, this has a bad rap, at least when it is applied to anything other than physics. Even Soddy didn't go there – he made key contributions to both quantum physics and economics, but it appears that he didn't try to combine the two. And today, while this too is beginning to change, most self-respecting social scientists are well aware that they should give the word a wide berth – and physicists stand ready to police its use, as anyone who dabbles in the area will soon discover. The physicist Sean Carroll, for example, declared in his portentously titled 2016 book *The Big Picture: On the Origins of Life, Meaning, and the Universe Itself* that 'No theory in the history of science has been more misused and abused by cranks and charlatans – and misunderstood by people struggling in good faith with difficult ideas – than quantum mechanics.'[23] However, the fault for misunderstanding is partly with physicists.

One thing is that many physicists actively dislike some aspects of quantum mechanics, and deal with this dislike by adopting a highly formal and abstract way of presenting the subject. Albert Einstein, for example, wrote in 1924: 'I find the idea quite intolerable that an electron exposed to radiation should choose of its own free will, not only its moment to jump off, but also its direction. In that case, I would rather be a cobbler, or even an employee in a gaming house, than a physicist.'[24] He later commented that the theory reminded him of 'the system of delusions of an exceedingly intelligent paranoiac, concocted of incoherent elements of thoughts',[25] and spent years trying to show it was wrong or incomplete. More recently, the physicist Steven Weinberg said in an interview that quantum mechanics 'has a number of features we find repulsive ... What I don't like about quantum mechanics is that it's a formalism for calculating probabilities that human beings get when they make certain interventions in nature that we call experiments. And a theory should not refer to human beings in its postulates.'[26] (Perhaps, then, it works better as a model of human beings.)

While physicists tend to claim ownership over the interpretation of quantum mathematics, they themselves have never reached a settled interpretation of what it all means. As physicists José Acacio de Barros and Gary Oas note, 'researchers agree with the theory's predictions, but there is substantial disagreement as to what the theory has to say about the physical systems it models. For example, is the theory about what the system actually is (ontological) or about what we can tell about the system (epistemological)?'[27] The notion of wave function collapse seems intuitively obvious in quantum economics, where it refers to a model of price measurement through a transaction, but in physics it leads to all kinds of quandaries, which is why physicists continue to debate it, or come up with alarming alternatives such as the Many Worlds hypothesis where instead of the wave function collapsing, the universe splits off into alternative paths.[28]

Most physicists handle these problems by adopting the 'shut up and calculate' approach mentioned in Chapter 2. When I studied the subject as an undergraduate, I found it odd that concepts such as superposition and entanglement were presented as dry equations rather than as fascinating conjectures about the nature of reality. It made for a particularly striking contrast with the arts courses that I was taking, where we could spend weeks analysing the meaning of a sonnet. (Mathematics in my university could be taken as part of the Arts programme – no hard/soft dichotomising there.)

Physicists also tend to see quantum physics as a special kind of theory, which underpins the nature of reality but at the same time is limited to a very particular domain. This disconnect is illustrated by the explanations for the uninitiated that one frequently comes across, such as this one from a university website: 'It's OK to be a bit baffled by these concepts, since we don't experience them in our day-to-day lives. It's only when you look at the tiniest quantum particles – atoms, electrons, photons and the like – that you see intriguing things like superposition and entanglement.'[29] I have even met physicists who think they *invented* the word entanglement. As we will see, entanglement is the quantum version of Newton's concept of gravitational 'action at a distance' – a mysterious connection (or Sympathetic Magic) that exerts itself across space, and is endowed with a dangerous whiff of the occult.

A side effect of this formal approach is that science is often conflated in the public mind with a particular reductionist viewpoint, as if the quantum revolution never happened. In his 2018 book *Alchemy: The Dark Art and Curious Science of Creating Magic in Brands, Business, and Life*, the marketing expert Rory Sutherland, for example, writes that 'because reductionist logic has proved so reliable in the physical sciences, we now believe it must be applicable everywhere – even in the much messier field of human affairs. The models that dominate all human decision-making today are duly heavy on simplistic logic, and light on magic – a spreadsheet leaves no room for miracles. But what if this approach is wrong? What if in our quest to recreate the certainty of the laws of physics, we are now too eager to impose the same consistency and certainty in fields where it has no place?'[30]

Quantum models might use non-classical logic and emphasise uncertainty, but these attributes are not popularly identified with science. Quantum physicists discovered that the universe was magic, and then somehow made that fact vanish. Part of the trick is to describe any applications of the theory outside physics as reducing to magical thinking.

SOFT SCIENCE

While the highly abstract and formal treatment of quantum phenomena is enough to deter most non-physicists from exploring the area, a related obstacle is our worries about what philosopher Slavoj Žižek called, in a 2002 book, 'New Age obscurantist appropriations of today's "hard" sciences which, in order to legitimize their position, invoke the authority of science itself'.[31] In other words, adopting a quantum approach in the social sciences amounts to a kind of power grab. While quantum economics does sound like physics envy taken to its logical conclusion, I have four remarks.

The first is that many or most people who work in the area have a background in physics, for the simple reason that they have a head start with the mathematical techniques (I am an exception, since while I studied quantum physics at an undergraduate level, my area is applied mathematics). Most of the results we will discuss here have been published in physics journals, rather than social science journals. So physics envy doesn't seem quite the right term.

Secondly, the identification of physics as a 'hard' science comes with some historical baggage. While economists have long benefited from their association with the financial sector, for physicists the sugar daddy has always been the military. Following the Trinity test, as the science historian Daniel J. Kevles observes, 'American physicists became a kind of secular establishment, with the power to influence policy and obtain state resources largely on faith and with an enviable degree of freedom from political control. What brought them to power is, to a considerable degree, what kept them there for most of the last half century – the identification of physics with national security.'[32] One reason why the multibillion-dollar Superconducting Super Collider project, which I worked on for several years, was cancelled in the 1990s was because the research couldn't convincingly be framed as leading to 'an enhancement of our national security', as one senator put it.[33]

If physicists have spent the last century emphasising the 'hard' nature of quantum physics, with its awesome power to build nuclear devices that can destroy the world many times over, then it is unsurprising that they are upset to see social scientists applying the same ideas to something as soft and cuddly as human relations (cultural appropriation of the worst kind). However, while in some ways quantum mechanics is a prime example of a 'hard' science, as already discussed in Chapter 2, an interesting thing about it is that it points always towards the 'soft'. A quantum wave equation, when written out in mathematical symbols, looks as hard as they come. But it's an equation of a wave, which is soft. The same could be said of features such as superposition, interference, or entanglement. Could our resistance to quantum ideas have something to do with these soft properties as well – and the tendency noted by Akerlof for economics to 'favor the "hard" and disfavor the "soft"'? And could this explain the constant refrain from physicists that quantum physics – which, again, was developed mostly by young men – is fundamentally incomprehensible to those outside the brotherhood? Yes, the mechanics get tricky when applied to physical systems – and subatomic particles *are* weird – but as seen in the previous chapter, the core mathematical ideas aren't so bizarre or difficult.

The third point is that social scientists have always based their models on physics – it was just the wrong sort. An example is the area of quantitative finance, which as discussed later was developed in part by the many nuclear physicists who switched to finance after the war. However, while there is no shortage of model abuse in economics, physics envy is not the main problem. Instead it is institutional pressures that encourage the use of models that look good based on the aesthetic criteria of mechanistic science but have so many parameters and moving parts that they can give any answer you want. This is why economist Paul Romer, in a 2016 paper called 'The trouble with macroeconomics', described that field as a pseudoscience (he was later awarded the Nobel Memorial Prize, but not for that paper).[34]

If we are going to discuss how physics-based models have been 'misused and abused' in the social sciences, to use Carroll's phrase, then the place to start is not with quantum models, but with what quantitative analyst Paul Wilmott and I called the 'industrial-scale abuse of mathematical models' by the financial sector that led to the crisis of 2007/8.[35] (Anyway, I always thought the greatest abuse of quantum models was by physicists when they built the bomb, and the bomb after that, and all the many other bombs which followed.)

Finally, there is no need for social scientists to claim any direct connection with physics, because quantum models are mathematical tools. This is a somewhat subtle point because it can be argued that the fact that the universe is quantum suggests that, ultimately, social interactions are quantum too. But when physicists first adapted mathematical techniques to model quantum phenomena, they were really just taking things off the shelf to see what worked.* There is no a priori reason, just because we live in a quantum universe, to believe that those mathematical techniques will work at the social level as well, or that a model of say option pricing should be based on quantum methods; but at the same time, there is nothing to stop social scientists using a 2-norm rather than a 1-norm in their equations, especially since they are dealing with things like the exchange of information rather than the trajectories of cannon balls. The test is whether such methods outperform classical ones.

Physicists themselves seem a bit confused about this, and exhibit a Platonic tendency to equate their aesthetically beautiful models with reality. I wrote about this in my 2012 book *Truth or Beauty*, where I predicted (somewhat riskily at the time) that elegant creations such as supersymmetric string theory would never be experimentally confirmed, and (much more riskily) that 'dark matter' might be an artefact due to model error (apparently a taboo in physics circles).[36] So while physicists may be the go-to experts on most things quantum, mathematical models are neither identical to nor tethered to

---

* As Richard Feynman said of Schrödinger's wave equation, 'Where did we get that from? It's not possible to derive it from anything you know. It came out of the mind of Schrödinger.' (*The Feynman Lectures on Physics*, 1964.) At the same time, though, it was a standard differential equation.

a unique physical application, and social scientists can have a turn at them too. They just need to prove that they work. That isn't magical thinking – it's the opposite. We return to this in Chapter 9 for the question of entanglement.

SPOOKY

One problem with a taboo-busting approach, obviously, is that there is little point in developing new theories if no one is willing to put them into practice. And as one central bank economist advised a colleague, 'if you're trying to convince mainstream economists that your ideas have merit then be careful to make the connection with the existing literature in the top econ journals. Orthodox economists spook easily at new ideas.'

It certainly seems reasonable that, in order to make progress, people should be conciliatory and go through the proper channels. Authors in quantum finance and economics tend to publish instead in those physics journals which tolerate excursions into the social sciences, such as the rather non-economics-sounding *Physica A: Statistical Mechanics and its Applications*.[37] The only specifically economics-related venues I have published in (several times) are *Economic Thought*, and *Wilmott* magazine. The former, which is run by the World Economic Association, is about as non-orthodox as they come, and was set up after the financial crisis with the specific aim of addressing the shortcomings in mainstream economics. (Its co-founder, Edward Fullbrook, complained of receiving 'hate mail, some of it quite nasty' from neoclassical economists, which is usually a sign that you're on the right track.[38]) The latter is a specialist mathematical publication, aimed at people in quantitative finance, which *Esquire* called the most expensive magazine in the world. (The overlap of contributors, or for that matter readers, for these publications is quite small – in fact I may be it.)

However, the idea that 'top econ journals' (to use the central banker's phrase) are the impartial and unbiased adjudicators of scientific credibility is wearing a little thin. As the hetero-dox economist Steve Keen wrote in 2019, 'The "top journals" remain impenetrable to any approach which is not rooted in Neoclassical equilibrium thinking', which would rule out a quantum approach, for one.[39] And while economics was once considered to be the queen of the social sciences because of its apparent emphasis on mathematics and academic rigour, today it sounds like an abusive but increasingly insecure and irrele-vant tyrant, occupied more by controlling transgressions and enforcing taboos than by the task of making genuine progress.

In a 2020 blog post – described by an Institute for New Economic Thinking piece as 'a cri de coeur, a protest, and a warning' – the economist Claudia Sahm, who was formerly a section chief at the Federal Reserve, noted that elite university departments and the journals they run 'are the gatekeepers of the economics profession ... They decide what is cutting-edge research.'[40] However, these elites 'punch down and attack those with opinions different than theirs'. The resulting 'lack of diversity and inclusion degrades our knowledge and policy advice. We hurt economists from undergraduate classrooms to offices at the White House. We drive away talent; we mis-treat those who stay; and we tolerate bad behavior ... Everyone who is privileged enough to hold a PhD in economics should reflect on our toxic culture.' The Chilean physicist César A. Hidalgo, whose work at MIT in complexity economics I cited in *Quantum Economics*, echoed Sahm in 2021 when he described 'an academic world of exclusion, fear, and deception' in which 'toxicity consumes the minds of younger students'.[41] A 2015 investigation of the economics department at the University of Manitoba called it simply 'a toxic tyranny of the majority'.[42]

Places obviously vary, but it all sounds like possibly not the best atmosphere in which to foster new thinking, engage with current developments, and generally keep up with the times – which might explain why in 2018 one UK economics student could report in *Nature*: 'I went to university and was stunned by the irrelevance of what I was being taught.'[43] Quantum economics in particular is a genuinely new paradigm, which is based on a completely different form of probability and logic, so for mainstream economists, adopting it would be like throwing out their sacred texts and learning a new language from scratch all at the same time – better to ignore it.

The idea that 'orthodox economists spook easily at new ideas' is therefore not quite right. It would be more accurate to say that they don't even notice new ideas. And you can't be spooked by a ghost if it is invisible.

THE QUANTUM TABOO

While, as I reported in my book *Economyths*, many heterodox economists, who make up maybe 10 to 15 per cent of the profession, have long been pushing for change, most don't see the need for any radical shift in direction, and some will resist it strongly.* As former central banker William White said in a 2014 interview, the 2007/8 crisis barely made a dent: 'Far from thinking, gee wiz we have to think this through from the

---

* One reviewer said of that book that it 'Must be good as I've had hate mails from economists for writing a positive review of it'. Charges against me include behaving like 'climate change deniers' and propagating 'conspiracy theory', though not, so far, witchcraft or consorting with the devil.

basics, it's just more of the same.'[44] A number of 'rebuilding' or 'rethinking' initiatives did emerge, but as discussed later, these were often more about retouching (an exception is the student-led Rethinking Economics organisation).[45] It was something of an understatement when doctoral student Devika Dutt reported in 2020 (after receiving the obligatory 'torrent of abuse' including 'hate mail, and a death threat' for an article questioning the latest Nobel Memorial Prize award to two old-white-rich-male economists for their work on game theory) that 'Economics is, contrary to the apparent perception of many economists, very resistant to change'.[46] Indeed, it is remarkable how neo-Aristotelian ideas about equilibrium have managed to persist as long as they have, and how the field remains resistant or impervious to both criticism and new ideas. For a profession which celebrates innovation in the economy, it isn't very good at producing it itself.

This points to an array of highly conservative forces, but I would suggest that the most powerful is the field's attitude towards money. On the one hand, mainstream economists downplay or ignore this substance whose complex properties elude their reductionist models. On the other hand, the field prizes its well-paid role as cheerleader for the financial sector, which is happy to keep money out of the picture.[47] After all, if markets are efficient, then companies such as Goldman Sachs are doing 'God's work' as then-CEO Lloyd Blankfein said in 2009.[48] (As a small demonstration of the power of said sector, firms including Goldman, the high-frequency trading outfit Citadel, and a range of banks paid Janet Yellen $7.3 million in speaking fees in the two years prior to her nomination as US Treasury Secretary, where her tasks include ... overseeing the regulation of banks.[49]) 'Were the quantum metaphor to be imported into economics,' speculated the scholar Philip

Mirowski in 1989, 'it would precipitate mistrust and perhaps full dissolution of the vaunted neutrality of the economic scientist with respect to the social object of his research, and hence force consideration of the interaction of the economist with the pecuniary phenomenon.'[50] If quantum models and approaches are adopted it might get even more interesting.

The perilously insecure and divided state of mainstream economics can be considered as both a problem and an opportunity for quantum economics. Mainstream economists are not going to rush out and embrace quantum ideas – but it is becoming increasingly obvious that economics is incapable of reforming itself, so change can only come from outside anyway. (This is true of other areas: as the ecologist Allan Savory noted, breakthroughs nearly always come not from the centre of a profession, but from the fringe: 'The finest candlemakers in the world couldn't even think of electric lights.'[51]) And none of these mainstream ideas or models, with their emphasis on classical logic, equilibrium, and independence, will survive contact with quantum computers, which work in terms of superposition, interference, and entanglement. Viewed this way, the stasis in economics is related to the quantum taboo. As Fullbrook pointed out in a 2012 article, the quantum approach in physics is inherently pluralistic, because it incorporates uncertainty and is open to different interpretations.[52] If quantum ideas had been adopted earlier by the social sciences, say a hundred years ago, economics would look very different today – and economists wouldn't react to every irritation by sticking another pin in their voodoo doll.[53] One effect of quantising economics will be to attract smart and creative people who have been dissuaded from entering the field by its adherence to an antiquated philosophy.

So no, quantum economics won't be progressing through the proper channels, at least by the standards of economics.

Instead it is forging new paths, and none of them start from neoclassical assumptions because those routes don't exist. While quantum economics is still a minority pursuit – you probably won't have much luck trying to find a university course in it, though it is sneaking into the curriculum in some select places[54] – it is also a growing one, as shown by Figure 4.1. It is too soon to tell whether it's a sign of a significant cultural shift, and I can't speak for quality, but one thing seems clear: the quantum taboo is finally lifting.

Quantum cognition and quantum social science are getting closer to critical mass in terms of journal publications and conference panels. Wendt and colleagues received a grant from the Carnegie Foundation to host a series of 'quantum boot-camps' for social scientists. These are held at The Ohio State University's Mershon Center for International Security Studies,

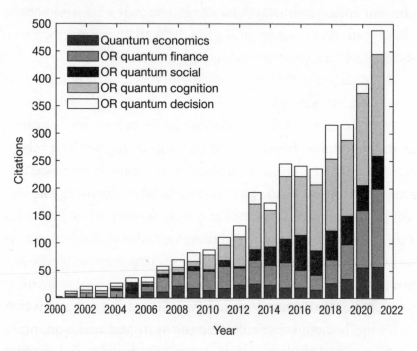

FIGURE 4.1 Plot of Google Scholar citations over two decades using related search terms. The data for 2021 is projected from August.

and taught by an eclectic group whose specialities include philosophy, psychology, physics, political science, and applied mathematics (I present a section on quantum economics).[55] The phrases 'quantum social scientist' and 'quantum economist' have been used in a non-ironic way, which is something of a milestone.[56] And one group which certainly sees potential in quantum ideas is the specialist area of quantitative finance – as evidenced in 2020, for example, by the *Financial Times* headline: 'Wall Street banks ramp up research into quantum finance'. You might not be able to get a degree in quantum finance, but jobs are available in financial centres around the world. As seen in Chapter 11, the reasons have less to do with economic theories or quantum physics than with the advent of quantum computers, for which quantum algorithms are native. The financial sector may continue to pay economists to recite familiar incantations and blessings about the invisible hand, efficient markets, supply and demand, and so on, but the models they rely on will increasingly be quantum.

MAGICAL REALISM

To sum up, quantum economics by its nature broaches a range of difficult subjects that are often treated in science as taboo, including money, consciousness, gender, quantum reality, and even religion (we'll save that one for a later chapter). The reason for its transgressions is that it deals with phenomena which defy conventional reason and therefore appear magical. At the same time, these taboos seem rather strange, given that the one thing any child knows about the economy is that it involves money; the one thing any child knows about the universe is that he or she is a conscious participant in it; and while quantum ideas may not be child's play, they also happen to be our best description of how the universe works, and furthermore have been around for over a century so we should be getting used to them.

Physicists have long played up the idea that quantum behaviour is weird and somehow alien. Commonly attributed quotes include the observations that quantum mechanics is 'fundamentally incomprehensible' (Niels Bohr); 'If you think you understand quantum mechanics, you don't understand quantum mechanics' (Richard Feynman); 'You don't understand quantum mechanics, you just get used to it' (John von Neumann). But it is easy to imagine those men (and they do always seem to be men) saying the same thing about their spouses, or even their pets: 'No one truly understands George, my tabby cat. He is a mystery even unto himself.' As Žižek also observed (in 2012): 'A fact rarely noticed is that the propositions of quantum physics which defy our common-sense view of material reality strangely echo another domain, that of language, of the symbolic order – it is as if quantum processes are closer to the universe of language than anything one finds in "nature;" as if, in the quantum universe, the human spirit encounters itself outside itself' (researchers in the field of quantum natural language processing would agree).[57]

And again, quantum mechanics is not reality, it is a mathematical model of reality. Yes, its predictive track record in the realm of subatomic particles is impressive, but the theory still has a few wrinkles, such as incompatibility with general relativity, which is why physicists continue to look for new ones. Many of the tools were developed independently by mathematicians. And what the university website called 'intriguing things like superposition and entanglement' are part of our everyday reality. In fact, Bohr's idea of superposition and complementarity was borrowed from the late nineteenth-century philosopher and psychologist William James, who had remarked on the human ability to hold conflicting ideas in our heads at the same time.[58] We went from explicitly basing concepts on human behaviour, to denying that there could be any connection.

Perhaps the main reason why topics such as quantum theory, consciousness, and money are unsettling is because they all deprive us, in related ways, of our view of the world, long cultivated in science, as a machine that can be understood objectively. Quantum reality is magical, but so is social reality, and it is up to the modeller to decide which mathematical framework to adopt. Indeed, it is remarkable that the use of quantum ideas outside of physics has been repressed for so long. It is as if a UFO landed in downtown Manhattan and everyone looked away.

The reason this chapter is called 'The Vanish Trick' is because in economics the net result – and the purpose – of these restrictions and taboos is that, as seen in the next chapter, money and associated subjects such as its relationship with power have been effectively ignored. Like dark matter, money has been rendered invisible, as if by a magical invisibility cloak. Neoclassical economists have managed to make it go away. Yet its gravitational pull over the economy is as strong as ever. And the invisibility cloak isn't real, it is just a form of model error.

So, if you still want to continue, these are a few of the scary hobgoblins and fearsome monsters that surround quantum economics. Let's ignore their chattering for a while and get on with the question of how to safely defuse and disarm the ticking device that we have created, called the world economy. We start in the next chapter by contemplating the fissionable material that makes up the core of the money bomb.

CHAPTER 5

ATOMIC MONEY

The modern banking system manufactures 'money' out of nothing; and the process is perhaps the most astounding piece of 'sleight of hand' that was ever invented.
MAJOR L.L.B. ANGAS, 'SLUMP AHEAD IN BONDS', 1937

Most transformation programs satisfy themselves with shifting the same old furniture about in the same old room. Some seek to throw some of the furniture away. But real transformation requires that we redesign the room itself. Perhaps even blow up the old room. It requires that we change the thinking behind our thinking.
DANAH ZOHAR, *REWIRING THE CORPORATE BRAIN*, 1997[1]

Nuclear weapons obtain their power from highly radioactive materials such as plutonium, which is produced in government labs from uranium. The financial system obtains its power from another fissile substance, known as money. This chapter explores the alchemical process of money creation, using the paradigmatic examples of a medieval tally stick and an ancient coin; shows how the technology to refine this material has changed over the ages; and reveals why, as with atomic sorcery, the monetary sort has long been linked with the military.

At 5.30 a.m. on Monday 16 July 1945, the sky over the Jornada del Muerto (Journey of Death) desert in New Mexico lit up in a massive explosion, in the world's first test of a nuclear device.

The Trinity test, as it was called, was witnessed by scientists and observers from a camp ten miles away. In the official report on the test, the project's supervisor General Thomas Farrell described what he saw: 'The effects could well be called unprecedented, magnificent, beautiful, stupendous and terrifying. No man-made phenomenon of such tremendous power had ever occurred before. The lighting effects beggared description. The whole country was lighted by a searing light with the intensity many times that of the midday sun ... Thirty seconds after the explosion came first, the air blast pressing hard against the people and things, to be followed almost immediately by the strong, sustained, awesome roar which warned of doomsday and made us feel that we puny things were blasphemous to dare tamper with the forces heretofore reserved to The Almighty.'[2]

The *New York Times* journalist William Laurence described how the delighted scientists 'clapped their hands as they leaped from the ground – earth-bound man symbolizing a new birth in freedom – the birth of a new force that for the first time gives man means to free himself from the gravitational pull of the earth that holds him down'.[3] But as with the different visions of Soddy and Wells, not everyone saw it so positively; the test site director Kenneth Bainbridge said, 'Well, we're all sons of bitches now.'[4]

The Trinity test showed the world that quantum forces, which before had been thought to concern only the subatomic world, could scale up to affect our lives. The path from the discovery of nuclear fission to the testing of the atomic bomb had been remarkably fast. The uncharged particle known as the neutron, which along with the positively charged proton makes up the nucleus of atoms, had only been discovered by the British scientist James Chadwick in 1932. In 1938, experiments by the German scientists Otto Hahn and Fritz Strassmann showed that bombarding uranium with a beam of neutrons could cause the unstable atoms to split in half. This would convert some of their mass into energy, and also release new neutrons which could in turn collide with neighbouring atoms. 'What idiots we have all been!' exclaimed the quantum physicist Niels Bohr on hearing of the results. 'Oh but this is wonderful! This is just as it must be!'[5]

The nuclear chain reaction was demonstrated in a small experiment led by the Hungarian refugee physicist Leó Szilárd at Columbia University (he had already come up with the idea in 1933, and patented a design for a nuclear fission reactor in 1934). He showed that if the quantity of material present was above a certain critical mass, which for uranium-235 turned out to be just a few kilograms, the result would be a self-sustaining chain reaction that grew at an exponential rate. The process could be the basis for a nuclear fission reactor – or alternatively, it being 1939, a bomb. The moment he saw the experiment had worked, 'there was very little doubt in my mind that the world was headed for grief'.[6]

Szilárd's sense of urgency was compounded when he heard that the German army occupying Czechoslovakia had blocked all exports from the uranium mines in Joachimsthal. He asked his famous friend Albert Einstein to help, and composed a letter to President Roosevelt, which Einstein agreed to sign, warning that 'extremely powerful bombs of a new type may thus be constructed'.[7]

The letter initially had little effect, but in December 1941 the Japanese attacked Pearl Harbor, bringing America into the war. The Manhattan Project to develop a workable bomb started in earnest soon afterwards, and culminated with the Trinity test and, just three weeks later, the first use of the weapon against Japan on 6 August 1945.

When it came to reporting on the horror of that event, the professional witnesses suddenly seemed to lose their capacity for vivid and accurate description. 'NO RADIOACTIVITY IN HIROSHIMA RUIN' was the headline to Laurence's *New York Times* piece about the explosion on 12 September, in which it was reported that General Farrell 'denied categorically that it produced a dangerous, lingering radioactivity'.

Since then, the energy from the atom has also been put to less destructive uses. Fission reactors provide peaceful nuclear energy. Fusion reactors, which create energy by combining atoms rather than splitting them apart, are in development. We have learned how to exploit the quantum power of the atom in a different way, through information technology. In fact, it has been estimated that some 30 per cent of the United States' gross domestic product can be traced to devices such as microchips, GPS, lasers and so on which exploit quantum effects.[8] And then there is the race by companies and governments to develop quantum computers, which are explicitly based on quantum logic.

One of Niels Bohr's contributions to quantum theory was his correspondence principle, which states that classical physics and quantum physics should give the same answer when the systems become large. In other words, quantum effects may be important at subatomic scales, but they wash out at large scales. But quantum technologies are explicitly designed to scale up, and atom bombs don't wash out. This is seen also with that other quantum technology known as the money system.

MINING FOR DOLLARS

Joachimsthal is now a spa destination. In the late Middle Ages, however, it was more of a mining town. Its products included silver, and another substance, used by local glassmakers for its beautiful fluorescent glow, which was called *Pechblende*, from *Pech*, for bad luck, and *Blende*, meaning mineral.

Silver minted from the area was known as 'thaler', from a shortened version of the town's name, and coins minted from the silver were thalers. This became pronounced as 'dollars' – and spread around the world, most famously to the United States, as a name for money. In 1789, meanwhile, the chemist Martin Klaproth found that Pechblende contained a metallic substance that he called uranium, after the recently discovered planet Uranus (and the Greek god of the sky).

As we'll see, money is the social version of uranium. It is a store of massive quantities of energy – and its powers were first exploited to their fullest by the military.

Money is usually presented in economics textbooks as an inert substance that emerged naturally as a means of exchange. One Canadian textbook, for example, informs us that: 'If there were no money, goods would have to be exchanged by barter ... The use of money as a medium of exchange solves this problem ... All sorts of commodities have been used as money at one time or another, but gold and silver proved to have great advantages ... The invention of coinage eliminated the need to weigh the metal at each transaction, but it created an important role for an authority, usually a king or queen, who made the coins and affixed his or her seal, guaranteeing the amount of precious metal that the coin contained.'[9]

Similar accounts have been provided throughout history: by Paul Samuelson in his *Economics*; by nineteenth-century neo-classical economists Carl Menger and William Stanley Jevons; by Adam Smith in the eighteenth century; and so on. In fact, the story can be traced all the way back to Aristotle, who wrote in *Politics* that the 'more complex form of exchange [money] grew, as might have been inferred, out of the simpler [barter] ...

113

the various necessaries of life are not easily carried about, and hence men agreed to employ in their dealings with each other something which was intrinsically useful and easily applicable to the purposes of life, for example, iron, silver, and the like. Of this the value was at first measured simply by size and weight, but in process of time they put a stamp upon it, to save the trouble of weighing and to mark the value.'

While the story has remained remarkably constant over the centuries, it is not based on empirical evidence. In fact, as anthropologists have long pointed out, economies based purely on barter don't appear to ever have existed.[10] Instead, money has its roots in a virtual credit system created 5,000 years ago in ancient Mesopotamia, where debts were recorded on clay tablets in cuneiform. Amounts were specified in terms of shekels, which referred to a weight of silver; however, the silver itself did not usually change hands.

The first coins date to the seventh century BC, in the nearby kingdom of Lydia, and the idea quickly spread, first to the Greek cities of coastal Asia Minor, and from there to the mainland and surrounding islands. By the time of Pythagoras in the sixth century BC, most Greek city-states were producing their own coins as a sign of their independence. Since then, power over the money supply, and the right to dictate what is legal tender, have been defining attributes of statehood. The ancient Romans, for example, projected power over distant colonies through the images of emperors that adorned their coins.

Indeed, the main motivation for the spread of coin money appears to have had less to do with the needs of the market – which historian Michael Crawford calls an 'accidental consequence of the coinage' – than with those of the military.[11] Money had found its killer app, and it was war.

Coinage was introduced at a time when the largest expense of Greek rulers was the mobilisation of huge armies. Coins served as a device for payment, but also as a tool to both motivate the troops and control the general public. Soldiers and mercenaries were paid using metal that was mined or plundered; they spent the money on things like food and supplies; and the state then demanded some of the coins back as taxes. The fact that the general public had to get their hands on money in order to pay taxes, for example by feeding or housing soldiers, solved the logistical problem of how to maintain the army.

The system was perfected by Aristotle's former student, Alexander the Great. During his conquest of the Persian Empire, salaries for his army of over 100,000 soldiers amounted to about half a ton of silver per day. The silver was obtained largely from Persian mines, with the labour supplied by war captives, and was formed into Alexander's own coins. He would go on to invade the Babylonian empire in Mesopotamia, where he wiped out the existing credit system and insisted that taxes be paid in his own coins. Rather than emerging naturally from barter, the money system was a designed social technology that was imposed at the sharp end of a sword, and in many respects was an expression of power.

AN INSIGNIFICANT THING

Of course, just as nuclear power can be put to creative or destructive uses, so the money system is useful for many things other than running the military or invading countries, and the spread of coin money around the globe coincided with a cultural blossoming in art, philosophy, literature, architecture, astronomy, mathematics, democracy and, above all, commerce. Money has done more to shape human civilisation than possibly any other invention. It is therefore interesting that we seem to know so little about it, and treat it as if it were nothing more than a neutral medium of exchange. Which is rather like saying that uranium is just a fancy rock.

The two main theories of money are bullionism and chartalism. The first states that money only has value when it is backed by precious metal like gold or silver, the second that money gets its value because it represents government debt (as in Modern Monetary Theory). As the Austrian economist Joseph Schumpeter noted, the debate between 'the two fundamental theories of money' goes back to ancient Greece, when Aristotle argued that money needed to be a valuable commodity in itself, while Plato saw it as a symbol.[12] Each theory reduces money down to a single dimension, to metal that can be physically possessed, or an abstract rational calculation on a ledger.

Bullionists and chartalists are like two rival schools of magic, who regularly try to expose each other as fakes and frauds. There is also a third approach – which usually goes unstated, but with which most mainstream economists would agree – that pretends to be above all the petty bickering and has been even more influential than the other two, even though it is actually the strangest theory of all. This says that money has no unique or special qualities, but instead is defined by its roles, e.g. as a medium of exchange. Samuelson, for example, defined money as *anything that serves as a commonly accepted medium of exchange* (his emphasis).[13] In this picture, as one economist quipped, 'you could use chickens as money', as long as people are ready to accept them as payment.[14] The two sides of money – commodity and symbol – collapse down to an inert chip.

So what does this chip represent? Adam Smith, who is usually considered to be the founding father of economics, followed the bullionist approach in asserting that the value of money was determined only by its weight in precious metal, with the numerical stamp playing no role other than proof of inspection. However, he defined the exchange value of a good, not in terms of money, but as 'the quantity of labour which it enables [a person] to purchase or command'. Just as the mass in uranium can be converted to energy, so a mass of metal is equivalent to the energy-like quantity of work. (Later, as we'll see, the presumed source of this value switched from labour to utility, but this made little difference in practice.)

In a market economy, this value would be discovered by the market's 'invisible hand', which was the centrepiece of Smith's theory. There was furthermore a distinction to be made between what Smith called the 'real' and 'nominal' prices of goods. Like any other commodity, the cost of gold or silver depended on the labour needed to produce it, which in turn depended on factors such as the 'fertility or barrenness' of mines. An excess of money therefore translated into higher nominal prices. But the role of the economist was to focus on real prices, which stripped out the distracting effects of what Irving Fisher later called 'the money illusion'. Smith therefore interpreted the economy in terms of ideas such as the division of labour and the mechanics of exchange, rather than of money, which with a wave of his magic wand vanished in a puff of smoke.

This is why the economist John Stuart Mill could write in his 1848 *Principles of Political Economy*, which served as a standard text for over 60 years, that 'There cannot, in short, be intrinsically a more insignificant thing, in the economy of society, than money'. Or why Paul Samuelson, whose *Economics* was the bestselling textbook in the second half of the twentieth century, could write that trade 'largely boils down to barter'. Or why central bankers could point out in speeches, ten years after the financial crisis, that the mainstream models hadn't included money or the financial sector.

KEEPING TALLY

While mainstream economists treat money as an inert substance, or a metric for accounts, it is better described as a powerful and transformative technology. And as with uranium, this power is created by quantum processes.

The real/virtual nature of money is perhaps best illustrated by the way in which throughout history it has presented as either a real thing or a virtual number, alternating between one and the other on a timescale measured in centuries, while always retaining the qualities of both.[15] Money was born as a virtual accounting system in ancient Mesopotamia, when debts were inscribed on clay tablets, as described above. It switched to metal coins in ancient Greece and Rome, before reverting to a mostly virtual credit system in the early Middle Ages. The discovery of massive quantities of silver and gold in the New World kick-started what eventually became the international gold standard, and this lasted in one form or another until the rise of virtual fiat currencies in the last half-century.

The paradigmatic, and longest-lasting, example of a virtual credit system was the payment system introduced around 1100 by King Henry I of England. This was similar in principle to ancient cuneiform tablets, with the difference that it was based on wooden sticks called tallies. These were sticks of polished hazel or willow wood that were notched to indicate the value of a debt, as described in a twelfth-century treatise called *The Dialogue Concerning the Exchequer*: 'At the top of the tally a cut is made, the thickness of the palm of the hand, to represent a thousand pounds; then a hundred pounds by a cut the breadth of a thumb; twenty pounds, the breadth of the little finger; a single pound, the width of a swollen barleycorn; a shilling rather narrower; then a penny is marked by a single cut without removing any wood.'

The tally was then split lengthwise down the middle so that each side carried a matching record of the amount. The creditor kept one part, known as the stock, which was slightly longer, while the debtor got the shorter stub. When the debt was retired, the two parts were compared, with the grain of the wood acting as a proof against counterfeiting, and the tally destroyed.

The tallies were used by the Exchequer as a tool for collecting taxes for some seven centuries, but they also circulated as a form of money in their own right. For example, suppose the state held a stock representing a debt owed to it by a landowner. Then rather than wait for the landowner to pay up, it could use the stock to pay a supplier, perhaps at a small discount. The supplier could then collect later from the landowner, or could sell the stock to a broker who would collect the debt when it came due. A similar system also existed in China, with the difference that the tallies were made of bamboo.

Tallies were referred to in the Napoleonic Code of 1804 – 'Tallies correlative to their patterns afford proof between parties who are in the habit of thus verifying commissions which they make and receive in retail' – and in England remained in use until 1826. However, they had fallen from favour as coin money made a comeback in the fifteenth century, courtesy of New World gold and silver, and took another hit after the founding of the Bank of England in 1694 – tallies were actually used to buy some of the initial stock of the Bank. In 1834 the final sticks were gathered together so that they could be disposed of. Casting around for a suitable location, notes the UK Parliament website, 'the Clerk of Works thought that the two underfloor stoves in the basement of the House of Lords would be a safe and proper place to do so.'[16]

I'm sure that many readers will be able to think of some episode from their own lives where it turned out to be less than wise to leave a collection of highly flammable burning objects unattended. In this case, the resulting 'Great Fire of 1834' burned down the palace of Westminster. The one you see today is a reconstruction. However, the energy in the tallies was not so much in the real material (even if it was combustible) but in the virtual debt.

ENTROPY

It might seem odd to compare a medieval tally stick with a quantum computer, but in fact the tally stick can be modelled in quantum terms, as shown in the quantum model for a debt relationship which is reproduced in modified form in Figure 5.1. The bottom qubit now represents the King, while the top qubit is the landowner who has to pay the debt. The initial state of the landowner's qubit is 0, but as described earlier it is flipped to a value near 1 by the action of the gate A.

The quantum circuit again represents a debt, but this time it is an involuntary debt imposed by the King on the landowner. The gate A therefore represents the coercion applied by the King on his subject. If there is no coercion, or the landlord simply can't pay, then the tally has no value. If there is a 5 per cent chance that the landlord will default, then this will affect the value of the tally, and an intermediary would only purchase it at a suitable discount. So in general, the value of the tally as a money object depends on the face value of the debt, but also on the probability of default, which reflects the coercive force applied by the King, as well as information about the borrower's creditworthiness.

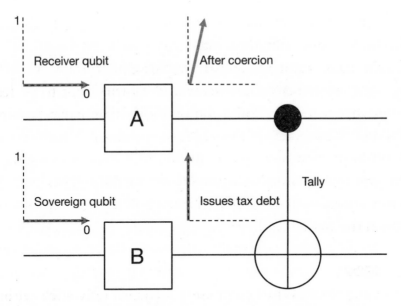

FIGURE 5.1 A two-qubit quantum circuit, identical to Figure 3.4 but now the upper qubit represents the person who receives the tally, the lower qubit represents the sovereign who issues the tally, the gate *A* represents the coercion asserted by the sovereign, and the entanglement gate represents the tally.

To assess the energy stored by the tally, we therefore need a way to express the energy required to change a person's mind, or in this case to make them pay a debt. In the nineteenth century, the new field of 'psychophysics' attempted to measure psychic quantities such as mental energy. The neoclassical economist Francis Edgeworth even suggested the idea of a hedonimeter which would register 'the height of pleasure experienced by an individual' or, more precisely, 'the psychical side of a physical change in what may be dimly discerned as a sort of hedonico-magnetic field' (and people think quantum economics is flaky).[17] Today, a neuroeconomist could put the person into a scanner to see if their brain centres for pleasure or pain lit up. But another way to express the effect is in terms of probabilities, and the concept of entropic force.

In physics, entropy is a kind of energy with a precise thermodynamic definition, but it can loosely be described as reflecting the degree of disorder in a system. The link between entropy, information, and force is illustrated by the puzzle known as Maxwell's demon, named for the nineteenth-century physicist James Clerk Maxwell who conceived it. This involves a container with two compartments, each filled with a gas at the same temperature; and an imaginary demon who sits at a small window in the dividing wall. When the demon sees a fast-moving atom in the left compartment, he opens the window to let it pass to the right; conversely, slow-moving atoms in the right compartment are allowed to pass to the left. After a while, particles in the left compartment will be slower on average than those in the right compartment. Since temperature is a measure of average particle speed, this means that the left side will be cooler than the right. It would then be possible to extract energy from this heat difference, which would appear to violate the principle of energy conservation.

The solution to the puzzle, which was proposed in 1929 by the ever-inventive Leó Szilárd, is that the demon is doing a kind of work, by manipulating information in a way which counteracts the randomness of the system. In this sense the demon is like an office worker, who doesn't do actual physical labour, but just manipulates virtual symbols.

But if information can do work, then it follows that other kinds of work might be related to information. As an example, imagine a box containing a quantity of a gas, where any given particle has an equal chance of being found anywhere within that box. This situation is illustrated in the top panel of Figure 5.2. The 'probability density' is a constant inside the box (meaning that each horizontal position is equally likely), and zero outside it. Since the distribution is stable and not

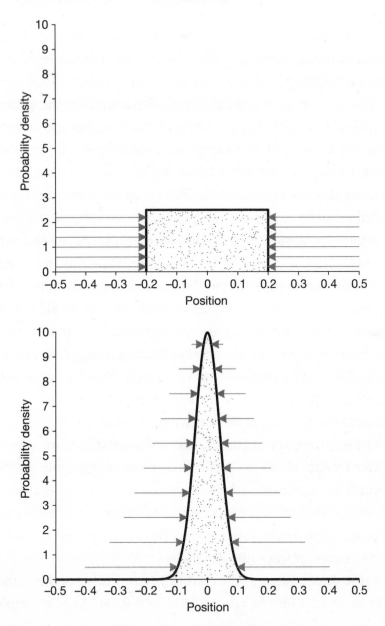

FIGURE 5.2 Top panel shows a uniform probability distribution over a particular range. Inside the range, the probability of finding a particle is a constant, while outside the range it is zero. The bottom panel shows a more localised distribution. A particle has the highest probability of being found near the centre, so there is more information about its location. The arrows represent the lines of entropic force, which confine the probability distribution to the particular region.

spreading out with time, it follows that there must be a force, indicated by the arrows, which is balancing the random motion of the particles.

The force here has an obvious mechanical interpretation, because it is supplied by the walls of the box. But more generally, the principle of maximum entropy in physics, which was first proposed by physicist Edwin Jaynes in 1957, states that a system tends to evolve towards states that are statistically more probable, so have higher entropy. The evolution can be viewed as being driven by a force, known as the entropic force.

In the bottom panel, for example, the likely location is now localised near the central point. This could represent an ensemble of particles constrained by a force, but we could equally interpret it as representing the propensity for a certain result, which again is a form of information. The propensity at any point can be described by a wave function, and has the same meaning as the propensity for the coin toss in Chapter 3. The difference is that instead of collapsing to heads or tails, the wave function collapses to a position; and the possible outcomes are not binary as for the coin toss, but cover a continuous range (though the total probability still adds to 1). As seen in the next chapter, a similar plot can be used to model a person's price estimate for something like a house.

The entropic force approach has seen wide use in physics: to describe, for example, heat dispersion, or the behaviour of the long molecular chains known as polymers. In 2009, the physicist Erik Verlinde even argued that gravity can be explained as an entropic force, which arises as the result of information associated with the positions of material bodies.[18] While this interpretation is controversial, a more obvious application is to the way that we think and make decisions. After all, there is no need to hypothesise a fictitious demon sorting particles to realise that things like financial transactions are subject to the push and pull of mental forces, or the flow of information. And because we are dealing with economics, we can use price as a measure of position, and derive other terms such as force and energy in terms of that.

So imagine that you are handed a wooden stick with some notches on it. Your initial impression would be that the value of the stick is approximately zero, unless you think it will serve as firewood. But then you are informed that, as unlikely as it might seem, the stick is actually worth the exact amount of a tax obligation, only in a negative sense. In order for you to agree with this assessment, some serious work will have to be done in rearranging the propensity curve which describes your view of the price of a stick.

In physics, the quantity of work required to counteract the entropic force depends on the relative change in the propensity, as expressed by the logarithm (which reflects relative change) of the ratio of final and initial propensities. This echoes the finding from nineteenth-century psychophysics, known as Weber's law after the physician Ernst Weber, which notes that what counts in psychological terms is not absolute change, but relative change. It also puts the concept of mental energy onto a much firmer basis, as a function of probabilities – and you don't need a hedonimeter to measure it.

We will return to this formula later, but the point for now is simply that the entropic force approach allows us to write down an expression for the mental effort needed to alter one's propensity; or equivalently the amount of energy that someone else needs to expend – through encouragement, advertising, or simple brute power – to change your mind, in a probabilistic sense, about the value of something, in this case a wooden stick. Here, energy is measured not in physical units, but in units of currency (though, as explored later, these are related). To be clear, we are not trying to draw a direct link between physics and 'psychics', as Victorian economists called mental phenomena; instead we are seeking a consistent way of expressing the changes in propensity that shape our decisions.

When the money is made of precious metal, such as gold or silver, rather than wood, an obvious advantage is that less coercion is required on the part of the sovereign in order to get it recognised as money, since the coins are already valuable in themselves. (Alchemists associated gold ♂ with that other nuclear energy source the Sun ☉, while silver ☽ was associated with its pale reflection, the Moon ☾.) And the closer the market price of the metal is to the face value of the coin, the greater the likelihood of the coin being accepted. The energy needed to mine the coin, which in ancient times was usually supplied by slave labour, therefore gets added to the power exerted by the sovereign, meaning that the coins may be accepted even in places where the sovereign holds little sway. It follows that the energy required to forge money could be supplied in two ways: by procuring and controlling precious metal, or by exerting social power through debt collection. This highlights the way that virtual energy, as projected through legal and military methods, is convertible with a real mass of metal – and it also points again to the inherently dualistic nature of money, which is what gives this substance its confounding properties.

Of course, readers may still worry that social systems can never be reduced to equations, and economics has a long history of abusing concepts from physics such as force and energy. As the philosopher Lin Yutang wrote in his 1937 book *The Importance of Living*, 'human personality is the last thing to be reduced to mechanical laws; somehow the human mind is forever elusive, uncatchable and unpredictable, and manages to wriggle out of mechanistic laws or a materialistic dialect that crazy psychologists and unmarried economists are trying to impose upon him.' But economists do need to express some aspects of human behaviour using equations, and if something is left out, like power, then it tends to be ignored. In neoclassical economics, the model depicted in Figure 5.1 would not need to feature entanglement with the debtor's state of mind – the two qubits would not talk with each other – because, as will be seen in Chapter 8, the possibility of default is usually absent. And the problem with neoclassical economics is not so much that its founders expressed their ideas in terms of forces and energy, but that they based these on the abstract concept of utility rather than on something that could actually be measured.

In contrast, the approach here starts from the idea of a propensity which can often be measured or inferred. The field of behavioural economics, for example, relies on experiments which assess the probability of a person making certain decisions, which is the discrete case of a propensity function. And as seen in the next chapter, we can define a curve to describe the propensity to buy or sell as a function of price. The propensity function will not be perfectly stable but can still be used to describe a particular situation: marketers study consumers' propensity to purchase with the aim of manipulating it, and the propensity to purchase is very evident in financial markets. The entropic force – along with the related expression for energy – is derived from the propensity function, so is just another way of describing the same thing (in fact all that counts from a computational standpoint is the probabilities). Human behaviour cannot be reduced to mechanistic equations, or lines of force, or fluxes of energy, but we can still use mathematics as a language to describe and predict observations about financial transactions.

THE STRONG FORCE

The strongest known force in nature is the appropriately named strong force, which binds the nucleus of an atom together. According to one theory, it too can be viewed as an entropic force.[19] If so, there must be a great deal of information at the heart of an atom of uranium.

Like uranium, money can be viewed as a kind of ossified information, that can also be primed to explode under carefully controlled conditions. A strange feature about money is that while countless books have been written advancing various theories of the stuff, few concentrate on its defining property, which is its relationship with number and information. It is as if, while we are happy to talk about the effects of money, we are as afraid to inspect the source of its energy as we are to stare at the Sun.

So far, we haven't said much about why money should be modelled using a quantum formalism. The entropic force approach can be viewed in purely classical terms. The only reason this is a quantum model is because the state of the debtor is being treated as a superposition of default and non-default; honouring the debt signified by the stick or tossing it in the fire. However, as with the simple example of the coin toss, analysing transactions in terms of propensity pushes us towards adopting a quantum approach. This becomes clearer in the next few chapters, when we consider the mix of hard and soft forces which affect economic decisions, and the way in which money objects serve to measure prices through the actions of buying and selling – or what economists call supply and demand.

CHAPTER 6

NOT A CROSS BUT A WAVE

It is in this middle field that economics lies, unaffected whether by the ultimate philosophy of the electron or the soul, and concerned rather with the interaction, with the middle world of life of these two end worlds of physics and mind in their commonest everyday aspects.

FREDERICK SODDY, CARTESIAN ECONOMICS, 1921

———

Supply and demand are the bread and butter of economics. Every introductory textbook has the figure with two lines representing supply and demand that intersect in an X shape. The traditional approach assumes that supply and demand act as forces that magically drive the economy to equilibrium; however, the reality, as shown by gyrating prices for things like financial assets, appears somewhat different. This chapter draws on lessons from computational biology and quantum physics to motivate a new theory of supply and demand, in which these quantities are represented as not a cross, but a wave.

———

The world of magic has its stars such as Jean-Eugène Robert-Houdin, or later Harry Houdini (born Erik Weisz, his stage name was borrowed from his French idol), who invented many of the basic tricks, versions of which are still performed today. If there is a similar central figure in economics, it is the Scottish economist Adam Smith.

Smith was as eccentric a figure as any wizard or prophet. He was famously absent-minded: one friend called him 'the most absent man in Company that I ever saw, Moving his Lips and talking to himself, and Smiling'.[1] On one occasion, he accidentally walked into a tanning pit; on another, he went for a stroll in his nightgown and ended up fifteen miles outside town. He lived with his mother until her death at 90, six years before his own death (his father died when Smith was an infant). It doesn't seem that he had any serious romantic relationships, and he was dependent on a series of patrons for his income. In general, as his biographer Dugald Stewart put it, Smith was 'certainly not fitted for the general commerce of the world'.[2] But this didn't prevent him from changing the way that the world thinks about commerce.

Smith is best known for his amazing 'invisible hand' trick.[3] In this trick, prices are magically drawn to what economists call their 'intrinsic' or 'fundamental' value. (And if you ask what the intrinsic value is, they will say it's the price, thus proving their argument.) The story is that prices are a compromise between buyers and sellers, or consumers and producers. If the price is too high, then more producers will appear and/or consumption will decrease, and competition between sellers will drive the price down. But if prices are too low, then producers quit and/or consumption increases, and the remaining sellers can raise their prices. The price is therefore always being corrected back towards its equilibrium value, courtesy of the market's invisible hand.

Smith himself didn't much use the phrase 'invisible hand', which was popularised later by Paul Samuelson. The first time he used it was actually in an early work called *The History of Astronomy*, which had nothing to do with economics: 'For it may be observed, that in all Polytheistic religions, among savages, as well as in the early ages of heathen antiquity, it is the irregular events of nature only that are ascribed to the agency and power of the gods. Fire burns, and water refreshes; heavy bodies descend, and lighter substances fly upwards, by the necessity of their own nature; nor was the invisible hand of Jupiter ever apprehended to be employed in those matters. But thunder and lightning, storms and sunshine, those more irregular events, were ascribed to his favour, or his anger.'

So Smith's 'invisible hand' referred here to the magical actions of a god. It was only later that he repurposed it to describe the magical workings of markets. But really there isn't much difference.

The invisible hand wasn't really new, and similar ideas had been around since antiquity.[4] But Smith, writing at the dawn of the Industrial Revolution, as part of the so-called Scottish Enlightenment, was in the right place at the right time. The invisible hand eventually became synonymous with the self-organising ability of capitalism, not just to compute prices, but to generate an enormously complex range of goods and services in the first place. And it was later translated into mathematical code by neoclassical economists as the law of supply and demand.

X MARKS THE SPOT

The 'law of supply and demand' refers to the idea that supply and demand for a particular good can be plotted as two curves. The supply curve shows the number of units that producers will supply as a function of price, while the demand curve shows the number of units that consumers will demand. Supply increases with price, while demand decreases. The point where the two lines intersect represents the equilibrium point where supply equals demand, the market clears, and utility is optimised, as per Smith's invisible hand. As Harvard's Gregory Mankiw summarises in his bestselling *Principles of Economics*, 'At the equilibrium price, the quantity of the good that buyers are willing and able to buy exactly balances the quantity that sellers are willing and able to sell ... The actions of buyers and sellers naturally move markets toward the equilibrium of supply and demand.'[5]

The law is summed up by the famous cross-shaped diagram of supply and demand which graces every introductory textbook, informs economic decisions, appears in the form of equations in mathematical models, issues from the lips of commentators, and shapes the way we think about the economy. The figure is traditionally plotted with price on the vertical axis, but this is unusual outside of economics, so I have swapped the

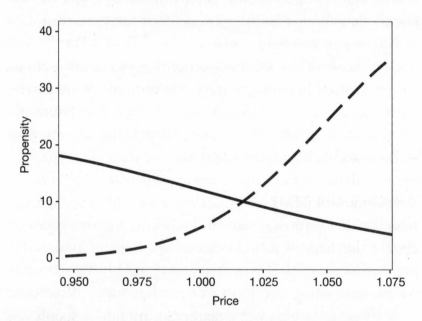

FIGURE 6.1 Intersection of a downward-sloping demand curve (solid line), and an upward-sloping supply curve (dashed line), of the sort used in neoclassical economics. The vertical scale is normally expressed as a quantity, but here it is called propensity.

axes around. In fact, this change is key to the whole story. The thing which distinguishes economics from the other social sciences is that it involves financial transactions, so price can be used as a measure of position, which usually goes on the horizontal axis.

Also, before proceeding, it should be pointed out that the entire approach is unusual outside of economics. While I am sure the method applies to some simple problems encountered in fields such as engineering, for my own part I have worked in a number of applied areas including electrical engineering, weather forecasting, biology, and so on, and have yet to come across a situation where people found it useful to analyse a complex dynamical system by drawing two curves and finding the intersection. It just isn't the way you do it, for the simple reason that it usually isn't possible to isolate the two parts of the system – in this case supply and demand – and treat them as if they were separate.

In the case of the economy, supply and demand are closely coupled, often in complex ways – luxury goods are coveted exactly because supply is constrained, expensive houses are desired because they may become more expensive, the price of oil has a life of its own – and can't be measured separately because all we have is transactions at particular price points. As the economist Ludwig von Mises wrote in 1949, 'it is important to realize that we do not have any knowledge or experience concerning the shape of such curves. Always, what we know is only market prices – that is, not the curves but only a point which we interpret as the intersection of two hypothetical curves.'[6]

This explains why, while textbooks are full of supply and demand curves, they are never based on actual empirical data. The economist Stephen Levitt summed up the approach in 2016 by saying, without irony, that 'we completely and totally understand what a demand curve is, but we've never seen one'.[7] A 2021 survey of five leading textbooks concluded that 'none of these tomes provides a single picture, table or graph of an *actual* demand curve, supply curve, or equilibrium. Not even one!'[8] (The state of affairs was also captured by a note in an online draft of an economics textbook: 'IF ANYONE KNOWS OF AN EMPIRICAL SUPPLY AND DEMAND MODEL THAT HAS PERFORMED WELL OVER TIME AND/OR SPACE PLEASE LET ME HAVE A CITATION.'[9]) This also explains why the theory doesn't seem to apply to industries such as real estate, financial services, or the resource sector, which basically rules out the Canadian economy for one.

So to quote the Steven Seagal character in the insightful 1992 film *Under Siege*, 'What kind of babbling bullshit is this?' The drawbacks of the supply and demand approach have been raked over many times by critics (see for example my book *Economyths*) so I won't repeat the arguments here, except to point out that the theory both relies on, and appears to justify, the assumption of an underlying equilibrium, as represented by the intersection of the two curves. If we view the economy not as a mechanical system but as a living system characterised by complex dynamics and feedback loops, then this assumption seems rather unsafe. In biology, for example, the only systems that are at equilibrium are dead.

Of course, the equilibrium assumption is useful from a mathematical viewpoint exactly because it removes the need to consider dynamics. The neoclassical economist Alfred Marshall, who first popularised the supply and demand diagram in his 1890 textbook *Principles of Economics*, wrote that 'the Mecca of the economist lies in economic biology' but continued that 'biological conceptions are more complex than those of mechanics; a volume on Foundations must therefore give a relatively large place to mechanical analogies, and frequent use is made of the term equilibrium which suggests something of a static analogy'. Or as Paul Krugman explained more recently, 'dynamics are hard, whereas looking at the presumed end state of a dynamic process – an equilibrium – may tell you much of what you want to know.'[10] So some 130 years later, the static analogy is still around, which is certainly a remarkable demonstration of equilibrium. But for most dynamical systems of the sort encountered in other areas – say cancer biology, or epidemiology, or weather prediction – a modelling approach that starts with the idea of equilibrium would be rather unhelpful, and the economy is no different. Can we do better?

THE PROPENSITY TO TRADE

The neoclassical model of supply and demand conflates two things: the desire for an individual agent to transact at a particular price, and the number of agents in the market. For example, the supply curve is supposed to increase with price in part because at higher prices more suppliers will enter the market, while lower prices will cause some to exit. However, these decision for firms to enter or exit a market depend on complex processes that unfold over long timescales.

A related problem is that, while an individual person or firm may have a version of a supply or demand schedule in their head, things get messy when we look at the total aggregate behaviour over a large number of agents. In fact, it turns out that the curves can take on pretty much any shape imaginable. So let's look first at a better-defined problem, which is the tendency for individual agents to transact over a particular trading period as a function of price.

Smith argued that the 'propensity to truck, barter, and exchange' was inherent in human nature. The economist John

Maynard Keynes later wrote, in 1936, of our 'propensity to consume', which was balanced by a 'propensity to hoard'.[11] The same can be said, in a more general sense, of chemical systems. In chemistry, when molecules from two chemical species interact, there is a certain probability that they will combine to form a compound. This probability is called the reaction propensity and will depend on factors such as the temperature. Adopting a similar approach, we can therefore reinterpret supply and demand curves not as fixed schedules, but rather as propensities for an individual buyer or seller to value the item being traded at a particular price. In fact, this is already done in marketing where the technique known as 'propensity modelling' is used to simulate how a customer's willingness to purchase an item is affected by attributes including price.[12] Note again that this works in economics, as opposed to the social sciences in general, because money is involved, and we can use price as an independent variable. Instead of assuming that supply and demand determine price, as in neoclassical economics, we assume that price determines propensity. And the fact that price is just a number, as opposed to something real and immutable, is exactly what introduces the uncertainty that makes the quantum approach suitable.

For example, if we ask a homeowner to put a probabilistic value on their house – and so answer the quantum question 'how much?' – the propensity curve could look like the ones in Figure 6.2, which compare with Figure 5.2 from the previous chapter. If we choose the curves to be a so-called normal distribution (also known as a Gaussian distribution, or bell curve), then the centre of the distribution (here 1 for $1 million) would be their best estimate, while the width (or standard deviation) would be a measure of their uncertainty or flexibility. The top panel shows the case where the owner has a relatively high

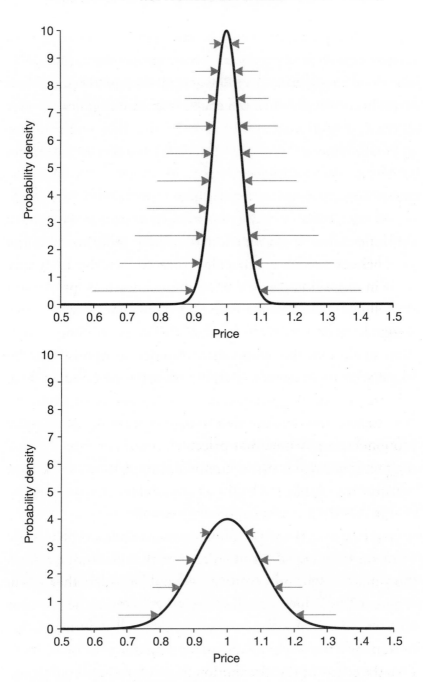

FIGURE 6.2 The curves show propensity as a function of price, measured in millions of dollars. Both are centred at $P = 1$, but the panel on the bottom has a higher level of price flexibility. The arrows indicate the strength and direction of the associated entropic forces.

degree of confidence in their estimate, while the bottom panel shows a case where the person is more open to negotiation. The horizontal axis is price (actually it is better to use the logarithm of price, which again expresses relative changes, but we can ignore that here).

For each price, the value of the curve indicates the probability density (so relative probability) of the person valuing the item at that price. As seen in the previous chapter, propensity can be interpreted as being produced by an entropic force – a kind of organising principle, based not on mechanics but on information – which in this case pushes the valuation towards the central estimate of $P = \$1$ million. For prices lower than P, the force pushes to the right, while for prices higher than that amount it pushes to the left, as shown by the arrows. The effect of the entropic force is therefore to corral the range of all possible prices into a narrow band around P. Something like infectious greed, or perhaps loss aversion, which shifts the distribution towards higher prices, can be viewed as a constant entropic force pushing to the right.

In the figure, the strength of the force is indicated by the length of the arrows. For a normal distribution, it turns out that the entropic force is identical to the force equation for a perfect spring. It is as if the owner has a kind of spring in their head which is at rest when the suggested price is at their expected value of $1 million. If a realtor suggests a small adjustment to the price, the owner will probably go along; if they come up with what seems like a completely unrealistic number, the owner might argue or look for someone else to represent them. The strength of the restoring force will also depend on the narrowness of the propensity curve: it is stronger for the top panel, which makes sense since the shape implies a higher degree of organisation and a more exact or informed price estimate.

In the context of a market transaction between a buyer and a seller, the only part of these curves to be active will be the parts where they intersect. This is illustrated in Figure 6.3, which shows a zoomed view of the intersection of two propensity curves representing a buyer (on the left) and a seller (on the right). In each case the propensity curves have been chosen to be part of a normal distribution, with the peak at the ideal price for that person (low for the buyer, high for the seller). The lines can be seen as representing the person's strategy. A buyer, for example, commits to a high chance of buying at prices near their ideal price, but will assign less demand to overly expensive prices. The case where the supplier fixes the price and refuses to negotiate is handled by assuming an infinitely thin propensity curve located at the sale price.

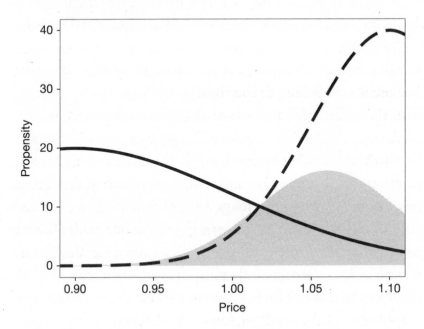

FIGURE 6.3 Intersection of a buyer's propensity curve (solid line) and that of a seller (dashed line). These propensity curves compare with the supply and demand lines in Figure 6.1. The shaded area shows the joint propensity curve, which is a product of the buyer and seller curves.

Together, these curves specify the probability of a buyer and seller each valuing the item at a particular price. So applying the laws of probability, to compute the chance of each agreeing on a particular price, we just need to multiply these two numbers together. The result is the joint propensity curve shown by the shaded area. It also turns out, after some mathematics, that the entropic force corresponding to the joint propensity curve is just the sum of the supply and demand forces, which act in opposite directions. The net force again acts like a spring: when prices are too high it acts to lower them, and when prices are too low it raises them. The entropic interpretation therefore gives real meaning to these market forces, in terms of the probability of transactions.

This figure differs from the classical one (Figure 6.1) in a number of respects. One is a shift in perspective: instead of seeing price as the deterministic result of supply and demand, the price emerges from the propensities of the buyer and seller. In the classical diagram, the equilibrium price is the point where the supply and demand lines intersect. In the probabilistic version, there is no unique equilibrium, but simply prices with lower and higher probability. Nor does the price with the highest probability conform to the classical equilibrium price; in this case the asymmetry between the buyer and seller propensity curves means that it is significantly higher. The classical model assumes that the market clears at the equilibrium price, while the probabilistic model just gives the chance of a transaction at each price. Finally, instead of being static, the quantum model responds to forces and changes in propensity.

THE PRICE OSCILLATOR

As pointed out by the Russian physicist Anatoly Kondratenko – who developed a similar model of market transactions, though without the entropic force interpretation[13] – the probabilistic approach is already more realistic than the traditional model, and can be used to make simulations that include the effects of stochasticity (i.e. randomness). Such models are akin to the stochastic models used regularly in computational biology to simulate the interactions in living cells (many of which involve a small number of molecules and are influenced by random effects).[14] In economics, a relatively straightforward step is to replace the deterministic supply/demand equations in conventional models with probabilistic versions, for example in agent-based models which simulate transactions between individuals.[15] Another advantage of using the probabilistic framework, though, is that it allows us to say something about the dynamics of the system.

In neoclassical economics, supply and demand are typically described as forces, which drive the price up or down, but the nature of these forces has been mostly unexplored. Instead, as with efficient market theory (discussed later), or for that matter Aristotelian physics, economists dodge this problem by just assuming that the system goes straight to equilibrium and the market clears. This is equivalent to assuming that motion is instantaneous, and there is no concept of mass or inertia to slow things down. For neoclassical economists such as Jevons and Fisher, the only role for mass was as a measure of the quantity of a commodity.

As seen above, though, the forces of supply and demand can be modelled as spring-like entropic forces, which reflect the probability of a transaction. In the classical picture, this wouldn't seem very realistic, because the price would just bounce back and forth around the central value, and in the absence of friction it would do so indefinitely and never come to a halt, like Adam Smith's invisible hand bouncing a yo-yo.

Of course, we know that prices don't behave this way, which is perhaps one reason why neoclassical economists didn't explore classical dynamics further. But fortunately there is a way to fix it – which is by going quantum. As computer scientist Scott Aaronson notes, quantum methods are adapted to handle 'information and probabilities and observables, and how they relate to each other'.[16] Since supply and demand seems a pretty good example of information, probabilities, and observables (in this case through transactions) it seems like a suitable approach. And it also provides a rather neat way to address the probabilistic and dynamic nature of something like a price negotiation.

The quantum version of an ideal spring is known as the quantum harmonic oscillator, which in physics is used to model a variety of phenomena such as molecular vibrations, or even the creation of particles out of the void.[17] It is also one of the few quantum systems that can be solved exactly, so it is often used as an approximation to more complicated systems. It differs from a classical spring in a number of respects, perhaps the most remarkable being that it does not have a state with zero energy.

For a classical spring, if the spring is still at its equilibrium point, so is not compressed or extended, then the energy is zero. It just sits there and doesn't move. This corresponds to the equilibrium in neoclassical economics. If you extend the spring and let it go, then it will bounce back and forth with an energy that depends on the size of the initial displacement. For the quantum version, in contrast, the energy can only take on a certain set of discrete values – and the state with the lowest energy, known as the ground state, is characterised by a normal probability distribution. The energy can never be zero, because this would violate the uncertainty principle (put simply, if it were zero, then we would know exactly what it was). The ground state therefore represents not an oscillation as such, but rather the potential for an oscillation.

Since the propensity curve for a price negotiation is a normal distribution and is generated by the same entropic force as an oscillator, it follows that we can model the potential transaction between buyer and seller in the same way. The resulting quantum model of supply and demand, published in *Physica A: Statistical Mechanics and its Applications*, then captures the probabilistic nature of the exchange, in a manner that also reflects the dynamic nature of the negotiation.[18] Better yet, as seen below, it allows us to assign meaningful units to things like force and mass.

As in physics, the assumption that the propensity is normal, which gives a linear entropic force, can be viewed as a first-order approximation to a more complex system. Of course, many things can be described by normal distributions (they are normal after all) and we don't model them as little quantum springs, or see them as the result of entropic forces, or talk about their mass. But recall that the assumptions used to generate the model of human decision-making – a propensity function, measured using a 2-norm – were minimal; and yet out popped the equation for an archetypal quantum system. As seen above, people talk about social and economic forces all the time. And the idea of having weight in a negotiation is not unfamiliar. So another way to look at it is that perhaps subatomic reality isn't quite as strange or abnormal as we have been led to believe; and perhaps the creation and observation of particles has something in common with the creation and observation of a thought, an idea, a point of view, or a decision, not necessarily because they are all based on the same physical processes, but because they are reflections of one another. As we'll see, quantum models in general turn out to be very useful for capturing how we think and make choices.

Propensity curves can be observed through things like surveys of buyer intentions, but their traces can also be seen in the order books of stock markets. Figure 6.4 is a snapshot of open buy and sell orders for Apple stock over a time period of one hour.[19] The horizontal axis shows the relative deviation from the average price, while the vertical axis shows the proportionate number of orders at each price. The figure resembles two normal distributions, for buyers to the left and sellers to the right, with the central section cut out. So-called market makers maintain a separation by posting one price at which they will

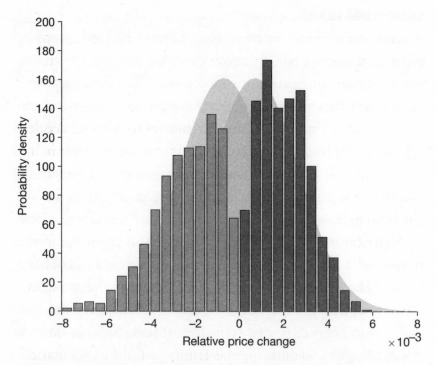

FIGURE 6.4 Plot of buy (light grey) and sell (dark grey) orders for Apple stock over a one-hour period. Also shown for comparison in the background are two symmetrical normal distributions, which represent the underlying propensity functions for buyers and sellers.

buy, another (higher) price at which they will sell, and profiting from the spread between them. Orders which execute are immediately removed from the order book. Buyers who are willing to transact at higher prices, or sellers who will accept lower prices, will not necessarily want to advertise that fact, so that information is missing. Indeed, people must be willing to deal outside these ranges, which do not overlap, since otherwise there would be no transactions. The order book is a classical phenomenon – these are posted orders with no uncertainty – and gives only a partial picture; however, it still reflects the underlying group propensity functions of the market (seen lurking like ghosts in the figure background).

QUANTUM MASS

A common criticism of neoclassical economics is that, unlike physics, it doesn't pay attention to units. Mankiw's textbook, for example, can feature a chapter on 'The market forces of supply and demand' without asking what units these forces are to be expressed in, how they act on masses to produce acceleration, or other basic questions of the sort you encounter in high school physics. This is a shame, because dimensional analysis is one of the most powerful tools in science – if only as a reality check to make sure that you haven't messed up an equation.

For example, one way to work out the equation for the period of a pendulum is to take all the relevant variables – namely the mass of the weight, the length of the string, and the acceleration due to gravity – and combine them in such a way that the answer has units of time (it turns out that the mass doesn't matter).[20] Following the Trinity test, the mathematician G.I. Taylor estimated the energy in the atomic explosion by applying the same dimensional trick but with quantities energy, air density, radius of the explosion, and time. His resulting guess that it was equivalent to around 17 kilotons of TNT was not far off the actual value of 22 kilotons.

For the quantum model, the mass of the buyer or seller depends on the strength of the 'spring' that informs their thinking, which as seen above depends on the width of the propensity curve. Referring to Figure 6.2, the narrow distribution on the top panel represents a greater mass than the one on the bottom. A person whose propensity is narrow and well-defined therefore carries a greater mass than one whose propensity is wide and relaxed. In a negotiation, the average price shifts towards the party with greater mass. This is why the peak probability price in the negotiation depicted in Figure 6.3 is to the right of the classical equilibrium – the supplier's mass in the negotiation is greater than that of the buyer. Of the two parties, they are the harder to move.

Similarly, the mass associated with the price for a particular asset depends on the shape of the joint propensity function. A price which is uncertain and ill-defined has lower mass than one which remains within a tight band as if weighed down by a heavy anchor. The quantum model therefore allows us to connect price, which is information, with mass, which is normally thought of as a mechanical quantity. Like money, it binds the virtual and the real in a single package. For example, it turns out that the price discovery process can be interpreted in information-theoretic terms as aligning supply with demand in a particular way that minimises entropy (so maximising the degree of order in the system). The normal propensity curves in Figure 6.4 satisfy this entropy-minimising property.[21]

This mass is certainly not a fixed number, since it will depend on market conditions. It can also be manipulated through financial wizardry. In a nuclear device, mass is transformed into energy according to Einstein's famous equation

$E = mc^2$. In quantum economics, any scheme that generates a continuous stream of money also involves a similar trade-off between mass and energy, in the sense that the mass of the source depletes over time.[22] This conforms to the quantity theory of money, which says that inflation is directly related to the quantity of money in circulation. The reason that, in Hartlibian money creation schemes of the sort discussed in Chapter 1, money supply can expand exponentially with little effect on inflation, is because the new money is crystallised in the form of real estate. It is equivalent to wealthy people being given a bonus in gold bars which they have to hide under their floorboards or bury in the garden. Only if that money is all released around the same time may people discover that it doesn't weigh what it used to.

THE UNCERTAINTY PRINCIPLE

A basic feature of quantum models is, of course, that they deal with individual quanta, which take the form of discrete parcels of energy. The energy in a beam of light does not come as a continuous flow but as what Einstein called 'a finite number of energy quanta localized at points in space, moving without dividing and capable of being absorbed or generated only as entities'.[23] Economic transactions are similarly quantised because they consist of discrete events. When you purchase gasoline for your vehicle, there is an indicator showing the price ramp up as the fuel flows from the pump. However, the actual payment is a single transaction involving two parties: you and the vendor. And instead of flowing out of your credit card, it jumps. Schrödinger once said, 'If we have to go on with these damned quantum jumps, then I'm sorry that I ever got involved'; but with money it happens all the time.

As discussed later, cognitive decisions are also quantised because of subjective factors which lead to a threshold effect. These subjective forces create a kind of mental barrier which must be overcome in order for a deal to take place. In the quantum model of supply and demand, the gap between energy levels represents the energy gap needed to break this barrier. In the ground state – which, again, is the state with a normal propensity function and the lowest possible energy – the model represents a potential transaction between two parties, just as in physics the ground state of a quantum harmonic oscillator might represent a potential micro-flash of light in the form of a single photon. Higher energy levels represent an excited state, where participants are changing their minds and their positions on the fly, and the propensity function moves in a complicated dance. In the extreme case, the oscillator behaves like a classical spring, swinging from one extreme to the other.

While this chapter has focused on using the oscillator model to simulate the transaction process, similar models have independently been used by researchers in the area of quantum finance to replicate things like the statistics of stock price fluctuations. One 2017 study found, for example, that a quantum oscillator model outperformed other approaches when used to fit historical price changes in the Financial Times Stock Exchange (FTSE) All Share Index. The model was in its base-energy ground state most of the time, with the next two energy levels contributing the remaining few per cent.[24]

More generally, the quantum approach is useful because it correctly models transactions as a measurement event. For example, Algostox Trading, headed by Jack Sarkissian, who trained as a quantum physicist, uses a version of a propensity function to model stock price dynamics and analyse areas such as trade execution modelling, large order pricing, and risk valuation for illiquid securities.[25] And as will be discussed in Chapter 11, the quantum oscillator model can be used to analyse and predict the price and volume of transactions for financial derivatives. Interest in such methods will only increase as investment banks pour billions of dollars of research funds into quantum computing. As one commentator wrote in 2021, 'it is likely, even plausible, that there are already financial-services companies using quantum technology to guide their trading strategies';[26] and what better way to exploit quantum technology than with quantum models?

At a more fundamental level, though, the quantum model is interesting because it tells a completely different story about how markets behave. Since the time of Adam Smith, economics has been dominated by the idea that the invisible hand of the market drives prices to an equilibrium level which corresponds to intrinsic value. Neoclassical economists formalised this approach with the law of supply and demand, and focused on equilibrium rather than the mechanics of how equilibrium was attained. The efficient market hypothesis applied the same idea to financial markets, but asserted that prices adjust immediately, so dynamics are irrelevant. Models used by economists to simulate the large-scale economy make the same assumption, but add epicycles in the form of external shocks and various 'frictions' in order to explain how equilibrium reacts to perturbations. And throughout, the role of money is downplayed or neglected entirely, on the basis that the economy is no more than a glorified barter system.

This barter model seems particularly crusty and old-fashioned in an era when most of the value traded in major exchanges – and an estimated 90 per cent of the S&P 500 index – is derived from intangible assets such as intellectual property, software licences, business rights, research and development, and other forms of information (the latest being 'non-fungible tokens' which assign digital rights to things like artworks). Or rather, on the legal limits and boundaries which control that information.[27] Even when you buy something tangible like a house, the value isn't so much in the physical building, or the land, as it is in the information encoded by rules and regulations – such as the ones that restrict your neighbours from converting their houses into a tower block or a chemical factory – along with things like social status.

As economist Peter Radford wrote, mainstream economics 'speaks of capital and labor and not of information and energy. It is still intensely material rather than digital. Its practitioners grapple with modern issues, but through a lens designed for an earlier era.'[28] The quantum model, in contrast, sees transactions as a measurement of a quantum system which is never truly at equilibrium. Even in its ground state, the system has a non-zero energy which corresponds with the uncertainty principle. In efficient market theory, the random nature of price changes is assumed to occur because market participants have perfect information and react immediately to all perturbations. In the quantum version, the randomness is due to indeterminacy, which is the very opposite of perfect information. Because the model is based on a quantum wave function, it can incorporate effects such as interference and entanglement, which, as will be seen later, characterise financial decisions. Finally, while the neoclassical model sees prices as the natural result of impersonal forces, the quantum approach highlights the role that power plays in a negotiation. In particular, when producers are in charge – for example when they limit supply or collude to fix prices – they effectively have more mass in the transaction.

A classic problem in economics is why diamonds are more expensive than water, even if they are less useful. The usual answer is that they are scarce – but one reason for that scarcity is the fact that companies like De Beers have the power to limit their supply.[29] Another example is the quandary of why interest rates on things like US Treasury bills have fallen over recent decades to the point where they are effectively zero. In classical economics, this is explained in terms of supply and demand, so economists argue that supply of loans must be high and demand low. In quantum economics the explanation is much simpler: short-term interest rates are low because the government, which has the controlling mass, sets them that way; and longer-term interest rates are low because investors think that the government will continue with that policy into the future, in part because any slight departure would threaten setting off financial bombs.[30]

THEORY BLINDNESS

Einstein said in 1926 that 'Whether you can observe a thing or not depends on the theory which you use. It is the theory which decides what can be observed.'[31] A graphic example is provided by supernovas, those massive stellar explosions which release a burst of radiation lasting months or even years. The first observations of such events by Western astronomers were in 1572 (recorded by the astronomer/alchemist Tycho Brahe) and then 1604 (recorded by his associate Johannes Kepler). However, Asian astronomers had known about them for centuries. The reason it took so long for the West to catch on was because astronomers there were blinded by Aristotelian science, which said that the planets rotated around the earth in spheres made of ether, and the heavens were immutable. Brahe also tracked a comet and showed that it would have smashed through those crystalline spheres, had they existed. Today it is the imaginary crystalline spheres of supply and demand which need to be smashed. As already seen, nowhere is the role of power more clear than in the debt relationship; and in order to prevent what one article called the 'supernova of a debt collapse', you need to be able to see the problem in the first place.[32] We return to this in the final chapter.

In science, the traditional test of a theory is whether it can make accurate predictions, and economists like to selectively draw on the prediction test to determine whether a theory offers something new. However, the core prediction from mainstream theory is only that prices reflect intrinsic value – which of course is untestable. And the efficient market theory's sole prediction is that price changes are unpredictable. It is a theory of non-prediction.

In the quantum approach to supply and demand, the lack of predictability can be ascribed in part to the uncertainty principle, which may not seem more useful. However, as will be seen in Chapter 11, we can still use the model to make some predictions of interest. More generally, as with the quantum theory of money, the model points the way to a deeper analysis of the economy in terms of its real drivers – money and power. In the next chapter we explore another aspect of money's confounding, dualistic nature, and an even more striking example of theory blinding us to reality.

CHAPTER 7

THE UTILITY SWITCH

*Man needs money and cannot exist without it. The
diabolic magic of money is here clearly visible. It has
helped mankind to make immense strides in economic
development, and has at the same time enslaved him.
Regression to a moneyless condition, or the modern
method of exchange by means of money – any kind
of money, but still money – these are the alternatives.
Money plays the role of the sorcerer's apprentice –
created to serve a master who cannot now rid himself
of his indispensible sprite. It is the master now.*
HJALMAR SCHACHT, *THE MAGIC OF MONEY*, 1967

———

In the nineteenth century, neoclassical economists decided that
value was best seen as a measure not of labour, as classical economists such as Adam Smith had long assumed, but of something
they called utility. Since then, mainstream economics – as opposed
to other areas of inquiry such as say psychology, or literature, or
folk wisdom – has been based on the notion that we act rationally to optimise this utility, which has been variously described as
a form of pleasure energy, a measure of happiness, or simply a
ranked preference. This chapter shows how – by means of a subtle
sleight of hand that magicians call a substitution trick – economists
perpetuated one of the greatest magical illusions of all time: that
human behaviour is rational.

———

As discussed in previous chapters, money has two sides. One corresponds to a virtual number, the other to a real object. The first is objective, in the sense that numbers are objective; the second is subjective, since it relates to ownership of a valued thing. At the birth of coin money in ancient Lydia, the coins were stamped with a symbol, such as the head of a lion, on only one side, so we can associate heads with the virtual aspect, and tails with the real aspect. The purpose of the money system is to put hard numbers on the fuzzy concept of value; heads on tails. This process can be modelled using the quantum concept of wave function collapse, which reduces a probabilistic wave to a fixed measurement.

Note again that we are using quantum ideas not in the sense of a metaphor, but rather in the sense of a mathematical model, which is not the same thing. Neoclassical economics, for example, gets its strength because it uses mathematical models that are based on mechanistic physics. (If it just used mechanistic physics as a metaphor, it probably wouldn't have done nearly as much damage.)

As mentioned in Chapter 2, the Pythagoreans associated that which is unified with the right hand, and that which is dissolved with the left hand. In their list of opposites, right was on the side of good, and left on the side of evil. Today, we know that the left hand is controlled by the right hemisphere of the brain and vice versa. As the psychologist Iain McGilchrist explains in his 2009 book *The Master and His Emissary: The Divided Brain and the Making of the Western World*, experiments performed since the 1960s – including ones on 'split-brain' patients whose corpus callosum, whose role is to connect the hemispheres, had been severed as a treatment for epilepsy – show that the two hemispheres play very different roles in cognition: the left hemisphere searches for closed, fixed answers, while the right hemisphere takes an open, holistic stance, and deals in possibilities. The right hemisphere therefore deals in a kind of psychological wave function, which 'needs to be "collapsed" into the present' by the left.[1]

An important feature of the left hemisphere, according to McGilchrist, is that 'its concern, its prime motivation, is *power*'.[2] Money can therefore be viewed as a kind of powered prosthetic for the left brain, which adds to its reach and grasp by collapsing the fuzzy quality of value to the hard quantity of price; and its invention was a major contributor to what McGilchrist identifies as a shift in 'hemispheric balance' that occurred around the same time, where the left hemisphere (right-handed, so good in the Pythagorean scheme) began to usurp the role of the right hemisphere.

Our discomfort in dealing with quantum duality is therefore ironic given that the most obvious physical feature of the human brain is that it is split down the middle into two parts, whose complementary roles find an intriguing parallel with both the dual nature of money, and with wave/particle duality. However, given the taboo nature of these topics, it may not be surprising that, as McGilchrist notes, the brain's 'deeply divided structure has remained largely unexplained and even unexamined' by scientists.[3]

Behavioural economists, for example, have advanced a number of models of human cognition which involve two separate processes. Daniel Kahneman and Amos Tversky proposed a fast System 1, which relies on rough-and-ready heuristics, versus a slow System 2, which takes the time to do the math. Richard Thaler proposed a planner-doer model along similar lines, with the planner attempting to make rational decisions, and the doer focusing more on the present moment. And so on. In fact, one author of a paper reviewing such models complained that 'So many authors have appealed to dual processes in so many different ways that it has proved a complex and challenging task to draw together any coherent overview of this topic'.[4] However, these dual-system models rarely (if ever) seem to make the obvious connection with hemispheric roles (hint: the left hemisphere does the calculations). To our list of scary no-go topics that so far includes gender, transmutation, the role of consciousness, and so on, we can therefore add the issue of brain hemisphere specialities.

According to McGilchrist, the brain should be seen not as 'a cognitive machine, a computer that is fitted with a *rule-based programme* for structuring the world' (his emphasis), but rather as 'an embodied, living organism'.[5] While that is certainly true, when it comes to making a model of cognition, perhaps the problem is that we have just been using the wrong operating system.

SLEIGHT OF HAND

As discussed in the previous chapter, classical economics in the eighteenth century was based on a labour theory of value. Implicit in this theory was the connection between money and power. The philosopher Thomas Hobbes wrote in his 1651 *Leviathan* that 'The power of a man, to take it universally, is his present means to obtain some future good.' His friend Adam Smith agreed that 'Wealth, as Mr Hobbes says, is power ... the power of purchasing a certain command over all the labour, or over all the produce of labour which is then in the market.' It followed that 'The exchangeable value of everything must always be precisely equal to the extent of this power which it conveys to its owner.' On the other hand, the value of a tally is a function of the sovereign's ability to exert power, and claim a portion of a subject's labour in the form of a tax payment.

In the nineteenth century, however, neoclassical economists performed what magicians call a substitution trick, where one thing is surreptitiously swapped for another. They substituted the notion of hard labour with something that was more like its opposite – namely pleasure or utility.

The idea of utility goes back to the philosopher and social reformer Jeremy Bentham, who defined it as that which appears to 'augment or diminish the happiness of the party whose interest is in question'.[6] According to Bentham, the aim of social policy was to maximise (a word he invented) social utility, leading to 'the greatest happiness of the greatest number'.

The concept was later picked up by economists such as William Stanley Jevons, who assumed in their models that people and firms would always act to optimise their own utility. According to Bentham's 'felicific calculus', the pleasure or pain of an event depended on a number of factors, including its intensity, its duration, and its certainty or uncertainty. As Jevons pointed out, this meant that utility had two dimensions, corresponding to strength and duration, and furthermore had a probabilistic aspect, since 'When it is as likely as not that I shall receive £100, the chance is worth but £50'.[7] What therefore counts is the expected utility, i.e. what a person might expect to gain, on average, from some transaction which has an uncertain outcome.

The task for economists therefore seemed well-defined. 'Pleasure and pain are undoubtedly the ultimate objects of the Calculus of Economics,' wrote Jevons. 'To satisfy our wants to the utmost with the least effort – to procure the greatest amount of what is desirable at the expense of the least that is undesirable – in other words, to maximise pleasure, is the problem of Economics.' The economist Francis Edgeworth spoke about the 'Calculus of Pleasure', and wrote that *the conception of man as a pleasure machine* may justify and facilitate the employment of mechanical terms and Mathematical reasoning in social science' (his emphasis).[8] (The behavioural economists Daniel Kahneman and Amos Tversky echoed him a century later when they wrote of 'the human organism as a pleasure machine'.)

The switch from labour to utility as the basis for value was motivated by the development of sophisticated financial markets, which seemed to sever the link between earnings and actual work. Jevons, for example, relied in part on investments to support himself. In an 1864 letter, he told his brother Herbert that 'railway dividends also are improved up to six per cent, so that I shall have an income of about £170, which fully covers expenses'.[9] Jevons was fascinated by the business cycle, and developed a theory that it was driven not by investor sentiment, but by sunspots. As he wrote in 1875: 'If the planets govern the sun, and the sun governs the vintages and harvests, and thus the prices of food and raw materials and the state of the money market, it follows that the configurations of the planets may prove to be the remote causes of the greatest commercial disasters.'[10] (The fact that the average business cycle, which he put at 10½ years, didn't match perfectly with the sunspot cycle drew him into a long argument with astronomers over the quality of their observations.)

In a world where you could live off your investments, which were listings in an exchange whose prices were at the mercy of events happening some 93 million miles away on the surface of the Sun, it is easy to imagine that a labour theory of value may not have appeared fit for purpose. Which is perhaps what led Jevons, in the second paragraph of his 1871 book *The Theory of Political Economy*, to announce that 'Repeated reflection and inquiry have led me to the somewhat novel opinion that value depends entirely upon utility'. After all, if the Sun comes out and the value of your investment portfolio goes up, then so does your utility, no work required.

While the switch to utility was done in a transparent way, it also amounted to a subtle sleight of hand. Just as money puts a number on the fuzzy concept of value, so economists replaced the 'soft' concept of pleasure with a 'hard' number. And just as classical economists removed money from the analysis, so neoclassical economists removed the question of power. This switcheroo seems a textbook example of how what McGilchrist calls the 'unopposed left hemisphere' has usurped functions better left to the right. It is what allowed the mathematisation of economics, at least in terms of classical mathematics. And the result was that economics could present itself as a hard science, disguise the importance of power, and still claim that 'Economics is about happiness', as a leading economist once wrote (where exactly is the joy in being handed the short end of a tally stick?).

It was a magic trick of the first order. In the magic show that is money, the role of the economist may be that of the famulus or assistant, but as always, they play a vital part in maintaining the illusion.

THE UTILITY OF UTILITY

One question concerned how exactly all this lovely pleasure was to be measured, given that detection of what Edgeworth had called the 'hedonico-magnetic field' was proving elusive. Another approach, though, was to simply assume that utility is reflected by price. Or as Jevons put it: 'just as we measure gravity by its effects in the motion of a pendulum, so we may estimate the equality or inequality of feelings by the decisions of the human mind. The will is our pendulum, and its oscillations are minutely registered in the price lists of the markets.'

Of course, this turned utility into a somewhat circular concept. As the economist Joan Robinson observed in 1962, '*Utility* is the quality in commodities that makes individuals want to buy them, and the fact that individuals want to buy commodities shows that they have *utility*' (her emphasis).[11] But it did seem to hold out the possibility that economics could be put on a rational scientific basis.

This job was taken up by the applied mathematician John von Neumann, who was ideally suited to the task. After spending years trying to reduce all of mathematics to a basic set of propositions or axioms (he thought he had succeeded, but then the Austrian mathematician Kurt Gödel proved that for any set of axioms, there will always be a statement that cannot be proved to be true or false without adding another axiom), and then developing quantum mathematics (he managed to unify the matrix approach of Werner Heisenberg with the wave equation approach of Erwin Schrödinger, but this time his thunder was stolen by the English physicist Paul Dirac, whose proof was more accessible to physicists), von Neumann turned his attention to economics.

After learning from an economist friend about the efforts being made to turn economics into a proper (i.e. 'hard') mathematical subject, von Neumann realised that economic transactions could be viewed as a kind of game, where the buyer and seller each adopted strategies to optimise their utility – and games usually have rules. In collaboration with the economist Oskar Morgenstern, he began work on a paper which eventually became a 600-page tome called *Theory of Games and Economic Behaviour*. This aimed 'to find the mathematically complete principles which define "rational behavior" for the participants in a social economy, and to derive from them the general characteristics of that behavior'.

Their theory laid out four axioms which defined a rational decision-maker. For example, the Completeness axiom assumes that the agent has well-defined preferences and can always choose between two alternatives, while the Transitivity axiom assumes that the agent always makes decisions consistently. In other words, to qualify as rational, people don't have to behave in a manner which strikes an impartial observer as particularly clever or well-informed; they just have to be consistent in a technical sense.

The book, when it came out in 1944, was an academic and popular hit. The *New York Times* even featured it on the front page of its Sunday edition, reporting that 'A new approach to economic analysis that seeks to solve hitherto insoluble problems of business strategy by developing and applying to them a new mathematical theory of games of strategy like poker, chess and solitaire has caused a sensation among professional economists'.[12]

Mathematical results don't usually grace the front covers of newspapers, and as the game theorist Ariel Rubinstein observes, one reason for the sensation around game theory was its clever framing. 'Von Neumann was not only a genius in mathematics, he was also a genius in public relations. The choice of the name "theory of games" was brilliant as a marketing device. The word "game" has friendly, enjoyable associations. It gives a good feeling to people. It reminds us of our childhood, of chess and checkers, of children's games. The associations are very light, not heavy, even though you may be trying to deal with issues like nuclear deterrence.'[13]

Again, the 'soft' domain of games was usurped by 'hard' mathematical theory. Indeed, another reason for game theory's success was that it removed the whole question of subjectivity from economic decisions. It didn't matter why someone preferred one thing over another, all that mattered was that they had fixed preferences which needed to be satisfied.

We return to the topic of game theory later, but for now, how useful is the concept of utility? And are people really defined by 'rational behaviour', as von Neumann assumed?

UNIVERSAL BOGEY

Critics have long mocked the concept of rational economic man, which underpins much mainstream theory. Thorstein Veblen compared him in 1899 to 'a lightning calculator of pleasures and pains who oscillates like a homogeneous glob-ule of desire of happiness under the impulse of stimuli that shift him about the area, but leave him intact'.[14] Economists in turn have always replied that their theory is much more sophisticated than critics believe – as the British economist Lionel Robbins wrote in 1932, 'if it were generally realised that Economic Man is only an expository device ... it is improbable that he would be such a universal bogey' – and accuse those critics of attacking a straw man.[15]

In the post-war era, though, rational economic man only took on a larger role in economics, beginning with a starring turn in the so-called 'invisible hand theorem' of Kenneth Arrow and Gérard Debreu.[16] This used a result from game theory to prove that a free market economy would automatically lead to a kind of optimal outcome, in the sense that nothing could be changed without making at least one person worse off (a con-dition known as Pareto optimality). However, to accomplish this remarkable feat, economic man had to be not just rational, but also endowed with infinite computational power and the ability to devise plans for every future eventuality. The model naturally assumed that the economy was effectively based on barter and didn't feature money.

While this was certainly impressive, rational economic man achieved even greater heights in the 1960s with Eugene Fama's efficient market hypothesis. This theory, which underpins the field of quantitative finance, argues that the actions of rational investors mean that the price of a financial asset reflects its utility in terms of expected future earnings. If an asset price gets out of whack, these rational investors act instantaneously to restore it to its correct level. A spin-off was the Black–Scholes model for computing the price of options, discussed later. The only role for money was to assume that investors had access to infinite credit, so they could exploit any inefficiency by borrowing funds to buy assets.

So-called 'rational choice theory' extended the influence of rational economic man into other areas such as psychology, sociology, and politics; and economic modellers became committed, as economist J.W. Mason wrote in 2018, to 'the idea that the economy can be thought of as a single infinitely-lived individual calculating the trade-off between leisure and consumption over all future time. For an orthodox macroeconomist – anyone who hoped to be hired at a research university in the past thirty years – this approach isn't just one tool among others. It *is* macroeconomics.'[17] One mathematical economist cited a review of one of his papers which simply read: 'We do not see the point of not assuming an agent knows the perfect model of the economy. This is not economics.'[18]

Far from being a 'universal bogey' or a 'straw man', rational economic man was looking more like a kind of magical totem that could be summoned to make sense of any problem. (Meanwhile, the 2015 investigation into the economics department at the University of Manitoba, mentioned earlier, described the straw man defence as 'gaslighting', which sounds like an apt summary of much of mainstream economics.[19]) The field's central narrative – which goes back to Adam Smith, was codified by Arrow and Debreu in their invisible hand theorem, and reached its apogee in efficient market theory – had long been that by taking rational decisions, economic agents guide the economy to a societally optimal outcome, in which price reflects intrinsic value. The utility of something is therefore just its price, as Jevons had argued, and the system was rational.

Economists were therefore as surprised as anyone by the 2007/8 financial crisis, which seemed among other things to call into question the idea that people always behave rationally, or have perfect insight into the future, or correctly and instantaneously allocate resources so that prices perfectly reflect intrinsic value.

ADD SOME EPICYCLES

A recurrent theme in this book is that when economic theory collides with reality, it adjusts not by revising any of its basic assumptions – as Paul Krugman put it, 'Neither the financial crisis nor the Great Recession that followed required a rethinking of basic ideas' – but by adding epicycles.[20] And to explain the behavioural lapses of economic man, it had a shiny new set of such devices standing ready, in the form of behavioural economics.

The field of behavioural economics began with the work of the psychologists Daniel Kahneman and Amos Tversky in the 1970s, who developed an approach known as prospect theory. Some of its main insights were summarised in a 1977 report that was funded in part by grants from the US Department of Defense and was supervised by the Office of Naval Research. The connection with military decision-making was made explicit in the introductory summary, which noted that 'The application of scientific methods and formal analysis to problems of decision-making originated during World War II from the need to solve strategic and tactical problems in situations where experience was either costly or impossible to acquire'.[21]

As the authors pointed out, standard decision theory was based on von Neumann's expected utility theory. Indeed, 'most students of the field regard the axioms of utility theory as canons of rational behavior in the face of uncertainty, and they also regard them as a reasonable approximation to observed economic behavior'. In practice, though, 'actual decisions under conditions of uncertainty do not obey the axioms of utility theory'. For example, people tend to frame problems as gains or losses which they treat differently. And instead of weighting different outcomes in terms of their probability, decisions are affected also by attitudes towards uncertainty, such as risk aversion.

Prospect theory therefore attempted to correct for these effects, as shown in the plots below. The value function (top panel) shows the psychological value of an event (vertical axis) as a function of monetary gains or losses (horizontal axis). The centre represents a reference level, according to which gains or losses are experienced. For example, if a house like your own sold recently for a particular price, then that price may become a reference point, so selling your own home for less than that will feel like a loss. The phenomenon known as loss aversion means that a loss of a certain amount is felt more than a similar gain (dotted lines).

The uncertainty weighting function (bottom panel) shows how an outcome is weighted by its probability. In expected utility theory, the uncertainty weighting of an event simply equals its probability (dashed line). In prospect theory, the curve is concave near 0 and convex near 1 (solid line). This reflects, for example, the empirical observation that people tend to attribute too much weight to events that have a very low probability of occurring, so a small increase in risk has a big effect.

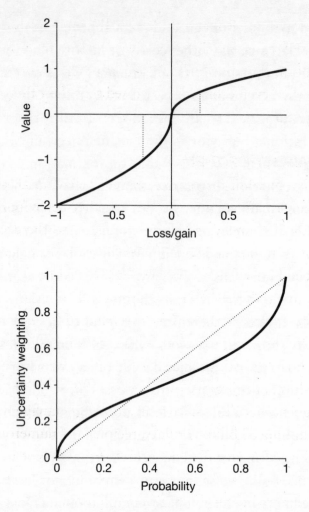

FIGURE 7.1 The top panel shows a plot of the value function for a hypothetical person. The bottom panel shows the uncertainty weighting function.

Kahneman and Tversky later came up with increasingly refined versions of prospect theory, and along with other behavioural economists discovered hundreds of 'cognitive biases' which make us behave in a less than perfectly rational manner. Kahneman was later awarded the 2002 Nobel Memorial Prize in Economics for their work (Tversky had died), as were other contributors to behavioural economics, including George

Akerlof (2001), Robert Shiller (2013), and Richard Thaler (2017). However, the theory had very little in the way of public recognition or impact on mainstream practice until the 2007/8 crisis, when even economists realised that their theory needed a few tweaks.

THE FAIREST OF THEM ALL

There is a puzzling disconnect between behavioural economists and mainstream economists over whether behavioural theory is a radical change, or just an extension to the economists' toolbox. On the one hand, Thaler for example has frequently described himself as a 'renegade' and his work in behavioural economics as 'heretical' or 'high treason'.[22] On the other hand, he wasn't burned at the stake, or even forced to suffer any grievous career setbacks – indeed, as the economist John Cochrane noted, he is 'a Distinguished Service professor with a multiple-group low-teaching appointment at the very University of Chicago he derides, partner in an asset management company running $3 billion dollars, recipient of numerous awards including AEA vice president, and so on'.[23] Not to mention recipient of the Nobel Memorial Prize.

Thaler credits his initial revelation to an incident where he decided that guests were eating too many cashews before dinner, so he took the bowl away, and was surprised when they thanked him, thus demonstrating how quirky humans are.[24] He writes about how he met Robert Shiller in 1982 and convinced him to 'embrace the heretical idea that social phenomena might influence stock prices as much as they do fashion trends. Hemlines go up and down without any reason; might not stock prices be influenced in other similar ways that seem to be beyond the standard economist's purview?' But in an age when the value of Dogecoin, a dog-themed cybercurrency itself invented as a joke, surges because Elon Musk jokes about it on Twitter, such observations – which might seem 'heretical' in the economics department common room – come across as rather anodyne to the rest of us, and are not quite in Frederick Soddy or Alexander Wendt territory.[25]

The conventional viewpoint would be to say that, after putting up spirited resistance, mainstream economics eventually shifted in order to absorb behavioural approaches, so that 'We're all behavioral economists now', as the title of one paper put it.[26] Another, though, is to say that describing behavioural approaches as 'heretical' and its proponents as 'renegades' is a useful piece of marketing that makes them look more interesting, and the mainstream more progressive and tolerant, than they actually are. As evolutionary economist David Sloan Wilson wrote, 'so far, behavioural economists have merely compiled a list of "anomalies" and "paradoxes" that are anomalous and paradoxical only against the background of the general equilibrium model, like satellites that cannot escape the orbit of their mother planet. They have not put forth a general theory of their own.'[27]

My own take on the subject (see my book *Behavioural Economics: Psychology, Neuroscience, and the Human Side of Economics*[28]) is that behavioural approaches have led to genuine advances in our understanding of human behaviour; shed light on topics such as forecasting and marketing; changed some areas of economics, such as finance; and, as discussed later, helped lay the empirical ground for quantum cognition. However, it is true that they have had much less impact on core models. For example, the *Oxford Review of Economic Policy*'s 'Rebuilding Macroeconomic Theory' report stated in 2018 that the 'two critical assumptions' underpinning mainstream macroeconomic models are 'the efficient market hypothesis, and rational expectations'.[29] While it recommends 'relaxing the requirement of rational expectations', it also remarks that 'there is not yet a new paradigm in sight'. And the general view seems to be that behavioural effects are interesting and important in particular situations, but tend to come out in the wash.

As law professor William Hubbard wrote in a 2017 paper, 'In the realm of physics, the Correspondence Principle tells us that Newtonian mechanics is basically wrong, but it's a pretty good approximation at the scale of human society, most but not all of the time. The analogous principle in behavioral economics is that neoclassical economics is basically wrong, but it's a pretty good approximation at the scale of human society, most but not all of the time.'[30] Or as Cochrane puts it: 'People do a lot of nutty things. But when you raise the price of tomatoes, they buy fewer tomatoes, just as if utility maximizers had walked into the grocery store.'[31]

The real reason that behavioural economics has been easily absorbed by mainstream practice, then, is that it is treated as an epicycle that can be wheeled out to fit particular empirical phenomena such as loss aversion or uncertainty aversion, while keeping the core of the theory intact. As Krugman (whose position as a public figure makes him something of a go-to source for this kind of thing) wrote in 2018, 'We start with rational behaviour and market equilibrium as a baseline, and try to get economic dysfunction by tweaking that baseline at the edges.'[32] A corollary is that economic problems can be treated using small 'nudges' to tune people's behaviour and make it closer to the rational sort assumed by models, as described by Thaler and law professor Cass R. Sunstein in their 2008 book *Nudge*.

However, as already argued, just as quantum effects scale up in nuclear devices, so the complex properties of money scale up and affect the global economy in a manner which can't be addressed by tweaking a curve or adding an epicycle. And as seen in the next chapter, it also turns out that there is a wide class of cognitive phenomena whose quantum nature eludes a behavioural approach.

Just as neoclassical economics replaced labour with utility, quantum economics shifts the focus from utility to propensity. Prices are measured by transactions, which in turn depend on the propensity curves of buyers and sellers. While utility can't be measured, we can at least infer something about the probability of people buying or selling. And the shift to a probabilistic framework is where quantum effects such as interference and entanglement come in.

Before getting on to that, though, it is worth pausing for a moment to reflect on the awesome power of neoclassical Magick to produce a kind of mental distortion field. The theory of expected utility, coupled with the assumption of rational expectations, may be the most influential mathematical model of human behaviour to have ever been devised – and one of the greatest deceptions played on the human species. For example, it implies, as quoted above, that people are capable of 'calculating the trade-off between leisure and consumption over all future time', including effects on their future descendants. This assumption feeds directly into government policy about things like pensions and retirement planning. Yet according to one analysis, the median working-age American couple has saved about $5,000 for retirement, which is a couple of unplanned expenses away from zero (this goes up to $17,000 for those on the 'cusp of retirement').[33] Our descendants may disagree with the notion that their utility has been optimised into the infinite future, as they deal with the consequences of structural inequality, climate change, and unexploded financial bombs. And behavioural nudges alone won't fix these problems.

Business schools, drenched as they are in neoclassical theory, teach the idea that startups must develop a convincing value proposition which can be measured using metrics such as productivity or revenue. But value has two components, the subjective and the objective – and often the value proposition is really a rationalisation of the former. Consider, for example, a new piece of business collaboration software which gets everyone communicating together on a shared platform rather than through separate emails (so a competitor for services such as Slack). The official value proposition could be that it will improve productivity and reduce the need for meetings. The subjective reason, on the other hand, might be that people like using it, but also (and this part is not said out loud) that managers in particular like it, because it gives them more control over their subordinates by making it easy to track their interactions – and they are the ones making the purchase decision. The business plan is therefore right, but for the wrong reasons. Conversely, a business plan which looks good on paper might fail in practice, because it doesn't take into account subjective factors.

One of the most important lessons of the quantum approach is that we need to be more humble – both about our understanding of the economy, and about our own capabilities. Like the witch in Snow White, we look at ourselves in the mirror of mainstream economics and see the fairest and most rational of them all (just a few tweaks and we'll be perfect!). As seen next, the quantum looking glass breaks this spell, and casts us in a more realistic light.

CHAPTER 8

OF MIND AND MONEY

*We recognise insanity, or madness in a man or woman,
by erratic, unpredictable, irrational behaviour that is
potentially damaging to the sufferers themselves or to
others. But that is exactly how financial markets have
behaved in recent years. They have been erratically
manic at one moment, unreasonably depressive
at others. The crises that have hit them have been
unpredicted and, to most observers, surprising.
Their behaviour has very seriously damaged others. Their
condition calls urgently for treatment of some kind.*

SUSAN STRANGE, *MAD MONEY: WHEN MARKETS
OUTGROW GOVERNMENTS*, 1998

While the field of behavioural economics adjusted mainstream
theory to accommodate a degree of psychological realism, a number of so-called paradoxes and anomalies, caused for example by
mental interference when considering conflicting ideas, continue to
elude it. As seen in this chapter, the main problem is that economics
is based on a classical operating system, while our minds seem to
prefer a quantum approach, which combines 'hard' objectivity and
'soft' subjectivity in a manner which defies conventional reason.
Nowhere is this quantum nature more apparent than in the magical
interactions between mind and money.

In 1947, two years after the Trinity test, the King of Denmark
conferred on Niels Bohr the country's top honour (known as

the Order of the Elephant, long story). The physicist needed a coat of arms to display at Frederiksborg Castle, and the design he chose featured a yin-yang symbol and a motto in Latin: *contraria sunt complementa* (opposites are complementary), which captured his principle of complementarity. This refers to the idea that quantum systems have complementary attributes, such as position and momentum, which cannot both be measured at the same time. In particular, quantum entities such as an electron have both wave and particle properties.

One can measure the location of an electron, as if it were a particle, but it also has a frequency, as if it were a wave. Neither description is complete in itself. An electron is singular and dissolved at the same time. The wave-like aspect is captured by something known as the Schrödinger wave equation. According to standard interpretations of quantum mechanics, the system prior to measurement is in a superposition of all the possible states. Only at the time of measurement does it somehow 'collapse' down to a specific state. The amplitude of the wave function at each position, when squared (this again is the 2-norm of quantum probability), gives the probability that the electron will be detected at that point, but the state is uncertain until measured.

As with other waves, the wave function displays features such as interference. This was most famously illustrated by the double-slit experiment, which is one of the most magical experiments in physics.

Physicists had long debated whether light was a particle or a wave. In the fourth century BC, Democritus said that light was made up of discrete *atomos*, or atoms. Aristotle countered that it was a wave in the ether. In the seventeenth century, Newton saw it as a stream of particles, while physicists on the Continent preferred the wave option.

In 1801, Thomas Young performed an experiment in which light from a source passes through two slits in a screen. He found that the light diffracts at each slit and forms an interference pattern, which is picked up by detectors on a second screen. The appearance of this pattern seemed to prove that light was a wave.[1] Waves have crests and troughs, so when two waves interfere with one another, there will be points where the crests reinforce one another, and other points where a trough is formed.

The debate, however, found new life when Einstein showed that light was a stream of photons. Finally, in 1909, Geoffrey Taylor repeated the experiment using an extremely weak light source, and demonstrated that even when individual photons are passed through the slit, the interference patterns are still reproduced.[2] The crests correspond to places with a high probability of seeing a photon, while the troughs are places with a low probability. Even though individual photons only pass through a single slit, they somehow react to the presence of the other slit. However, if another detector is used to determine which slit the photon passes through, then the system behaves in a classical fashion, and the interference pattern disappears.

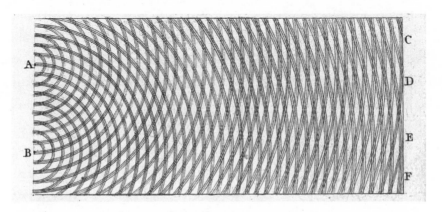

FIGURE 8.1 Thomas Young's sketch of interference patterns for light waves, formed when the light passes through two slits, labelled A and B.

This trick on the part of nature is so impressive that the physicist Richard Feynman famously said that the double-slit experiment 'has in it the heart of quantum mechanics. In reality, it contains the only mystery.'[3] However, duality is not limited to the subatomic domain. Yin-yang was invented for humans, not particles (though Lin Yutang did describe 'the male, active, positive or *yang* principle, and the female, passive, negative or *yin* principle' as 'really no more than a lucky, shrewd guess at positive and negative electricity').[4] Bullionists and chartalists have long debated whether money is a real thing or a virtual idea (of course, it is both). And the human mind is capable of producing mysterious effects and paradoxes of its own, which demand a similarly quantum approach.

MENTAL INTERFERENCE

An early example of a cognitive 'paradox' known as the disjunction effect was presented in a 1992 paper by behavioural scientists Amos Tversky and Eldar Shafir. This described an experiment in which the researchers asked a group of students whether they would purchase a non-refundable Hawaiian vacation if they were told that they had passed or failed an important exam, compared to a situation where the exam outcome was unknown.[5] The results showed that more than half the students chose to buy the vacation package if they knew the outcome, whether it was pass (54 per cent chose to buy) or fail (57 per cent). However, if they did not know the outcome, this dropped to 32 per cent. From a classical perspective, this makes little sense, since the outcome has to be either pass or fail.

The disjunction effect gets its name because in logic, disjunction refers to the OR statement, and in this experiment people were more likely to buy the vacation if they knew they had passed OR failed. Classical computers have OR gates which output a 1 if either of the input bits are in the state 1. There is no exact quantum analogue, for the reason that in a quantum computer, gates are always reversible. A classical OR gate involves a loss of information, because knowing that the output is 1 does not tell you which input was 1. Quantum computers retain information up until the moment of measurement.

Tversky and Shafir explained the disjunction effect as being caused by 'the loss of acuity induced by the presence of uncertainty', which could apply to just about any economic decision, where little is usually certain. However, another way to look at it is not in terms of a loss of information or acuity, but instead as the result of quantum interference.

A diagram of the experiment would look like the top panel of Figure 8.2. In the first stage, the person is faced with a test, which has two possible outcomes, pass or fail. In the second stage, they then have to make a yes/no decision about whether to buy a vacation.

If we assume that each person has a 50 per cent chance of passing the test, then from a classical perspective we can compute the possible outcomes by analysing each path separately. Referring to the figure, half the people take the top path, passing the test. Of them, 54 per cent decide in favour of the vacation. Half the people take the bottom path, failing the test. Of them, 57 per cent decide in favour of the vacation. So if we don't know whether a person has passed or failed, the chance of them buying the vacation should just be the average of these, which is 55.5 per cent.

In the quantum model, this is only true if we assume that the test result is measured and known, because otherwise the person is not in a single definite state, but is rather in a superposition state, which opens up the possibility of interference. The situation is therefore like a simple version of the double-slit

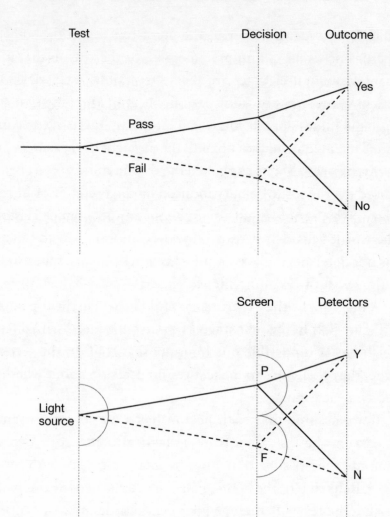

FIGURE 8.2 Top panel shows a schematic diagram of the disjunction effect experiment. Bottom panel shows a similar diagram for the dual-slit experiment.

setup (bottom panel) with two detectors. The event of taking the test acts as a kind of splitting device, which creates two possible paths. Even if the test result is not known, the mere existence of the test affects the mental state of the participant. The decision to purchase the vacation then acts on each aspect of this superposed state – the part which passes and the part which fails – in different ways, leading to interference. This is why the probability of purchasing the vacation drops to 32 per cent. However, if the test result is measured, then the path is known, the system behaves classically, and the interference magically disappears.

ENTANGLEMENT CIRCUIT

Just as we can simulate classical cognition using a classical computer, so we can simulate quantum cognition using a quantum circuit. The easiest way to do this is with the circuit shown in Figure 8.3. The upper qubit is acted on by a gate which positions it to reflect the probability of passing (1) or failing (0) the test. If we chose this gate to be a Hadamard gate, then there would be a 50:50 chance of passing or failing. The lower gate represents the probability of deciding to take a vacation. The two are entangled by the C-NOT gate.

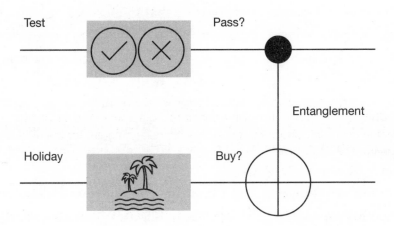

FIGURE 8.3 A quantum circuit for a decision to buy a vacation (lower qubit) following a test result (upper qubit). The shaded boxes now represent general quantum gates which position the qubit to reflect the probability of passing the test or buying the vacation, and the C-NOT gate represents mental entanglement.

To compare with the dual-slit setup, the top qubit therefore encodes the test result, whose measured value represents pass or fail, while the second qubit represents the vacation decision. The C-NOT gate, like a quantum if-then statement, entangles the two by making the vacation decision conditional on the test result. When the circuit is run, and the output is measured, exactly the same interference pattern is produced. We will spare the mathematical details, but note the similarity with the credit circuit that we have already seen in Figure 3.4, which illustrates the connection between mind and money. The difference is that the quantum gate on the lower qubit is no longer restricted to just flipping the qubit as in the credit circuit. Also, the entanglement gate represents not a contract between two people, but the internal entanglement of a subjective context (the test) and a final decision (the vacation). The inclusion of this entanglement gate is exactly what differentiates quantum cognition from classical logic.

We return to the topic of entanglement in the next chapter, but for now it is interesting to note that Figures 8.2 and 8.3 are two different ways of representing the same thing. In the former, a single qubit is being measured twice, for the test result and then for the vacation decision, while in the latter the test and vacation are represented by separate qubits that are measured at the end; but both methods yield the same probabilistic results when measured. The use of the entanglement gate is therefore a modelling choice.

One advantage of the quantum approach, in either representation, is that it allows us to separate out the relative contributions of the objective and subjective components of a decision. In the example of the disjunction effect, the test result isn't directly relevant to the question of whether or not to buy a vacation, so its influence is purely subjective. This is shown by the fact that if the test result is known, then whether it is pass or fail has little effect on the purchase decision. However, when the result is not known, the test does play an important role by creating uncertainty. In fact, one way to interpret the interference effect in this case is as a measure of aversion to uncertainty.

In a classical model, the probability of taking a decision can be computed just by calculating the objective expected utility. In the quantum model, we also need to take into account the subjective component, which creates the interference term. In general, of course, we don't know how large this subjective term will be until we test it. However, a good starting point, in the absence of other information, is to guess that the two components are of roughly equal magnitudes. If we measure the propensity of an outcome (i.e. the probability of it being chosen) on a scale of 0 to 1, then the objective part and the subjective part are equally important; however, their contributions don't add in the usual way because of interference. If the two parts add in a constructive manner, as in the crest of a wave, then the total propensity is 0.75, while if they subtract, as in the trough of a wave, this reduces to 0.25. The result is what quantum decision theorists Didier Sornette and Vyacheslav Yukalov call the quarter law.[6] It states that the interference term adjusts the probability of a particular decision up or down by about 25 per cent, depending on whether the option is considered subjectively attractive or not.

For example, in the case of the disjunction effect, where the interference is negative, the probability of choosing the vacation when the test result was known was on average 55.5 per cent. When the result was not known, this dropped to 32 per cent, which is a difference of about a quarter. The quarter law has in fact been tested in a wide range of cognitive experiments and has proved to be quite robust.

MOVING MOUNTAINS

The disjunction effect, which has also been tested for a range of different experiments, is an example of how a shift in context can affect the process of decision-making. In this case, the context is the event of taking an exam, and learning or not learning the result. The same approach can be used to model the so-called order effect seen with survey results, where the order in which two questions are asked affects the outcomes, because the first question establishes a context for the second.[7] In Figure 8.3 the top qubit would represent the response to the first question, while the bottom qubit represents the response to the second question. Another example is the phenomenon of preference reversal.

A core assumption of equilibrium-fixated neoclassical economics is that preferences remain fixed and stable. As Nobel Memorial winners George Stigler and Gary Becker wrote in 1977, 'tastes neither change capriciously nor differ importantly between people. On this interpretation one does not argue over tastes for the same reason that one does not argue over the Rocky Mountains – both are there, will be there next year, too, and are the same to all men.'[8] In the real world, though, it seems that people change their minds.

This had already been officially demonstrated in a 1971 paper by psychologists Sarah Lichtenstein and Paul Slovic.[9] Experimental subjects were told that a roulette wheel with 36 sectors will be spun, and they must choose to take one of two bets. In bet A, eleven of the 36 sectors give a win of $160, while the remaining 25 lose $15. In bet B, 35 of the 36 sectors give a win of $40, while one sector gives a loss of $10.

These two bets were chosen so that they give almost exactly the same expected payout ($38.47 for A versus $38.61 for B), but they have very different risk profiles. Bet A is the exciting bet with the chance to win big, like investing in a risky stock, while bet B is more conservative, like putting your money into a safer bond. In the experiment, most people preferred B because of its safety. However, they were then asked how much they would charge other people for tickets to play these games. In this case, they charged a higher price for A, probably because they focused on the possibility of the larger prize. So when asked to play a game themselves they preferred B, but when selling tickets to others they preferred A. If they were an investment advisor, they would be pushing their clients into technology startups while stashing their own earnings in a savings account.

As the economists David Grether and Charles Plott pointed out in a 1979 article, this phenomenon of preference reversal was again inconsistent with classical logic, since it 'allows individual choice to depend upon the context in which the choices are made'.[10] Taken at face value, it would imply that 'no optimization principles of any sort lie behind even the simplest of human choices'. As usual, they hastened to point out that just because classical theory is 'subject to exception' does not mean it should be discarded, especially since 'No alternative theory currently available appears to be capable of covering the same extremely broad range of phenomena'.

Indeed, as Kahneman later noted, the paper had 'little direct effect on the convictions of economists'.[11] In a 1990 paper, he argued that preference reversal can be explained using prospect theory, by saying that the change of context forces subjects to switch from System 1 to System 2 thinking.[12] When choosing the bet for themselves, they are operating in System 1 mode and prefer game B because it feels safer; when pricing the game, they put on their System 2 hat and do the math, so select game A.

While this certainly sounds like a reasonable explanation, it also confuses matters. As discussed earlier, the main results of prospect theory are summarised by the value function and the uncertainty function (Figure 7.1). In those plots, System 2 thinking can be represented by a straight line; so, for example, the value of a gamble is just equal to the payout. Prospect theory therefore already incorporates a mix of System 1 and System 2 effects. In the classical picture, the only way to accommodate preference reversal is to introduce an additional ad hoc epicycle that differentiates between the two contexts.

In another 1990 paper, Tversky and Thaler concluded that: 'First, people do not possess a set of pre-defined preferences for every contingency. Rather, preferences are constructed in the process of making a choice or judgment. Second, the context and procedures involved in making choices or judgments influence the preferences that are implied by the elicited responses. In practical terms, this implies that behavior is likely to vary across situations that economists consider identical.'[13] But if preferences aren't fixed, then it becomes impossible to optimise utility, which is the basis of mainstream economics.

As seen with the disjunction effect, though, another approach is to realise that any decision is a mix of objective and subjective components, with the latter often sensitive to context; and that what counts is not abstract utility, but observed propensity.

DON'T BRING FACTS INTO THE ARGUMENT

Returning to the circuit diagram above for the disjunction effect, imagine that the upper gate corresponds not necessarily to a test, but to a general subjective context which prepares the ground for a decision. Then this context will again create interference, positive or negative, which affects the decision. If we use the quarter law as a first approximation, then when the subjective context adds to the objective calculation, the total propensity will be around 0.75, while when it subtracts, the result will be around 0.25. In terms of a ratio, the difference between these is therefore a factor of three.

A corollary is that subjective factors create a kind of threshold which objective utility must overcome before it can change a decision – and while utility can often be measured on a continuous numerical scale (such as price), the subjective context is more of a switch-like effect. So if, for example, the subjective context favours a particular decision, then any reversal of the decision will rely on the objective utility calculation making up that gap. When you do the math, this suggests a similar factor of three difference in the objective utility, as measured, for example, by money – a result known in quantum decision theory as the preference reversal criterion.

Now, it might seem ridiculous to say that objective factors need to change by on average a factor of three in order to overcome subjective preferences – especially since, in the classical model, the threshold would be zero, because what counts is only objective utility. On the other hand, though, it does help to explain why rational argument seems to have so little impact on questions such as who is a good political leader, or what we should do about climate change. When subjective forces are at play, the joking expression 'Don't bring facts into the argument!' may be correct.

In fact, this preference reversal criterion has been empirically tested and again shown to be quite robust. It is also related to a number of other cognitive effects studied by behavioural economists. An example is the endowment effect, which refers to the observation that we value something more highly if we own it than if we don't own it. This has been illustrated by behavioural economists many times, the best-known experiment being one in which subjects were given a mug and then offered the chance to sell or exchange it. The researchers found that people demanded a median selling price of $7.12 in exchange for the mug, but only were willing to spend a median buying price of $2.87 to purchase the mug themselves. As with the roulette example above, the change in context – in this case, from owning to not-owning – is enough to change the person's mind about the object's worth. The relative difference in prices is a factor of about 2.5, which is not far off the value of three predicted by quantum decision theory (especially when compared with neoclassical theory, which suggests the difference should be 'negligible').[14]

UNDER WATER

While such cognitive effects are usually demonstrated under controlled conditions using experimental subjects, a natural experiment for preference reversal was provided by the observed rate of strategic default during the US housing crisis. According to objective utility maximisation, default makes sense if the costs associated with staying in a home exceed the costs associated with selling it; and a quarterly survey of US households from December 2008 to September 2010 found that roughly 30 per cent of respondents said they would default if the shortfall was more than $100,000, and a 64 per cent majority said they would default if it exceeded $200,000.[15]

However, the actual statistics for foreclosure paint a very different picture. By mid-2009, over 16 per cent of US homeowners had negative equity exceeding 20 per cent of their home's value, but strategic defaults remained at only 1 to 2 per cent of all mortgages.[16] The main cause of default, it turned out, was not utility optimisation, but unemployment leading to an inability to maintain payments. According to one estimate from the Federal Reserve, the 'median borrower walks away from his home when he is 62 per cent underwater'.[17]

On the face of it, this behaviour seems irrational, since even given the various costs of foreclosure, the best option from a narrow utilitarian point of view would often be default. For example, one paper describes the case of a hypothetical home-owner who bought an average home in Miami at the peak of the housing market for around $360,000: 'That home would now be worth only about $159,000, and, assuming a 5% down payment, the homeowner would have approximately $170,000 in negative equity. Assuming he intended to live in the house for five years, he could save approximately $147,000 by walk-ing away and renting a comparable home ... The advantage of walking away is even more starkly evident for the large percent-age of individuals who bought more-expensive-than-average homes in the Miami area – or in any bubble market for that matter – in the last five years. Millions of U.S. homeowners could save hundreds of thousands of dollars by strategically defaulting on their mortgages. Homeowners should be walking away in droves. But they aren't.'[18]

As it turned out, home prices in Miami bottomed in 2012 according to the S&P/Case-Shiller FL-Miami Home Price Index, and have since recovered their pre-inflation losses, but of course few people expected that at the time (defaulters in early 2010 could have invested their savings in the stock market and tripled their money over the next decade, but that wasn't a popular option either).

Applying the preference reversal criterion, one might expect prices to drop by about two thirds before an owner will walk away from their home. This is not far from the Federal Reserve estimate of a 62 per cent shortfall. The mortgage crisis can therefore be viewed as a kind of giant natural experiment which demonstrates the quantum nature of preference reversal. According to classical theory, homeowners should default as soon as it becomes clear that they are likely to lose money by staying. Surveys showed that homeowners agreed, at least when they were answering questions in a survey. When they were faced with the actual prospect of default, though, they experienced a cluster of emotions such as fear of uncertainty, shame at reneging on their debt, attachment to their home, sorrow at losing it, and so on, which loomed much larger than any objective calculation of utility.

If you want a simple handle, remember that decisions are the product of the two hemispheres of the brain working together. The left hemisphere is good at math, so we can give it the role of the accountant working out a statement of profit or loss. However, the right brain takes in the big picture and is sensitive to context. If we assign each a roughly equal role in decision-making, but with a degree of context-dependent interference, then this gives you the preference reversal criterion. Superposition is the window that lets the right brain in. Of course, the interplay between hemispheres and the dynamics of cognition are incredibly complex, but if the test is predictive accuracy, then this very basic model of cognition would seem to beat the classical utility approach, which emphasises only the objective side such as price.

Subjective factors don't just affect our mental decisions, they also affect our bodies, as in the magical placebo effect from medicine. The first public medical trial of this was carried out in 1784, by a royal commission that included Benjamin Franklin (then serving as American ambassador to France), and concerned the work of Franz Anton Mesmer, who claimed to be able to endow objects with an 'animal magnetism' with curative powers. After handling a specially treated ('mesmerised') object or substance, his clients would enter a 'crisis' marked by convulsions, fainting, and so on, after which they were pronounced cured. The commission found, however, that some patients experienced a crisis after touching plain water which they were told had been mesmerised, while others did not react to treated water which they were told was plain. They concluded that any effects were due to 'imagination'. While mesmerism has gone out of fashion, the placebo effect and the power of subjective beliefs and imagination are alive and well. For example, sleeping pills are usually blue because that colour enhances the placebo effect (except, apparently, for Italian males, who associate blue with their national football team).[19] There might be what Wendt calls a taboo on subjectivity in the social sciences, but in medicine it is harder to ignore, which is why clinical trials must be designed to show that treatments beat a placebo.

THE QUANTUM THRESHOLD EFFECT

In physics, the existence of quanta was first proposed by Max Planck in 1901 as a kind of trick to explain why something called ultraviolet catastrophe didn't occur in practice. It was known that the energy carried by a beam of light depended on its frequency, which for visible light corresponds to colour. Blue light has a higher frequency than red light, so is more energetic. Invisible ultraviolet light has a higher energy still. The problem was that, according to classical theory, the energy would become unbounded at high frequencies. Ultraviolet light would do more than tan, it would fry. Planck found that the problem went away if he assumed that the energy was transmitted in discrete parcels, or quanta.

The fact that quanta were more than a mathematical convenience was demonstrated by Einstein in 1905 using the photoelectric effect. This refers to the tendency of some materials to emit electrons when light is shone on them. According again to the classical theory, the energy of the emitted electrons should depend only on the intensity (i.e. brightness) of the light source; but in practice, it turned out that what really mattered was the frequency. Furthermore, each material had a cut-off frequency, below which no amount of light would work. It seemed that an electron must receive a certain threshold of energy in order to be dislodged from an atom. In a 1905 paper, Einstein showed that the photoelectric effect could be explained by use of Planck's quanta.

The mortgage crisis is similar, with the difference that, instead of computing the quantum of energy required to dislodge an electron from an atom, we are computing the quantum of debt required to dislodge a homeowner. And if the idea of a quantum was originally introduced in physics to explain why the ultraviolet catastrophe didn't occur in practice, the threshold effect in economics explains the non-occurrence of a less dramatic but still very expensive disaster of a different sort. If underwater borrowers had reacted like rational economic agents and engaged in mass default, then according to an estimate from First American, it would have cost some $745 billion, or slightly more than the size of the 2008 bank bailout, to restore the lost equity. The fact that this didn't happen can be put down to the quantum threshold effect.

Going back to the discussion in Chapter 1, the same effect might explain why it was that Canadian lenders in 2021 were so eager to make highly leveraged loans in the middle of a pandemic and a recession: the banks knew that when it came to the crunch, homeowners would do anything in their power to honour their debts. In other words, they were performing their calculations in a manner consistent with quantum economics, rather than classical models, which in any case don't usually include the financial system or the possibility of default.[20]

As we will discuss later when considering the dynamics of financial transactions, the resemblance between something like a mortgage crisis and the photoelectric effect runs even deeper. For now, though, it is worth noting that subjective effects play a key role in money creation. Returning to our circuit diagram of a tally stick, the reliability of the tally as money depends on the degree of coercion applied by the money lender. Again, the coercion will be a mix of objective and subjective factors. Interference between these effects implies that we might expect money objects to show a kind of threshold behaviour themselves. Like much else in life, they work until they (suddenly) don't. They are the product, not just of law and the threat of force, but also of intangible factors, which might be described as faith in the sanctity of the money supply.

Any belief system needs priests to help keep the faith alive, and in the modern economy this task falls to economists and central bankers. Economists really don't like being compared to priests, since obviously it doesn't mesh with the field's image as an objective science. As will be seen later, though, much of their activity boils down to maintaining a kind of holy story about money and markets. In the next chapter, we turn our attention to another source of quantum magic: the miracle of entanglement.

CHAPTER 9

ENTANGLED CHOICES

Much discussion of money involves a heavy overlay of priestly incantation. Some of this is deliberate. Those who talk of money and teach about it and make their living by it gain prestige, esteem and pecuniary return, as does a doctor or a witch doctor, from cultivating the belief that they are in a privileged association with the occult.

JOHN KENNETH GALBRAITH, *MONEY: WHENCE IT CAME, WHERE IT WENT*, 1975

Would our probability of survival be greater if we believed that individuals and groups were conscious and entangled agents who are capable of transforming cultures and systems at scale?

KAREN O'BRIEN, *YOU MATTER MORE THAN YOU THINK: QUANTUM SOCIAL CHANGE FOR A THRIVING WORLD*, 2021[1]

———

A key axiom of rational choice theory, and the mathematical area known as game theory, is that people act independently. The reality is that we are influenced by other people, both directly through things like herd behaviour, and indirectly through shared social norms and beliefs. As seen in this chapter, entanglement is a standard trick of quantum systems, including both the physical and the social sorts, and is an important feature of quantum computers. Games designed to be played on quantum computers are upending not only game theory, but the way that we think about human behaviour.

———

Chemistry was not the only scientific field to emerge from alchemy. Newtonian physics is often presented as the triumph of a rationalist, mechanistic worldview, but it didn't start that way.

Newton himself spent far more time on mystical pursuits such as Kabbalism, searching for prophetic passages in the Bible, attempting to unlock the secret code of the pyramids to determine the date of the apocalypse, and so on than he did on science. He wrote an entire 300,000-word tract on the book of Revelation, which is about 30 times longer than the book of Revelation. He was also a serious alchemist: even while writing his masterwork *Principia Mathematica*, according to his secretary, he kept up with the alchemy, his fire blazing throughout the night until 'he had finished his Chymical Experiments, in the Performances of which he was the most accurate, strict, exact'.

Newton saw his scientific and mystical work as different aspects of the same approach. In fact, just as Soddy's interest in alchemy may have primed his insights into radiation, it was probably Newton's mysticism which made it possible for him to conceive his theory of gravity in the first place, given that it relied on an instantaneous action at a distance, which doesn't seem very mechanistic. As he explained in a letter: 'Gravity must be caused by an agent acting constantly according to certain laws, but whether this agent be material or immaterial is a question I have left to the consideration of my readers.'[2] His contemporary Leibniz went so far as to accuse Newton of treating gravity as a kind of 'occult quality', i.e. not explainable by rational or mechanical means. In other words, as magic.

In magic, a transportation trick is one which involves magically moving something from one place to another, as when a coin passes from a hand to behind a person's ear, or a bird appears inside a light bulb. Newton's gravitational action at a distance does the same thing, by mysteriously transporting a force across space. Even in a 'hard science' like mechanics, there is always a place where the magic gets in – or the religion. According to the philosopher Andrew Janiak, 'Newton obviously thinks that God might be the very "immaterial medium" underlying all gravitational interactions among material bodies.'[3] And, even if he otherwise conceived of a clockwork universe governed by mechanistic forces, Newton also held out a role for the deity as the 'prime mover' who winds the clock in the first place.

Newton didn't think he actually invented his laws of physics, but believed that such truths had been revealed long ago by God, and were known to some of the ancients; however, they had long ago been lost, so he was just rediscovering them. An example was the idea that everything is made of atoms. As Newton wrote, 'That all matter consists of atoms was a very ancient opinion. This was the teaching of the multitude of philosophers who preceded Aristotle, namely Epicurus, Democritus, Ecphantus, Empedocles, Zenocrates, Heraclides, Asclepiades, Diodorus, Metrodorus of Chios, Pythagoras, and previous to these Moschus the Phoenician whom Strabo declares older than the Trojan war.' He was just restoring it to its rightful place.

Perhaps more remarkably, Newton also believed that Pythagoras knew the law of gravity but, being a good magician, had decided to keep it secret. The evidence was secretly encoded in Greek art, mythology, and even coins, in the symbol of Apollo's lyre. The lyre's seven strings were said to represent the main heavenly bodies (they missed Uranus and Neptune), and its music thus captured what the Pythagoreans called the Music of the Spheres, which according to them only Pythagoras, being a demigod, could hear.

As already mentioned, Pythagoras was the first to relate musical harmony to mathematics, and this was what inspired his idea that the universe was based on number. With a little experimentation he could have found that the tone produced by a string at a certain tension varies according to the square of its length. This was very similar to the law of gravity, which states that the gravitational force produced by one object on another decreases with the square of distance. So according to Newton, the secret message encoded by Apollo's lyre was that 'the Sun by his own force acts upon the planets in that harmonic ratio of distances by which the force of tension acts upon strings of different lengths, that is reciprocally in the duplicate ratio of the distances'. Or more simply: the law of gravity corresponds to a law of music. The Pythagoreans knew the law, but 'loved so to mitigate their mystical discourses that in the presence of the vulgar they foolishly propounded vulgar matters for the sake of ridicule'.[4]

In 1693, Newton suffered some kind of breakdown, possibly brought on by mercury poisoning from his alchemical activities. He confided to his friend Samuel Pepys that he had 'neither ate nor slept well in the last twelve months' and was lacking his 'former consistency of mind'. In 1696, another friend shuffled him into what was supposed to be a comfortable position at the Royal Mint – however, he took on his new role with gusto, especially when it came to cracking down on counterfeiters, and continued to practise magic and alchemy of the financial sort full time as Warden, then Master of the Mint, until his death in 1727.

Following his death, Newton was survived by an enormous collection of papers and manuscripts, totalling some 10 million words. The breakdown was about 50 per cent religious, 30 per cent science, 10 per cent alchemy, and 10 per cent related to his work in finance. There were even useful tips on how to treat the plague. Of possible cures, he wrote, 'the best is a toad suspended by the legs in a chimney for three days, which at last vomited up earth with various insects in it, on to a dish of yellow wax, and shortly after died. Combining powdered toad with the excretions and serum made into lozenges and worn about the affected area drove away the contagion and drew out the poison.'[5]

After his state funeral, and his entombment in Westminster Abbey as a hero of the new age of science (actually, natural philosophy – the word 'scientist' wasn't coined for another century), his heirs had a look through the great man's manuscripts and were of course horrified by the contents. So they didn't exactly rush to get them published.

In 1936 – so two centuries later – the economist John Maynard Keynes bought a large batch of the papers at auction. In a lecture to celebrate the 300th anniversary of Newton's birth in 1942 – it was postponed until 1946 because of the war, but Keynes died three months earlier so the lecture was read by his brother, Geoffrey – he wrote: 'Newton was not the first of the age of reason. He was the last of the magicians, the last of the Babylonians and Sumerians, the last great mind which looked out on the visible and intellectual world with the same eyes as those who began to build our intellectual inheritance rather less than 10,000 years ago.'[6]

'Why do I call him a magician?' Keynes went on, rhetorically. 'Because he looked on the whole universe and all that is in it as a riddle, as a secret which could be read by applying pure thought to certain evidence, certain mystic clues which God had laid about the world to allow a sort of philosopher's treasure hunt to the esoteric brotherhood.' But this connection with magic was repressed and forgotten. Instead Newton became 'the Sage and Monarch of the Age of Reason'. This was of course ironic given that Newton's 'secret heresies and scholastic superstitions ... had been the study of a lifetime to conceal!'.

As Keynes and Newton knew, society is deeply uncomfortable with things like magic and alchemy, so tries to repress them (especially if the magicians are female – see witch burnings). Which, as we'll see, is one reason why so little is known or understood about the magical properties of money, and in particular the notion of entanglement, which Einstein famously referred to as 'spooky action at a distance' (and which more recently was called 'The God Effect' in the title of a book by science writer Brian Clegg).

In physics, entanglement refers to the apparently magical way in which particles can be connected even though they are at opposite ends of the universe. For example, physicists can entangle pairs of photons in the laboratory, so that if one is measured spin up, then the other can only be measured spin down. The spin is therefore indeterminate until measured, but correlated at the same time, which is perplexing since the electrons are not connected by hidden wires capable of instantaneous transmission. Telepathy may be a mainstay of magic shows, but as Einstein wrote in a 1942 letter, the idea that God 'plays dice and uses "telepathic" methods ... is something that I cannot believe for a single moment'.[7] (Subsequent experiments showed that the universe didn't care.)

As discussed in Chapter 3, entanglement is a characteristic feature of quantum mathematics, and it is key to the function of quantum computers. Given that the development of computers has gone hand in hand with the development of computer games, it is perhaps not surprising that one of the first applications of quantum entanglement was to a game whose history goes back to the founding of game theory.

GET OUT OF JAIL

After the invention in the 1940s of game theory, researchers at places like the policy think tank RAND (the name stands for research and development) began casting around for ways that the mathematically elegant theory could be usefully applied to the real world. One topic which seemed to be relevant to real-life situations, at least of the sort encountered in jail, was a game known as the prisoner's dilemma.

The game involves two imaginary members of a criminal gang, who have been arrested for a crime and are being held separately. The prosecutor offers each prisoner a choice: testify that the other person committed the crime, or remain silent. Their penalties will then be as follows:

1. If both prisoners remain silent, they each get two years on a reduced charge. Total jail time served for both prisoners is four years.
2. If only one prisoner defects and betrays the other, that prisoner gets off and the other gets the full five years. Total jail time served for both prisoners is five years.
3. If both prisoners betray the other, they each get four years. Total jail time served for both prisoners is eight years.

From the perspective of both prisoners taken as a whole, outcome 1 is the best because total jail time is only four years, while outcome 3 is the worst, with a total of eight years. Both prisoners should therefore remain silent. However, from the perspective of a single prisoner, classical utility suggests a different response.

If the first prisoner opts to betray the other, then they will get either four years or zero years, depending on the actions of the other prisoner. If they assume, in the absence of other information, that each possibility has equal odds, then the expected sentence is the average of these, which is two years. On the other hand, if the first prisoner opts to not betray, then the expected sentence is the average of two years and five years, which is three and a half years. The option with the best expected outcome is therefore to betray.

If both players choose to betray, neither player can improve their outcome by changing their own strategy unilaterally. For example, if A switches strategy from betraying to remaining silent, they get hit with the maximum five-year term. In game theoretic terms, this state of mutual betrayal is known as a Nash equilibrium. On the other hand, if both choose to remain silent, the strategy is Pareto optimal, because any change will make one of the players worse off.

A strategy	B strategy	A sentence	B sentence
silent	silent	2	2
silent	betray	5	0
betray	silent	0	5
betray	betray	4	4

THE DOOMSDAY MACHINE

Now, usually when scientists come up with an exciting new theory, they look for something safe to test it on, just to make sure there aren't any bugs that need to be ironed out. For example, when Leó Szilárd came up with the idea of a nuclear chain reaction, he didn't accumulate several kilograms of uranium to see if he could blow up his backyard. Instead he tried it out on a small scale using a tiny sample in his laboratory.

However, game theorists didn't do the social science equivalent, which would be asking their students to play the game. Nor did they go to an actual prison to see how the inmates behaved. If they had done either of these things, they would have discovered, as discussed further below, that people cooperate far more than the rational utility model would suggest. Instead, the mathematicians decided to skip this process and go right to the serious applications.

The game was related to the urgent question, then being pursued at RAND, of the optimal strategy to adopt in the face of possible nuclear conflict. In a face-off between two nuclear adversaries, each side had a choice to cooperate (not blow each other up) or defect (blow the other side up). RAND's consultants included game theory creator John von Neumann, who, because of his work on the nuclear bomb, was also a member of the US Atomic Energy Commission, and served as an advisor to President Eisenhower. In von Neumann's eyes, the contest between America and its Soviet adversary was a classic example of a two-person game, with well-defined rules and payoffs, which in this case happened to involve total destruction. And according to game theory, there was only one winning strategy – the US should strike immediately, before Russia had the chance to develop its own weapon.

However, while von Neumann managed to convince the secretary of state, John Foster Dulles, Eisenhower hesitated. Perhaps his right brain was giving him some signals. And when the Russians announced in 1949 that they too had a bomb, it was too late.

As a result, the Cold War became a stand-off characterised by another strategy from game theory, which became known as Mutually Assured Destruction. Von Neumann is said to have had a hand in the name. As one of the founders of computer science, he also worked on an early computer called the Mathematical Analyser, Numerator, Integrator and Calculator. It is ironic, but also somehow fitting, that these products of rational expectations theory became known by their acronyms, MAD and MANIAC. And that von Neumann, who used a wheelchair in the later years of his life, is said to have been the inspiration for the titular character played by Peter Sellers in Stanley Kubrick's 1964 film *Dr. Strangelove; Or: How I Learned to Stop Worrying and Love the Bomb*. Indeed, that character's explanation that 'because of the automated and irrevocable decision-making process which rules out human meddling, the Doomsday machine is terrifying and simple to understand ... and completely credible and convincing' does seem to capture the cold hard logic of classical game theory rather well.

TIED UP

Game theory obtained much of its own credibility in economics through its association with Cold War strategising – after all, there is nothing like having a role in nuclear conflict to bolster the impression of being a 'hard' science – and games such as the prisoner's dilemma are a staple of economics textbooks. However, the picture it paints of human nature, as a rational calculating machine driven only by the need to optimise personal utility, does seem a little on the bleak side. And as already mentioned, it doesn't jive with empirical observations of human behaviour. A range of experiments have shown that, in a one-shot prisoner's dilemma game, people typically choose to cooperate between a third and a half of the time. For example, a 1992 experiment by behavioural economists Amos Tversky and Eldar Shafir showed that 37 per cent cooperated.[8] Political scientist James Der Derian taught the game to convicts from Gardner State Prison in a world politics class he was holding there and found that decisions tended to be based on established prison norms, such as 'traditional codes of silence, pre-scripted stories, and intersubjective rituals of honor', which don't appear in the classical model.[9]

While game theorists have described the prisoner's dilemma as 'the *E. coli* of the social sciences' (presumably for its usefulness as a research tool, rather than any germ-like qualities), the reality, as the philosopher of science Robert Northcott notes, is that the game 'has been greatly overrated and over-studied: it explains almost nothing'.[10] And outside of specialised situations, such as the design of auctions, game theory in general doesn't seem very realistic or useful. The game theorist Ariel Rubinstein almost seems to take it as a point of pride that 'I categorically cannot see any case where game theory could be helpful'.[11] That would be fine if game theory was just an interesting intellectual exercise for academics, but in fact it plays a key role in some neoclassical theories (the Arrow–Debreu 'invisible hand theorem', for example, uses a game theoretic result to 'prove' the existence of an equilibrium) and exposure to it has no doubt also helped shape the attitudes of generations of economists.

Behavioural economists have tweaked game theory by taking into account effects such as limits in strategic thinking, the ability to learn, emotional factors, and so on.[12] However, while modellers can always add epicycles to a model to make it more realistic, a more direct approach is just to acknowledge that we do not behave as isolated particles, but are better seen as parts of a whole. In other words, we are entangled.

When you mention the concept of social entanglement to a physicist, they usually (not always) look unhappy, because entanglement is very magical and only affects teeny tiny particles, as opposed to real life which is supposed to be classical because it's big.[13] However, when we simulate something like the prisoner's dilemma using a quantum circuit, it just means that each prisoner's mental state is modelled as a superposition state (remember, that is how the uncertainty, subjectivity, and interference get in), but at the same time the states are correlated through what amounts to a mathematical version of a social contract.

The quantum version of the prisoner's dilemma was first proposed in a 1999 paper, and was demonstrated two years later by a team that managed to control a pair of entangled hydrogen nuclei with radio pulses to play the moves. Of course, trapped nuclei are a rather simplified model of real trapped prisoners, but they do seem an improvement over classical atoms.

The quantum circuit for the game has two qubits, which represent the two prisoners. These are initialised in the state 0 which represents the strategy to not defect, while 1 represents the strategy to defect. The two qubits are then acted on by a gate U, which entangles them. Again, this may sound a bit mystical, but it is a routine step in any quantum computer program. Each of these entangled qubits is then operated on by a gate which represents the person's individual strategy (but has implications for the other person because of entanglement). Finally, another gate (the inverse of U) reverses the entanglement in order to bring the two qubits back into their original frame, and the outcome is measured.

In order to replicate the classical version of the game, the entanglement gate can be set to the 'identity', which just means it has no effect, and the strategies can be set to either the identity or 'flip'. The former means that the qubit remains in the 0 state, so the prisoner does not defect, while a flip, as performed by a NOT gate, turns the 0 into 1 and indicates defect. In either case, the qubits are not in a superposition state, but are definitely 0 or definitely 1. The various outcomes then follow from the rules; so, for example, if both qubits are in the state 1, then each prisoner is choosing to betray with 100 per cent certainty and the penalty from the table above will be four years each.

The game becomes considerably more interesting, though, when we allow quantum moves. For example, suppose that we choose the entanglement gate to be the C-NOT gate $\oplus$; and instead of insisting that each prisoner make a binary decision on whether or not to defect, we allow moves that put them in a superposed state, such as the Hadamard gate which gives a 50 per cent chance of defecting, and a 50 per cent chance of not defecting. Because the C-NOT gate has the property that it has no effect on the initialised qubits, and is also its own inverse, the circuit reduces to the basic entanglement circuit seen already (and represented in this new iteration by Figure 9.1 below). The outcome in this case will be a balanced blend of the different possibilities with an expected penalty for each player of 2.75 years, which represents a Nash equilibrium. This compares with the Nash equilibrium from the classical game where each prisoner betrays the other and receives a four-year sentence. Other quantum versions of the game exist which produce a Pareto optimal equilibrium with an expected penalty of only two years. To quote David Meyer again, 'Quantum strategies can be more successful than classical ones.'

DEGREES OF ENTANGLEMENT

The level of entanglement depends on the choice of the gate U, and can be tuned from zero to complete. The observed statistics from experiments suggest that the degree of entanglement is fairly high. So what does this entanglement mean?

When computer scientists first developed quantum game theory, they assumed that the entanglement was provided because each player had access to some kind of quantum device, which allowed each to determine their strategy by measuring the state of their qubit. This might work when the game is played on a quantum computer, but seems unlikely down at the local jail.

Another interpretation is the physicalist approach, which asserts that the brain and consciousness in general are based on quantum processes, so we are literally what Alexander Wendt calls 'walking wave functions'.[14] As Wendt points out, this approach is bolstered by experimental evidence that quantum effects play a role in biological phenomena such as photosynthesis or avian navigation.[15] Scientists have hypothesised that consciousness could be encoded, for example, in the quantum properties of entangled molecules in the brain, or in biophotons which play a role in brain cell communication.[16] However, while such findings would certainly change the conversation around quantum effects in the social sciences, they do not directly help here, because showing that brain processes exploit quantum properties would not prove that prisoners have such properties too, or tell us how to model them, any more than knowing that birds exploit quantum neural effects to navigate would mean that avian migration patterns are best modelled using quantum mechanics. As physicist Robert Laughlin notes, the laws of hydrodynamics cannot be deduced from first principles – 'The reason we believe them, as with most emergent things, is because we observe them' – and the same is true of social phenomena.[17]

We return to this question of interpretation below, but the approach here is again to use entanglement in the context of a mathematical model. (Some quantum social scientists refer to 'quantum-like' approaches, but this doesn't work in terms of quantum mathematics – when I use calculus in a biology model, I don't say it is 'calculus-like'.) As with the quantum model of the coin toss in Chapter 3, what is being simulated is not the physical dynamics of the system, but rather its probabilistic state as computed using a 2-norm, which leads naturally to the concepts of superposition, interference and entanglement. As always, it is the prerogative of the modeller to decide what modelling technique is most applicable to a particular problem (and again, physicists don't hold a veto); so rather than appeal to physics as justification for taking a quantum approach, social scientists should take quantum social properties at face value – and let physicists and philosophers puzzle over why the subatomic world resembles the social one.

A key distinction of the quantum version of the prisoner's dilemma is that the strategies are superpositions rather than binary decisions, and the outcome is probabilistic. The strategies should therefore be viewed as propensities to act in a certain way. The entanglement means that these propensities for the two prisoners cannot be neatly separated. Instead of being perfectly independent, or joined at the hip, they are somewhere in between.

Another way to look at this is to note that, as with the quantum model of option pricing discussed later, what is being modelled is not the actual outcome of the game, but rather the expected outcome, seen from the perspective of a participant, as they play out the possibilities in their head. In this view, a player's strategy is entangled, not with the other player, but with their own subjective ideas about what the other player will do, based on things like shared social norms and behaviours.[18] The situation is therefore the same as for the uncertainty aversion in the disjunction effect from the previous chapter, with the difference that the uncertainty now arises from the unknown strategy of the other player.

If, as discussed above, we choose the entanglement matrix U to be the C-NOT gate $\oplus$, then the resulting circuit, illustrated in Figure 9.1, is equivalent to the basic entanglement circuit used earlier for the disjunction effect in Figure 8.3.[19] The prisoner's dilemma can therefore be interpreted as a version of the same problem, where the decision qubit on the bottom now represents a player's strategy, while the context qubit on the top represents their subjective ideas about the other player's strategy. The fact that versions of the same simple circuit can be used to model social entanglement, context-dependent decisions, and the debt relationship, again drives home the intimate, alchemical connection between mental and financial phenomena. Note that the circuit can again be expressed without the entanglement gate, as in Figure 8.2, which highlights the fact

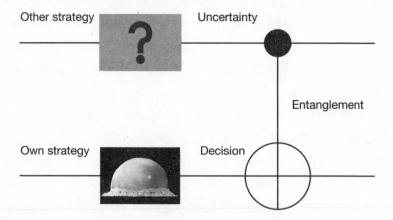

FIGURE 9.1 The basic entanglement circuit can be used to represent the prisoner's dilemma, where the lower qubit represents the person's own strategy (in this case, the nuclear option to defect), and the upper qubit represents their subjective beliefs about the other person's strategy. The uncertainty then leads, after entanglement, to interference effects when the qubits are measured on the right.

that the entanglement here is a modelling choice that is used in order to produce a desired effect.

Applying the quarter law, and using the observation that about 10 per cent of players choose to cooperate when they know the other person's strategy, suggests (if we assume that uncertainty increases the chance of cooperation) that 35 per cent should choose to cooperate in the presence of uncertainty, which is not far off the 37 per cent found experimentally by Tversky and Shafir. Of course, if participants act as if they are entangled, then this will affect the final result, so in essence the decision is being made by a kind of group mind.

THE PUBLIC GOOD

The prisoner's dilemma is just one example of a game where people should behave in a selfish way according to classical logic, but in practice tend to behave in a more altruistic fashion. A revealing quote from a 2018 survey noted that quantum games 'produce counter-intuitive outcomes such as a greater prevalence of altruism than in the classical game'.[20] Perhaps the greatest contribution of classical game theory to economics was the fact that it managed to convince generations of students that altruism is counterintuitive.

Another game which reveals a kind of social entanglement is the ultimatum game.[21] This gets its name because a prize of, say, ten dollars is awarded to one of two people, who must then offer a cut to the loser. If the offer is rejected, then they both get nothing. According to classical logic, the optimal choice would be for the winner to offer some nominal prize to the loser, on the basis that they will accept it because it is better than nothing. However, the experiment has been repeated many times in different countries, and the results consistently show that offers less than around three dollars tend to be rejected. The reason, of course, is that the loser feels that smaller offers are unfair, and is willing to sacrifice the payment in order to register their disgust (neuroscientists have shown that the part of the brain involved in this rejection of unfair offers is the bilateral anterior insula, which is associated with anger and disgust).

The existence of a minimum acceptable threshold can also be viewed as another example of the threshold effect caused by preference reversal. In a sense, because the winner is entangled with the loser, they are negotiating with themselves. The difference between the two rewards therefore reflects the preference reversal due to a change in context from price setter to price taker.

A related example is the public good game. In economics, a public good is a resource such as a lighthouse that can be used by anyone, and is non-rivalrous in the sense that its use by one person doesn't reduce its use by another. The term goes back to a 1954 paper by Paul Samuelson, which argued that public goods will be undersupplied in a free-market economy because even if they are beneficial, people won't pay for them.

In the game version, a number of people are given tokens and are asked to contribute some to a pot, which represents the public good. The tokens in the pot are multiplied by a factor greater than 1, which reflects the increased utility gained from the public good. The pot is then divided equally between the players. A player's final holdings therefore consist of the initial endowment, minus what they contributed to the pot, plus their share of the final pot.

According to classical game theory, the correct move for any individual player is to donate nothing to the public pot (the so-called free rider problem). However, as with the prisoner's dilemma or the ultimatum game, very few people take this approach. The typical contribution depends on the returns from the public good, but for a game with 40 players and a factor of 1.3 (so a return of 30 per cent) most people contribute around 50 per cent. Again, this seems reasonable given that most people are willing to pay taxes for the same reason. However, there is one group of people who seem particularly prone to the free rider problem. As the sociologists Gerald Marwell and Ruth Ames discovered, an education in economics has the effect of dropping the contribution rate from 50 per cent to 20 per cent – not that surprising given that they have been trained to see the world through the eyes of rational economic man. Referring to Figure 9.1, neoclassical economics removes the entanglement gate (and the resulting 30 per cent reduction is not far off a quarter).

The public good problem is related to the 'tragedy of the commons' – popularised by the ecologist Garrett Hardin in a 1968 paper[22] – which differs only in that now the public good is rivalrous, in the sense that it degrades with overuse. Hardin's example was a pasture shared by a number of animal herders. For each herder, rational self-interest dictates that they should exploit as much of the land as possible; but if they all do this, then the result is over-grazing, so no one benefits. The conclusion seems to be that such common areas must be managed, either privately or by the state. As the political scientist Elinor Ostrom argued, however, the evidence shows that commons – including forestries, fisheries, irrigation systems, grasslands, and so on – can be sustainably managed. After all, you don't need a quantum computer to realise that people are governed not just by laws or money or utility optimisation, but also by things like empathy and social norms. In fact, one could argue that in many cases it is exactly the encroachment of the money system into areas that were previously viewed as commons that is feeding the money bomb, and contributing to a real tragedy.

HEAVEN'S GATE

In physics, particles become entangled with each other through interactions. The net effect of many such interactions is that particles can never be viewed in isolation but are always entangled to a degree with their environment. One result of this entanglement is the phenomenon of decoherence, which means that systems lose their quantum nature and behave in a more classical fashion. The trickiest challenge in quantum computing is to avoid decoherence by reducing this environmental entanglement to a degree where the computer can be viewed as an isolated system.

In quantum decision theory, environmental entanglement can similarly make the system behave in a more classical manner. Indeed, experimental evidence shows that cognitive biases tend to reduce when participants exchange information by consulting with others.[23] Such an effect was seen for the case of strategic default discussed earlier. As one report found, people who knew someone who had strategically defaulted were 82 per cent more likely to declare their intention to default: 'This effect does not seem to be due to clustering of people with similar attitudes, but rather to learning about the actual cost of default. We find a similar learning effect from exposure to the media.'[24]

Of course, classical behaviour does not always mean stable or rational; effects such as herd behaviour are classical, but not necessarily rational when viewed from a broader perspective, as behavioural economists are fond of pointing out. And nor does decoherence mean that quantum effects wash out at the societal level. The reason, again, is that, in financial terms at least, the strongest form of entanglement is through the money system, which has been designed to scale up; and there isn't anything very mystical about a loan contract, or a financial derivative. We return to this topic later.

Before proceeding, though, many readers may still be sceptical about this idea that people can be socially entangled, or that we can choose to model them as if they were entangled; or they may just want something concrete to help visualise what an entanglement gate in a quantum computer is supposed to represent in terms of human behaviour. In my experience, the concept of social entanglement seems to arouse a level of discomfort that is right up there with the other various taboos discussed so far – which is perhaps why economics has long been based on the idea that people are unencumbered by social or financial entanglements. Again, one wonders whether there is a gender connection. Or at least Mary Midgley did. In a piece she wrote for BBC radio in the 1950s, which began with the sentence 'Practically all the great European philosophers have been bachelors' (see quote at start of Chapter 2), she wrote: 'Philosophers have generally talked as though it were obvious that one consciousness went to one body, as though each person were a closed system which could only signal to another by external behaviour, and that behaviour had to be interpreted from previous experience. I wonder whether they would have said the same if they had been frequently pregnant and suckling.'[25] (The piece was rejected because the editor thought it a 'trivial, irrelevant intrusion of domestic matters into intellectual life'.) So to add to the list of topics that should never be discussed in a book on science, here is one more: religion.

Given that a substantial fraction of people today and throughout history have religious beliefs, it follows that many are conscious of an all-seeing presence that might be called the eye of God. Long before the classical economists, the subject of monetary transactions was studied by churchmen such as Thomas Aquinas. According to Aquinas, money was not an end in itself – the pursuit of wealth was un-Christian – but 'was invented chiefly for the purpose of exchange'. The most important virtue, and the glue which held society together, was *caritas*, or charity, which was an expression of love. If entanglement in physics can be described as the 'God Effect', then here it was a signal from the heavens. (Again, the point here is not whether religious people are seen by such an eye, but the fact that they behave as if they are.)

Today we live in a world where our mental entanglements often tend to be financial, rather than spiritual, in nature. Our bond is with the bank. And from an economic or a mathematical modelling perspective, this designed entanglement through things like loans may seem more direct than entanglement through love or social connection. Indeed, the all-seeing Eye of Providence is right there on the back of every US dollar bill. But another way to look at this is that money interferes with *caritas*. As Pope Francis wrote, 'Now, more than ever, what is revealed is the fallacy of making individualism the organizing principle of society. What will be our new principle?'[26] If there is one thing that the COVID-19 pandemic has demonstrated, it is that we live on a connected planet. Vaccines are an example of a public good, where it isn't enough for a country to only vaccinate its own citizens when the virus may be mutating to a more virulent form in some other corner of the globe. And problems such as inequality and the climate crisis are similarly collective in nature.

To summarise, a key difference between neoclassical and quantum economics is that the former assumes that decisions are based on rational, independent utility maximisation, while the latter accounts for context-dependent effects. In terms of brain function, these are specialities of the left and right hemispheres respectively.[27] Neoclassical economics is like economics performed by a brain in which the corpus callosum, which links the two hemispheres, has been severed; quantum economics integrates the two points of view (Figure 9.2). This difference applies to things like purchase decisions but also to the credit relationship and the nature of money. One consequence is that the quantum approach emphasises the importance of money and power, which play little role in neoclassical economics. The change in perspective is a result of the shift from utility to probabilistic propensity. But understanding the role of entanglement in the economy can be elusive (comparing with subatomic particles doesn't really help), and seems to require something of an 'aha' moment, which again is a right-brain phenomenon.[28]

While mainstream economics emphasises the 'hard' particle aspect of behaviour, the quantum approach can also handle the 'soft' and entangling wave aspect, which can lead to very different dynamics – just as the binary yes/no logic of the

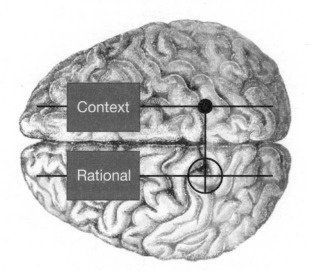

FIGURE 9.2 This is your brain on quantum economics. Context can represent a preceding event, presumed beliefs about another person (as in the prisoner's dilemma), or any subjective factor. In neoclassical economics, the context is assumed to have no effect on the decision process, so the entanglement gate is omitted.[29]

isolated bits in a classical computer behave differently from the entangled, multi-valued qubits of a quantum computer. In the next chapter, we take a look inside the complicated machines, whose roots go back to medieval magicians, that economists have constructed to simulate and predict the quantum social system known as the economy – and ask whether we need a quantum oracle.

CHAPTER 10

BRAZEN HEAD

The truth of the model is not the truth of the phenomenon. It is a common confusion between these two kinds of truth – the norm in magic – that sometimes sanctifies the model (which is regarded as part of the real world) and gives the scientist the role of priest.

ANTOINE DANCHIN,
THE DELPHIC BOAT: WHAT GENOMES TELL US, 2002

The test of science is its ability to predict.
RICHARD FEYNMAN, THE FEYNMAN LECTURES ON PHYSICS, 1964[1]

Magicians and their audiences have always been fascinated with the idea of automata that can do impressive tasks such as play chess, predict the future, or simulate a living being, and their construction was linked with developments in science and computing. Economists are equally entranced by the notion of a mathematical model that can simulate and predict the economy. This chapter takes a look inside these automata, reveals how they really work, shows why their prophesies and predictions are usually no better than random guesses, and argues for a more realistic alternative which accounts for quantum uncertainty.

As Alexander Wendt has noted, a foundational assumption in the social sciences, including economics, is the idea that causation is mechanical and local, so that social systems can be viewed as an elaborate machine. In principle, it should therefore be possible to understand and predict the economy by taking the machine apart, figuring out the forces which guide it, express as mathematical equations, and solve. Alternatively, one can let computers do the work for you, which is the idea behind the area of machine learning. However, the idea of building such a predictive machine, that exhibits an artificial form of intelligence, predates even Newtonian science.

In the thirteenth century, Saint Albertus Magnus was said to have spent 30 years constructing a 'brazen head', which was a brass replica of a human head, capable of thought. Unfortunately, it chattered incessantly, to the point where none other than Thomas Aquinas took a hammer to it, and shut it up permanently. As Aquinas wrote, 'only God can perform miracles, create and transform'. The story may have inspired their contemporary, the Franciscan friar Roger Bacon, to write a play which also featured a brazen head, though this one was less talkative.

Bacon lectured on Aristotle at Oxford, but also dabbled in astrology and alchemy, and may have been imprisoned for a time after a crackdown on such practices. Although it doesn't appear that he ever obtained a doctorate himself, after his death he was sometimes called Doctor Mirabilis (Latin for amazing or marvellous). He is credited with writing a number of works on Aristotelian philosophy, and in one year apparently wrote a million words, which puts him right up there with Newton. But he is most famous for his brazen head – an early version of what we today call a talking head, except that it answered questions about the future using only 'yes' or 'no' (if only economists would do the same), was made of brass (hence brazen), and wasn't on TV.

Bacon's version was described, in an anonymous sixteenth-century prose romance called *The famous historie of Fryer*

218

Bacon, as a replica of a 'natural man's head' that included 'the inward parts'. In other words, it was a functioning automaton. The purpose of the head, according to this account, was to help Bacon build a magical wall of brass (a brazen wall) around Britain, well before Brexit, as protection from invasions and illegal immigrants. The story goes that Bacon was having trouble getting it to say anything, so he summoned the Devil, who said it would speak eventually but first had to be powered up through 'the continuall fume of the six hottest simples' (plants used in alchemical medicine). So Bacon does as he is told, but at the key moment falls asleep and misses its oracular statement, which is: 'Time is', 'Time was', and 'Time is past'. It turns out that this was some kind of sign-off, because the head then explodes.

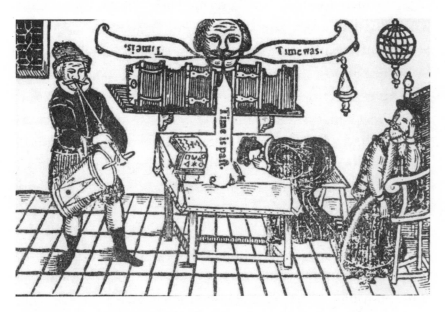

FIGURE 10.1 An Elizabethan woodcut of the scene from the later play *Friar Bacon and Friar Bungay* where the brazen head makes its announcement, while Friars Bacon and Bungay sleep, and Bacon's rather dim-witted assistant Miles plays the tambour.

CONVERSING WITH ANGELS

The same story appears around 1594 in a play called *Friar Bacon and Friar Bungay* by Robert Greene, with the difference that in this version the head is built with the assistance of 'necromantic charms' i.e. consulting with the dead. Bacon's reputation as a magician, which lasted well into the seventeenth century, was probably based on his work on optics (in Greene's play he has a 'magic glass' that allows him to see scenes from the future), or perhaps his fascination with early brass models of the cosmos (which were first used in order to predict the astrological positions of the heavenly bodies). In seventeenth-century London, as Daniel Defoe noted in his *Journal of the Plague Year*, the trade of astrology and fortune-telling 'grew so open and so generally practised that it became common to have signs and inscriptions set up at doors: "Here lives a fortune-teller", "Here lives an astrologer", "Here you may have your nativity calculated", and the like; and Friar Bacon's brazen-head, which was the usual sign of these people's dwellings, was to be seen almost in every street'.

This connection with sorcery might seem ironic, given that Bacon was a mathematician whose emphasis on experimentation is believed by some scholars to have helped lay the ground for the development of the scientific method. However, what Greene called 'magic, and the mathematic rules' were considered to be related at the time. An example was the English mathemagician John Dee, whose job as advisor to Queen Elizabeth I involved astrology, numerology, alchemy, and conversing with angels (though Robert Hooke later said this might have been a way of sending encrypted intelligence messages). He was said to have made, for a play, a giant mechanical dung beetle that could carry an actor on its back, which was so realistic that it gave him the reputation of being a magician. 'And for these, and suchlike marvellous arts and feats naturally, mathematically and mechanically wrought and contrived, ought any student and modest Christian philosopher be counted and called a conjurer?' he complained in his *Preface to Euclid*.

Mathematics too was considered to be a kind of witchcraft, and mathematics books were burned as 'conjuring books'. Today, of course, there is a clear distinction between science and the occult arts. In science, prediction isn't an occult practice, it's a key part of the scientific method. As physicist Richard Feynman said, 'The test of science is its ability to predict.'

Economists understandably aren't so keen — one, for example, wrote that 'Feynman is quite wrong. Explanation is the heart of science.'[2] As Keynes observed in 1936, economists have long been 'unmoved by the lack of correspondence between the results of their theory and the facts of observation;— a discrepancy which the ordinary man has not failed to observe'; and as we'll see, things haven't improved since then.[3]

A PURE MACHINE

The fascination with such automata did not, of course, end in the Middle Ages. An example which is perhaps closer to the spirit of modern macroeconomic models was the work of the French inventor Jacques de Vaucanson, whose 1739 invention the *Canard Digérateur*, or Digesting Duck, could drink water, raise itself on its legs, and quack realistically. The exterior was made of gold-plated copper and it had over a thousand moving parts, including the world's first flexible rubber tubes. Its main trick, though, was to eat kernels of grain from the hands of spectators, metabolise them, and (after a suitable period) defecate them out.

Vaucanson took the duck on tour and grew rich on the proceeds. Louis XV was so impressed that he gave Vaucanson a job as inspector of silk manufacture. The silk industry was being revolutionised in England and Scotland through the design of more efficient looms, and Vaucanson set about developing what would become the world's first fully automated loom, based on an existing punch-card system. This idea was later refined by Joseph-Marie Jacquard, and was adapted by the English mathematician and inventor Charles Babbage for his 'analytical engine', which is considered the forerunner of modern computers.

Unfortunately, Vaucanson's automated loom proved much less popular than the automated duck, especially among weavers, who on one occasion pelted him in the street with stones. As we are being reminded today, automation is cool as long as it isn't you being automated. In 1844, the magician Jean-Eugène Robert-Houdin inspected the duck to see how it worked, and determined that the defecation was actually 'a piece of artifice I would happily have incorporated in a conjuring trick'.[4] The turds were pellets made of green-dyed breadcrumbs that were kept in a separate compartment.

A different approach was taken by the Hungarian inventor Wolfgang von Kempelen in 1770, whose Mechanical Turk, aka Automaton Chess Player, consisted of a life-sized model of the head and torso of a bearded and turbaned man, dressed like an oriental sorcerer in Ottoman robes. Its left arm cradled a smoking pipe, its right hand rested next to a chess board atop a wooden cabinet. The cabinet had doors on each side which allowed people to peer into it to inspect the insides. This was a complicated assemblage of gears and cogs, with spaces so that viewers could look through from one side to the other as the presenter opened the doors, to prove that no assistant was hidden inside.

Kempelen took the automaton on a successful tour of Europe where it beat players including Benjamin Franklin. As with Vaucanson, though, Kempelen seemed to tire of his creation and preferred to concentrate on developing more sophisticated machines, including ones that attempted to replicate human speech. After his death in 1804, the machine was sold to a Bavarian musician called Johann Nepomuk Mälzel, who oversaw a successful match against Napoleon in Paris, before taking the Turk to London and over the ocean to the United States and Canada.

Edgar Allan Poe observed it and wrote in 1836 that 'we find everywhere men of mechanical genius ... who make no scruple in pronouncing the Automaton a *pure machine*, unconnected with human agency in its movements'.[5] He argued that such a thing was on a completely different level from something like Babbage's computer. 'Arithmetical or algebraical calculations are, from their very nature, fixed and determinate ... But the case is widely different with the Chess-Player. With him there is no determinate progression' because of the uncertain actions of the other player. As a master in the art of storytelling, though, Poe wasn't taken in, and argued that the machine was a carefully constructed fake.

Indeed, fans of magic shows might notice that quite a few tricks seem to involve cabinets or similar items which appear to be empty but also happen to be the right size to accommodate a human being. For the Mechanical Turk, the chess-playing assistant was seated on a platform which could scoot back and forth to get out of the way depending on which set of doors was opened. He or she could see the position of the chess pieces because they were linked to magnets, and control the Turk's arm to make moves.

FORTUNE TELLERS

Today we have grown used to devices that can talk, answer questions (just ask Siri), and thrash grandmasters at chess. In economics, modern versions of automata also live on in the form of mathematical models of the economy.

These models feature hundreds of moving parts. They are based on gold-plated and Nobel-certified economic theories. They produce what appears to be a realistic simulation of a real economy. But the answers that emerge like green-dyed pellets from the model's metaphorical posterior aren't the result of some natural metabolic process; instead they are added right at the beginning. And the calculations are not really impartial or objective but, like the Mechanical Turk, always contain the human element.

As will be discussed further in the next chapter, the great prediction of economists is that they cannot predict. Economist John Cochrane, for example, wrote in 2011 that 'It is fun to say that we did not see the crisis coming, but the central empirical prediction of the efficient markets hypothesis is precisely that nobody can tell where markets are going' (it wasn't that fun).[6] It is like a brazen head that, instead of saying yes or no, only says 'I don't know'. And doesn't explode, but keeps appearing on TV.

Still, just as Renaissance mathematicians constructed elaborate machines and automata, be they brass heads, dung beetles, or models of the cosmos, so economists enjoy building elaborate mechanistic models of the economy. An example is the dynamic stochastic general equilibrium (DSGE) models – the so-called workhorses of macroeconomics – that are used to simulate the economy and predict the effect of things like policy interventions.

As always in magic, where the patter is designed to conceal what is really going on, the words here are used in a highly misleading way. Really the only word used in the normal way is 'equilibrium', which is key to the story. The word 'dynamic' gives the impression that the model is being used to simulate a dynamic evolutionary system which changes and adapts as it goes along, like the real economy. What it really means is that the model has a feature that shows how its equilibrium should respond to an external shock, such as a policy change – which is not the same thing (who says there is an equilibrium?). The word 'stochastic' means that the model can accommodate random effects such as a change in oil prices, which again are assumed to come from outside. 'General' means that the model is supposed to include all the major markets. However, because economists have a problem with money, the models traditionally have not included the financial sector.

Early versions of these models were developed in the 1960s, and evolved slowly as more bells and whistles were added. The way they work is to represent producers and consumers using a handful of representative agents, who act to maximise their utility by trading some representative good. Agents are assumed to know how the economy works, and how to react if something changes. In the spirit of rational economic man, they are also assumed to live forever, to be perfectly rational, to have a perfect model of the economy in their head, and to have access to all relevant information. The result is that the forces of supply and demand drive prices to their unique and optimal equilibrium point. There may be an inflation term that is linked to output, and a central bank which sets interest rates, but otherwise money itself doesn't come into the picture.

Because the model is assumed to be at equilibrium, it follows that something like a recession is treated not as the result of the economy's internal dynamics, but as an unfortunate event imposed from outside. In other words, the picture is exactly the same as for the efficient market hypothesis, where a stable equilibrium is perturbed only by random shocks which come out of nowhere. Instead of 'time is, time was, time is past', we are told that time doesn't matter. The conclusion is known from the start.

More recent versions of these models do account for so-called frictions, which refer to things like the difficulty some firms have in raising funds, or the possibility that not everyone is perfectly rational. Again, though, the use of the word 'friction' betrays the mechanistic mindset of the modellers. Something like a financial crisis is not the result of friction – instead it is the opposite of friction, when the ground falls away beneath your feet, and you find yourself suspended in mid-air, financially speaking.

Of course, a main characteristic of economies is that they tend to expand, which seems to be in conflict with the idea of long-term equilibrium. Economists handle this by simply adding a new element. The so-called neoclassical growth model, for example, which earned its creator Robert Solow a Nobel Memorial Prize, computes the production output by multiplying terms representing the contributions of labour and capital (e.g. factories), raised to various powers that make no dimensional sense but can be adjusted to fit data, with a time-varying number that represents 'technical change'.[7] The latter was loosely defined by Solow as '*any kind of shift* in the production function. Thus slowdowns, speedups, improvements in the education of the labor force, and all sorts of things will appear as "technical change"' (his emphasis).[8] The exact mechanism remained vague, and was attributed to an unexplained 'residual' that another scholar, Moses Abramovitz, described as 'a measure of our ignorance'.

Seventeenth-century alchemists faced a similar enigma in the mysterious phenomenon of fire. They came to the conclusion that combustible substances contained a fire element called phlogiston, after the Greek word *phlogistos*, for flammable. The substance had negative weight, or, as the Marquis de Condorcet put it, was 'impelled by forces that give it a direction contrary to that of gravity', which was why smoke raised up when the phlogiston was released. Today, economists explain economic growth in much the same way, and can get whatever answer they want by adjusting its strength. The economist Paul Romer later introduced several other parameters in a variety of incompatible units in order to fit the effect of things like government stimulus, and earn another Nobel Memorial Prize.

After the crisis, which was characterised by neither equilibrium nor growth, economists of course tried to distance themselves from the whole business of prediction, which made sense given how bad they obviously were at it. As one group of scholars sniffily put it, 'We are not astrologers, nor priests to the market gods.'[9]

But it is like economists want to have it both ways. They want to be seen as serious scientists, but when it comes to prediction all they have is that the economy can't be predicted. Which also means – in their minds at least – that their theories can't be falsified. (Or as complexity economist Andri W. Stahel put it, '20th- and 21st-century economics has shown remarkable resistance to abandon its theories in the face of empirical falsification.'[10]) It really is the strangest kind of fortune-telling. So you might be wondering: if this is the case, why are their soothsaying services so much in demand?

The reason, of course, is that magic, as we have seen, is all about the story. People don't go to fortune-tellers or astrologers to actually get an ironclad prediction about the future. Instead they are seeking a story which helps to make sense of their lives and justify a decision. When the economist Kenneth Arrow, who was working as an Air Force weather forecaster during the Second World War, informed his boss that their long-range predictions were no better than random, the response was: 'The Commanding General is well aware that the forecasts are no good. However, he needs them for planning purposes.'[11] The models therefore don't need to be accurate, they just need to produce something that gives a feeling of meaning and closure. In economics, this is supplied by the notion of a stable and optimal equilibrium.

In magic shows, a perennial favourite is the restoration trick. This involves the destruction of an object, which is then miraculously restored to its original state – as when a watch is smashed and then restored, or an assistant is sawn in half, then miraculously returned to life (and here the assistant is being treated like an object, not a person). The trick plays with our ideas of robustness and persistence, our fear of damage, our desire to turn back time and make things right again, as well as our need to attain closure and restore order – every good story has a satisfying ending. The same narrative appears also in fiction, and in politics, in the perennial image of the hero who brings order to chaos. But the restoration trick is also about trust and power, because by destroying a precious thing, the magician is both asserting power over its owner and demanding the audience's trust in his ability to fix the problem. Economists are the masters of the restoration trick: even after something like the 2007/8 crisis, they are always ready with a glib explanation about how the forces of supply and demand will soon restore the economy to peace and balance. After all, it's there in the models.

One critic noted that 'It is no secret that the predictive power of rational-expectations DSGE models is a joke'; but sometimes, like with an old and familiar TV show, the pleasure of a joke is in hearing it repeated.[12] As heterodox economist

Steve Keen observes, 'This image of a self-regulating market system that always returns to equilibrium after an "exogenous shock" is a powerful emotional anchor for mainstream economists.'[13] And for their audiences.

THE MATHEMAGICIANS

Of course, some investors and hedge funds do seem to be able to predict market fluctuations, or at least derive enormous and consistent profits from them. An example is the hedge fund Renaissance Technologies, whose billionaire founder James Simons reputedly once bought an insurance policy for a restaurant just so that he could smoke with his meal.[14] These funds use automata of a different type.

The founder of the hedge fund industry was the mathematician Ed Thorp, who became interested in the mathematics of gambling while working as a professor at MIT in the 1950s. His ideas were shaped by two scientific collaborators, John Kelly Jr and Ed Shannon, both of whom worked at Bell Labs (Shannon also joined the MIT faculty).

Kelly had developed a formula, which became known as the Kelly criterion, to determine how much to bet at any round in a game of chance. In 1961, he was the first to attain Kempelen's aim of building a machine that replicated human speech, basing it on an IBM computer. He demonstrated the machine by getting it to sing the song 'Daisy Bell' – an event witnessed by Arthur C. Clarke, who used it for the computer HAL in his novel (and later screenplay) *2001: A Space Odyssey*.

Shannon was a mathematician who is considered to be the father of information theory, and invented the word 'bit' for the 0 or 1, yes/no basis of classical computer logic. On the side, he invented machines such as a juggling automaton and a flame-throwing trumpet, which sounds like good fun. He also kept what he called an 'ultimate machine' on his desk, which was a box with a switch. After you turned it on by pressing the switch, a lid would open and a hand would emerge, turn the switch back off again, and withdraw into the box. As Clarke noted, 'There is something unspeakably sinister about a machine that does nothing – absolutely nothing – except switch itself off.'[15]

With this dream team assembled, Thorp was ready to take on Las Vegas. His first idea was to predict the result of a roulette wheel, using what some consider to be the world's first wearable computer, which he developed with Shannon. This involved one person, with the computer hidden inside their shoe, tapping their toe to record the position of the ball and compute its likely trajectory, and communicating via an earpiece to a second person placing the bets.

The method did work, but suffered from technical problems, such as wires breaking or earpieces falling out – not to mention the risk of getting caught, at a time when the casinos were often run by organised crime. Thorp therefore switched to the safer and more tractable problem of blackjack. The idea this time was that by counting cards, it was possible to calculate the odds of winning a hand based on the composition of cards in the remaining deck. He publicised his technique in the best-selling book *Beat the Dealer*. Soon after its publication, casinos started doing things like increasing the number of decks, shuffling more often, and so on, to make life more difficult for card-counters who had read his book. As always, acting in a predictable way is a weakness, which is why living systems often evolve in such a way that they become unpredictable.

By this point Thorp himself had already moved on to a much larger kind of casino – the markets. Thorp's idea was that, rather than predict the market directly, one could look for arbitrage opportunities by comparing the prices of stocks and options. A call option, for example, gives you the right but not the obligation to buy a stock at a certain date for a set amount, known as the call price. Together with his collaborator/magician's assistant Sheen Kassouf from Columbia University, Thorp obtained an empirical curve which seemed to describe the relationship between stock price and option price. He could then look for cases where options seemed to be incorrectly priced. If, for example, the option looked too cheap, then they could purchase the option and sell (go short on) the stock. That way it didn't matter whether the stock went up or down, because they profited on the price difference either way. They published their system in a 1967 book called (naturally) *Beat the Market*, which helped create the hedge fund industry.

As a sidenote, in 1977 another mathemagician named Doyne Farmer worked with a group of scientist collaborators on a nearly identical roulette scheme. As *Wired* magazine reported in 1994 (apparently unaware of Thorp or his book), this again involved building 'a set of handcrafted, programmable, tiny microcomputers into the bottoms of three ordinary leather shoes. The computers were keyboarded with toes; their function was to predict the toss of a roulette ball.' Like Thorp, Farmer also ended up founding a hedge fund, called the Prediction Company. Unlike Thorp, he didn't publish his methods. As he put it, in a financial version of the Magician's Oath: 'We really have found statistically significant patterns in financial data. There are pockets of predictability. We have learned a lot, and I would love to be able to describe it all to the world, to write a technical book laying out the knowledge we have accumulated on how to extract the weak signals that exist in financial markets and trade on them – a kind of Theory of Financial Prediction. Maybe call it *How to Beat the Market*.

But given the quantity of money involved, I'm sure our partners will never let us do that.'[16]

HOW TO PREDICT THE FUTURE

Today, of course, there are thousands of hedge fund companies. The latest trend is to use artificial intelligence and machine learning to analyse 'big data' and spot price patterns that can be exploited for profit. Some companies are very successful at doing this, including the above-mentioned Renaissance Technologies. But the vast majority are less impressive. Instead of a brazen head, we have black boxes that do a great job of matching historical data, which is what they are trained on, but may be untrustworthy when it comes to consulting about the future. The limitations of such approaches is shown by the fact that the Eurekahedge AI Hedge Fund Index, which tracks the returns of thirteen hedge funds using machine learning, had an average annual return for the five-year period 2016–2020 of 5.5 per cent, which underperformed the broader S&P 500 index (at 12.5 per cent) by more than a factor of two.[17]

Those hedge funds which are successful appear to be able to predict markets, but really they are more like card counters at a casino – what they do is find a weak signal, or a persistent artefact of trading, then amplify it by using massive amounts of leverage. But while it may be possible to find such 'pockets of predictability' in data, this isn't much use for anyone who is actually trying to predict something useful, like the timing of a recession, or the impact of the economy on the environment.

The most gloriously complicated mathematical models are perhaps those which attempt to simulate the integrated economy–climate system, by combining economic models with climate models. In 2018 Yale economist William Nordhaus was awarded the Nobel Memorial Prize (that reliable marker of quality) for such a model, which, after laborious calculations, predicted the effects of climate change as follows: 'Including all factors, the final estimate is that the damages are 2.1% of global income at a 3°C warming, and 8.5% of income at a 6°C warming.'[18] While a decline of 8.5 per cent certainly sounds serious, it would take place over many years so would really represent a slowing of growth rather than a true crisis.

However, as I pointed out while discussing Nordhaus's integrated climate–economy model in my 2007 book *The Future of Everything*, neither climate models nor economic models are very reliable for making long-term predictions, and linking them together is unlikely to improve their forecasting skill. Also, the notion that six degrees of warming is just a speedbump for the economy relies on a suite of assumptions about the economic effects of global climate change that is strongly contested by environmentalists, or for that matter most people who are not on the economics Nobel committee. The Paris Agreement on climate change, for example, aims for a maximum increase of 1.5°C. Since Nordhaus's prize-winning work was presumably vetted by a coterie of leading economists, this backs up my conclusion at the time, which was that mainstream economists are incapable of grasping the true nature of the climate crisis. Or as ecological economist Richard B. Norgaard wrote in 2021, 'mainstream economists, and many economists in lesser streams, and those stuck in eddies as well, have become detached from the realities of Planet Earth'.[19] (It is fitting, in a way, that Alfred Nobel earned his wealth as the inventor of dynamite, since economists seem bent on blowing up the world in his name.)

So my vote for the most powerful predictive method in economics goes to the Black–Scholes formula for calculating the price of an option, which we look at in the next chapter. My reason for choosing it isn't because of its originality; in fact, it was already being used by Ed Thorp, who had correctly guessed the formula but kept it to himself. There is also some evidence to suggest that options in competitive markets traded at similar prices before and after Black–Scholes, which implies that the model only formalised what traders already knew.[20] Nor is it because I think it is true; the formula's proof is based on Old Magick tales such as the efficient market hypothesis. No, the reason I choose it is because it achieved a higher plane of quantum magic, which is to conjure up a group illusion of truth, in an example of what has been called the 'performative' nature of quantitative finance.[21]

One of the main lessons of the quantum approach, after all, is that the observer affects the system. If market participants think that the Black–Scholes model is correct, then they will trade accordingly. And by expressing option prices as the result of a mathematical calculation, the formula put everyone on the same page and allowed the development of increasingly sophisticated derivative products. The result is that prices do more or less conform to it, though with some anomalies that economists explain away by adding epicycles. The model therefore predicts the future, by helping to create it.

As we'll see, quantum finance does present a workable alternative to the Black–Scholes model. At a deeper level, though, the quantum economics approach does not leave much room for the construction of functioning automata that can make accurate predictions about the economy. As shown by quantum cognition, subjective forces mean that value can never be objectively pinned down (again, quantum finance may look like hard science, but in quantitative terms its message is often fuzzy in the extreme). The economy is not a mechanistic system, but a complex, organic, quantum system whose properties emerge from quantum interactions. And given that we can't predict the properties of water, let alone the weather, from our knowledge of a water molecule, there is little reason to think that we can build an accurate model of the economy. All we can hope for is those pockets of predictability, and hints on how to make the economy more fair, robust, and sustainable.

Investors, who after all have money on the line, have long known this, and some have intuited the connection with quantum reality. George Soros, who co-founded the famous Quantum Fund (which as far as I know had nothing to do with quantum economics), told the *New York Review of Books* in a 2014 interview that there is a 'remarkable similarity between human affairs and quantum physics' in the sense that 'subatomic phenomena have a dual character: they can manifest themselves as particles or waves. Something similar applies to human beings: they are partly freestanding individuals or particles and partly components of larger entities that behave like waves. The impact they make on reality depends on which alternative dominates their behavior. There are potential tipping points from one alternative to the other but it is uncertain when they will occur and the uncertainty can be resolved only in retrospect.'[22]

The financial analyst David Roche, who was formerly Morgan Stanley's chief global strategist, and now heads the investment research group Independent Strategy, takes a more explicitly quantum line. In a report titled 'Quantum Economics', he wrote that while the economy does not reduce to quantum physics, 'we can apply the logic of what quantum theory implies. Start by asking the question: why are our predictive models incapable of predicting any shock of any importance? ... Our economic models are based on the outdated perception of a stable universe of big solid objects.'[23] He argues that 'If quantum thinking changes one thing for strategy, it is the lesson never to think ... in terms of a seamless coherent universe. Because there isn't one out there.'

As mentioned above, living systems evolve in such a way that they become unpredictable. To quote biologist Antoine Danchin, 'Life is simply the one material process that has discovered that the only way to deal with an unpredictable future is to be able to produce the unexpected itself.'[24] And conversely, saying that you can predict something means you are denying it agency. It is ironic that we are eager to assign intelligence to things like computer programs, but not to living things like plants, an ecosystem, or even the economy. So when brazen-head economists present the results of their mechanistic, equilibrium-based models, they should be treated with the same scepticism we reserve for hucksters at a fair.

THE QUANTUM FORECAST

Of course, it is often possible to make useful predictions without having a complicated model. The main requirement is that you need to be able to see the most important factors that are driving the dynamics. One of the focuses in my applied mathematics career, while working with the UK computational biology company Physiomics, has been on developing mathematical models to simulate and predict the effect of anti-cancer drugs on growing tumours.[25] The models have been tested in over 70 projects to date and blind-tested by a number of companies. The approach we use, which employs methods from complexity science and systems dynamics, involves quite a few equations but a rather minimal structure, and aims to be 'sophisticatedly simple', to use a phrase from the economist Arnold Zellner. Something like the real estate-financial complex, which grows exponentially while sucking resources out of the local economy, shows the same kind of dynamics as a tumour (with the difference that doctors, unlike central bankers, are less prone to insist on more growth), and it should be possible to make similarly useful models by including things like money creation, social entanglement, and threshold effects.[26]

As in medicine, though, the need in economics is not so much about making accurate predictions for things like the timing of a crash – no one expects a doctor to put a date on a possible cardiac arrest – but instead being able to diagnose the underlying problem, warn of the potential consequences, and suggest treatments. We return to the topic of modelling in the next chapter, where we consider a narrower but still interesting application of quantum economics.

As for the brazen heads dreamed of by alchemists, perhaps the closest we have is quantum computers, which often come adorned with nests of thermally conductive gold-plated brass rods that are used to move cooling fluids. Researchers are already experimenting with quantum machine learning methods, similar to those that run on conventional computers but potentially much more powerful. The circuits for these algorithms are complex but the modules from which they are typically built are similar to the basic entanglement circuit of Figure 9.2, which describes how concepts are mapped from one mental framework to another. These modules are linked together through entanglement gates, so the output from one affects the context of another, like a series of nested and interconnected decisions. By adjusting the projection strengths, the circuits can be tuned to fit and predict data, in a quantum version of artificial intelligence.[27] Since similar circuitry can be used to describe both mental and financial phenomena, including the dynamics of supply and demand, it isn't hard to see that quantum computing offers not just a new computer architecture, but a new language for modelling the economy. And just as quantum behaviour is famous for being weird and wonderful, so such algorithms may prove superior at capturing the weird and wonderful behaviour of human systems.

Followers of panpsychism believe that consciousness is inherent in all matter, and some physicists, such as Roger Penrose, support the idea we encountered in the last chapter, that human consciousness is driven by quantum processes in the brain – which raises the question of what will emerge when we combine quantum technology with artificial intelligence.[28] Will quantum computers learn to feel, to want, to *value*?

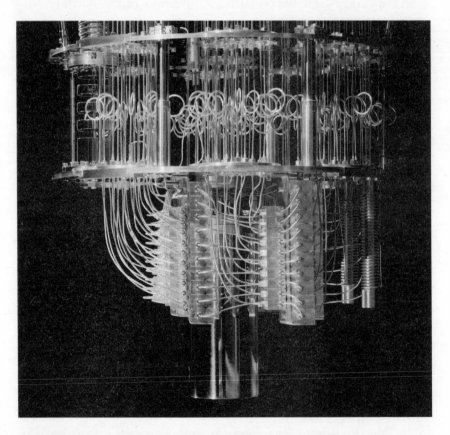

FIGURE 10.2 A brazen head, circa 2018: part of an IBM quantum computer. (Source: IBM)

As James Der Derian and Alexander Wendt note, there is 'a growing recognition – in some quarters an apprehension – as quantum artificial intelligence labs are set up by tech giants as well as by aspiring and existing superpowers that quantum consciousness will soon cease to be a merely human question. When consciousness becomes a chimera of the human and the artificial, not only new scientific but new philosophical and spiritual cosmologies of a quantum bent might well be needed if we are to be "at home in the universe".'[29] Or at home in the stock market, as human investors face off against quantum algorithms.

Or perhaps the real lesson of the quantum approach will simply be that the system is too complex to reliably simulate. It is often said that it takes a model to beat a model, so neoclassical economics will only be displaced by an alternative that makes superior predictions. Maybe quantum economics will be the model which teaches us to, at least some of the time, let go of models.

Either way, one somehow imagines that mainstream economics is going to struggle to cope. The greatest contribution of neoclassical economics to the world of economic forecasting is that it managed to hide, disguise, and generally render invisible the roles of money and power, which is what has long enabled the financial system to carry out its brand of monetary magic, not just unpredicted, but undetected. As seen next, nowhere has this magic been more powerful than in the area of quantitative finance.

CHAPTER 11

A QUANTUM WALK DOWN
WALL STREET

*The alchemy of trading volatility is not magic for the fool.
You must be the sorcerer and not his apprentice ... you
must control the spirits that you have called and to do so
means a deep understanding of one mystical truth that
encompasses the whole of global banking and modern
capital markets. It is the profound knowledge that on all
levels life is about hedging risks we fully understand and
in doing so assuming risks we cannot possibly fathom.*

CHRISTOPHER R. COLE, FIRST QUARTER 2012 LETTER TO
INVESTORS FROM ARTEMIS CAPITAL MANAGEMENT LLC

The essence of being a great financier is that you keep quiet.
G.K. CHESTERTON, 'THE LITTLE BIRDS WHO WON'T SING', 1935

The field of quantitative finance is based on the idea that asset price changes resemble what mathematicians call a random walk. The prices are therefore unpredictable; however, quantitative analysts, or 'quants', can still use mathematical models to compute the 'correct' price for financial derivatives such as options. While their ability to conjure profits out of thin air had quants being called the alchemists of Wall Street, these models all failed during the financial crisis of 2007/8 and indeed were a main cause of the crisis, since they gave traders a false sense of confidence. This chapter shows how financial firms are turning to a different kind of alchemy, in the form of quantum models – in part because these run on quantum devices, but also because they are a better match for how investors actually make decisions.

While, as mentioned earlier, the social sciences have been effectively quarantined from quantum science, there are some areas in which a neutered form has been admitted to circulate. As with a vaccine, it retains only harmless elements of quantum, in particular the notion of stochasticity, and discards the remaining features such as superposition, entanglement, and interference. In this safe version, systems are assumed to be random, as opposed to indeterminate, with the randomness being due to external perturbations. The paradigmatic example of this quantum-lite is the efficient market hypothesis, which economist Michael Jensen described in 1978 as 'the best established fact in all social sciences'.[1]

The efficient market hypothesis was first proposed in a 1965 doctoral thesis by Chicago economist Eugene Fama. He described efficient markets as places where 'competition among the many intelligent participants leads to a situation where, at any point in time, actual prices of individual securities already reflect the effects of information based both on events that have already occurred and on events which as of now the market expects to take place in the future. In other words, in an efficient market at any point in time the actual price of a security will be a good estimate of its intrinsic value.' He later noted that one can't actually test the 'intrinsic value' (or fundamental value, as it is also called), for example by summing up the present value of expected future returns, since those are affected also by things like the discount rate, but these details didn't detract much from the central message that the current price was the best estimate of that value.[2]

A corollary was that no one could beat the market because all the relevant information was baked in and changes were random. Or as Fama put it, 'I'd compare stock pickers to astrologers but I don't want to bad mouth astrologers.' (Hedge fund managers such as Ed Thorp begged to differ.) In this picture, bubbles do not exist (Fama once said, 'I don't even know what a bubble means') so historical episodes such as the seventeenth-century Dutch Tulip Bubble, the eighteenth-century South Sea Bubble (which cost Newton a fortune), the nineteenth-century Railroad Bubble (nearly bankrupted Downton Abbey), the Internet Bubble, the US Housing Bubble (Fama said that efficient market theory 'did quite well in this episode'), and so on have all been horribly misnamed. (Bitcoin is a bit of an odd case as well, since according to Fama it is 'not a store of value', which implies it is a bubble, but then those don't exist.[3])

The hypothesis, which is really an updated version of Smith's invisible hand applied to asset markets, is based on the assumption that financial assets are correctly priced at any time, so any change in price is due to new information. Since such news is inherently unpredictable (which is why it is called news), price changes follow what is known as a random walk. This gets its name because it is equivalent to following the motion of a person who randomly takes a step to the left or to the right at each time increment. The idea was later popularised by the Princeton economist Burton Gordon Malkiel in his book *A Random Walk Down Wall Street*.

One way to simulate a random walk is to assume that the direction of each step is decided by a coin toss. If the result is heads, the person steps right; otherwise, they step left. The process is illustrated in the top panel of Figure 11.1. In the trajectory shown by the arrows, the person starts at the centre, then tosses a coin to determine their next step. The result is

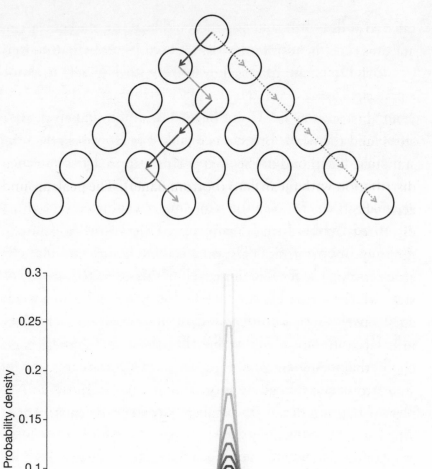

FIGURE 11.1 Top panel shows a schematic diagram of two random walks. The bottom panel shows a sequence of probability distributions for every tenth time step to a maximum of 80. The first (light grey) is a sharp peak, truncated in the figure, which is zero except for the two positions +1 and −1. The distribution spreads out slowly with time, with the shape converging to a normal distribution. The position in the horizontal axis can be interpreted as a relative price change.

tails, so at time 1 they step to the left. They toss the coin again, and this time the result is heads, so their next step, in time 2, is to the right. This is followed by two steps to the left, and one to the right, and so on.

If this process is carried out for a large number of time steps, and the whole process is repeated many times, then the statistical likelihood of the final position approaches a normal distribution with mean zero (bottom panel). The peak around zero reflects the fact that there are more ways to travel a short distance than there are to travel a large distance. For example, the only way to achieve the maximum distance would be to either toss heads at every time step, or to toss tails at every time step, which is very unlikely. The curve resembles the normal curves used to represent the propensity of buyers and sellers in Chapter 6, but grows wider with time because there is no counterbalancing entropic force to keep it stable. In fact, the standard deviation can be shown to increase with the square root of the number of steps taken, so after sixteen steps it is twice as big as after four steps.

The random walk model was actually first developed by another PhD student, Louis Bachelier, in his 1900 dissertation about asset prices in the Paris Bourse. His 'Principle of Mathematical Expectation' stated that the mathematical expectation of a speculator (i.e. what they gain or lose on average) is zero, while his 'Law of Radiation (or Diffusion) of Probability' described how the price uncertainty increased with the square root of time as prices performed a random walk. The theory was later modified so that it applied to proportional price changes, rather than the price itself, since what investors care about is the proportional gain or loss as a percentage of their investment.

While the random walk idea began in finance, it only gained scientific respectability after Einstein (who apparently did not know of Bachelier's work) applied the same mathematical technique to estimate the mass of an atom.[4] The random walk model was later used in the Manhattan Project to simulate the motion of neutrons in the core of an atomic device, and found its way back into finance along with a stream of physicists who had been trained during the war effort.[5] The association with cutting-edge mathematics and physics lent credibility to economics and mathematical finance as it was developed during the 1960s, and to the idea that efficient markets are drawn to a stable and optimal equilibrium where price equals value. Indeed, one can argue that the efficient market hypothesis – and much of quantitative finance in general – was an intellectual offshoot of the US nuclear programme.

At a deeper level, though, the efficient market hypothesis is an extreme example of classical thinking dressed up in probabilistic clothing. As Wendt pointed out, the five basic assumptions of the classical approach are materialism, reductionism, determinism, mechanism, and objectivism. Efficient market theory is materialist in that it treats price fluctuations as similar to the random motion of classical atoms; reductionist because it treats markets as being no more than the sum of their parts; deterministic because prices are governed by laws of efficiency; mechanistic because price changes are reactions to news; and objectivist because investors are assumed to be independent of each other and of the markets as a whole. The apparent randomness is not intrinsic quantum uncertainty, but is caused merely by external information. In this picture, the market itself is the magician's automaton, which always spits out the correct price when asked. Roger Bacon would have been impressed by this modern neoclassical version of his all-knowing brazen head.

Bacon, as we have seen, was an Aristotelian scholar. And it can be argued that while quantitative analysis does have an intellectual debt to quantum physics, its real roots do in fact go back to the ancient Greeks. In its strongest form, the efficient market theory states that prices adjust instantaneously to any perturbation from equilibrium. It therefore doesn't correspond to a classical mechanical system, which cannot move at infinite speed. Something like a self-closing door, for example, takes a while to react, and may overshoot. As with the mainstream standard theory of money, this theory is reminiscent not so much of Newtonian physics or quantum physics (where things do jump, but not to equilibrium), but of the Aristotelian variety. According to Aristotle, each of the separate elements of earth, water, air, and fire sought its own level, in the same order from bottom to top, and in a vacuum this adjustment process would take place instantaneously. He therefore concluded that a vacuum could not exist. Efficient market theory is the same, except that it asserts a vacuum does exist, and it is the markets.

THE SUBSTITUTION TRICK

According to its supporters, the efficient market hypothesis is proved true by the fact that markets do seem to be unpredictable. However, this is what amounts to another substitution trick. The test of the efficient market hypothesis would be that prices accurately reflect intrinsic value, which is impossible to prove. Economists therefore substituted the test that markets should be unpredictable. This is what Jensen was referring to when he described the hypothesis as 'the best established fact in all social sciences'. But the fact that [insert your own weather-, transport-, family member-, etc. related example here] is unpredictable obviously does not prove that it is efficient.

It might therefore seem that the efficient market hypothesis does little more than give an innovative excuse for why economists can't forecast the economy. However, if one assumes that market fluctuations follow a random walk, then it is possible to calculate the risk of future changes based on past variability. One may not be able to predict whether or not a stock will rise or fall in price by 10 per cent over the next year, any more than one can know whether a particular atom of radium will decay, but one can calculate the probability of it doing so, and therefore the odds for betting on a particular outcome. The random walk technique therefore pointed the way to what Paul Samuelson called 'the Holy Grail ... the perfect formula to evaluate and to price options', which, as mentioned earlier, give the purchaser the right but not the obligation to buy or sell an asset in the future for a particular price.[6]

This 'perfect formula' was developed in the late 1960s and published by the University of Chicago's Fischer Black (who initially trained as a physicist, and spent a summer at RAND) and Myron Scholes in 1973. Options had long been viewed as a rather disreputable way of gambling on stock price movements, and regulators attempted to ban them from time to time. That changed in 1973 with the publication of the Black–Scholes paper, which happened to coincide with the opening in April that year of the Chicago Board Options Exchange (CBOE). As its counsel explained, 'Black–Scholes was really what enabled the exchange to thrive ... it gave a lot of legitimacy to the whole notions of hedging and efficient pricing.'[7]

The formula also contained within it the promise of an automated system for making money. By dynamically hedging their bets, traders armed with the formula could exploit anomalies in bond and stock markets to make what appeared to be risk-free profits, just as hedge fund pioneer Ed Thorp had done, without needing to worry about the messy realities of the underlying company. Risk was therefore tamed and neutralised by the power of mathematics. As the derivatives trader Stan

Jonas noted, 'What a wonderful thing for exchanges to hear. The more we trade, the better off the society is because the less risk there is.'[8]

Quantitative analysts soon set about devising increasingly complicated financial derivatives – so-named because, like options, they derive their value from some underlying asset. An example was collateralised debt obligations, which bundled up loans such as mortgages into financial products at tailored levels of risk. Prices of these were calculated using the Gaussian copula model, which quantitative finance expert Michael Crouhy described as 'the Black–Scholes for credit derivatives'.[9] The result, as financial writer Aaron Brown notes, was a kind of 'black magic' which created seemingly secure assets 'by redefining the basis of value from cash or gold in the vault to risk equations'.[10]

CODE NAME ALCHEMY

The efficient market hypothesis has been influential, not just on the development of the financial sector, but on the way that we think about value in general. As an anecdotal example, an attendee at a social science workshop in 2018 argued that the social sciences cannot be in crisis, as some at the workshop had claimed, since the salaries of social scientists have increased in recent years, which was proof of their continued usefulness. In the US, economists' salaries did actually climb in the aftermath of the 2007/8 crisis; however, rather than reflecting utility, this may be more a function of institutional forces, which, as economist Narayana Kocherlakota notes, would 'help explain the lack of a paradigm shift in macroeconomic research'.[11] The international student groups which popped up in the wake of the crisis to protest the teaching of economics might agree.[12]

Indeed, while its fans might trumpet the efficient market hypothesis as 'the best established fact in all social sciences', one of the biggest international disasters in the social sciences, at least in monetary terms, must be the failure of economists to predict, warn of, or even properly understand the financial crisis, which was driven in large part by the collapse in instruments such as collateralised debt obligations. According to research from the Federal Reserve Bank of San Francisco, the ongoing economic impact in the US, for example, 'represents a lifetime present-value income loss of about $70,000 for every American', which would seem to argue against pay raises for economists.[13]

Again, when equilibrium-based mainstream models fail, economists do not discard their basic assumptions, but merely add epicycles in order to make the models look more realistic. In the case of the Black–Scholes model, quantitative analysts already had a name for this process: calibration. The Black–Scholes model relies for its accuracy on a single key parameter, the volatility, which is assumed to sum up everything you need to know about a security's behaviour. This is just the standard deviation of the price change distribution, normalised for a particular time period, such as a year. A volatility of 20 per cent for a particular stock means that it will typically vary by plus or minus that amount over one year, so is fairly risky. A safer asset, such as a bond, will have lower volatility.

Trading options therefore comes down, in the model at least, to trading opinions about volatility (in fact, market volatility expectations can even be traded directly, using the CBOE Volatility Index, or VIX). However, this volatility is a mathematical construction, which only applies to historic prices over a particular period, and does not remain constant in time. If a model such as Black–Scholes does not agree with market prices for options, then rather than conclude that the model is wrong, traders can simply assume that the input value of volatility needs to be adjusted. Thus calibrated, the model will be in perfect agreement with observed option prices, and can be used to calculate the prices of other options. Or alternatively, it can be used to give the answer that the modeller wants – for example, by implying that a particular instrument carries much less risk than it actually does, in order to close a deal and bank a commission.

As an example, after the crisis a civil complaint was launched against the Standard & Poor's rating agency for its part in mispricing financial derivatives. It claimed, based on the company's internal documents, that S&P would adjust the model results to suit its own business needs, by which they meant the $900 million or so it made on the deals.

While S&P had promised that its ratings would be 'objective and independent', the Justice Department alleged in a 2013 press conference that this was far from the truth. 'In the Justice Department, our codename for this investigation was "Alchemy". Centuries ago, medieval alchemists tried various methods to turn lead into gold. Here, we allege that S&P's desire to ensure market share, revenue and profits led it on a misguided venture to take securities it knew were lead and to tell the world through its ratings that they were gold. And in so doing, we believe S&P played a significant role in helping to bring our economy to the brink of collapse.'[14]

So it's official: derivatives equal alchemy. Or as anthropologist David Graeber noted: 'Financiers had managed to convince the public – and not just the public, but social theorists, too (I well remember this) – that with instruments such as collateralized debt obligations and high-speed trading algorithms so complex they could be understood only by astrophysicists, they had, like modern alchemists, learned ways to whisk value out of nothing by means that others dared not even try to understand.'[15]

So much for efficiency. In a 2015 settlement, S&P denied violating any laws, but agreed to pay a penalty of $1.37 billion. Of course, all the bankers avoided prison. In magic, that is called escapology – and escape artists such as Harry Houdini had nothing on the financial community.

MISCALIBRATED

In 2008, Alan Greenspan even blamed the financial crisis itself on what amounted to a calibration error: 'the data inputted into the risk management models generally covered only the past two decades, a period of euphoria. Had instead the models been fitted more appropriately to historic periods of stress, capital requirements would have been much higher and the financial world would be in far better shape today, in my judgment.'

However, while calibration works on paper, it is a bit like having a weighing scale which needs to be recalibrated every time you use it, and suggests a possible problem with reliability. Maybe we need a new weighing scale.

As with much economic theory, the efficient market hypothesis is ultimately a statement about the relationship between price and intrinsic value, which it says are the same (at least in idealised markets). A puzzling aspect of it, though, is that it assumes not just that markets follow a random walk, but that investors also think they will continue to follow a random walk. After all, if that isn't the case, then a formula based on the random walk won't work very well. The option pricing model is therefore based on a cognitive model which states that imagined future price changes follow a normal distribution.

The reason this is strange is that, if speculators really thought that prices behaved in this way, there would be no reason to buy stocks or options in the first place. It would make far more sense just to keep their money in cash and save the trouble of investing.

Also, the random walk model assumes that the standard deviation or volatility grows with the square root of time. For a particular asset with annual volatility of 5 per cent, price deviations after four years should only be twice as big, so 10 per cent. But people usually think of prices as changing up or down by a certain percentage each year, so if prices go up by 5 per cent in one year, then in four years they will go up by four times as much.

To summarise, the classical model assumes that investors view assets such as stocks as being boringly predictable. Prices stay clustered around a central point, bounded within a range that grows with a known and decreasing rate. But this seems like another attempt by science to produce what Einstein called a 'tranquilizing philosophy'. It is interesting to compare it with the remarks of derivatives trader Pablo Triana, who described markets as 'ferociously untamable. The randomness is not just wild; it's savagely uncageable, abominably undomesticated. No equations can subjugate it, control it, or decipher it. Where anything can happen, there are no mathematically imposed bounds.'[16]

In other words, traders are not purely objective, markets are not rational, and prices do not behave like random coin tosses – especially during times of market stress, such as crashes. Can a quantum model do better?

THE PARANORMAL DISTRIBUTION

The natural place to start for a quantum model of option pricing is with the quantum version of a random walk. This is known as a quantum walk, and is pictured in Figure 11.2. It starts with a superposed state, which is then acted on at each time step by a so-called quantum coin. A typical choice for the coin is the Hadamard transformation, introduced earlier, and since other choices give a very similar behaviour, we will stay with that.

The quantum walk differs from the classical random walk in a number of respects, one being that the walk itself isn't actually random. Instead, the position at each time step is described by a wave function which spreads out in a deterministic fashion with time. The randomness only comes in at the final step, when the system is measured to determine the position.

To see how this works, at time 0 the state of the coin is a balanced mix of up and down. We apply the Hadamard transformation, corresponding to the first quantum coin toss, which gives another mix of up and down. The up part moves to the left, the down part moves to the right, as if the walker has split in two parts. We then apply the Hadamard transformation to each of those in turn, which again splits them off in two directions, and so on, to create a kind of cascading probabilistic wave as shown in the top panel of Figure 11.2.

Another key difference between the classical random walk and the quantum walk is that with the former, the probability of ending up at a particular spot is calculated by adding up the probabilities of all the different paths reaching that point. As already mentioned, this is why the final probability distribution is highest near the middle, where there are more available paths. In the quantum version, however, paths can interfere with one another, so probabilities are not additive but may cancel out. The result, when the output is measured at the bottom for a number of simulations, is what may appear to be a rather strange probability distribution, which has two peaks near the

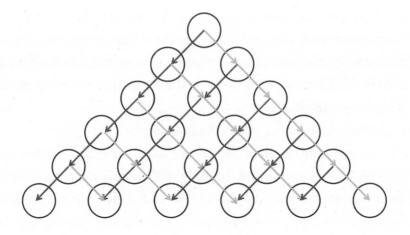

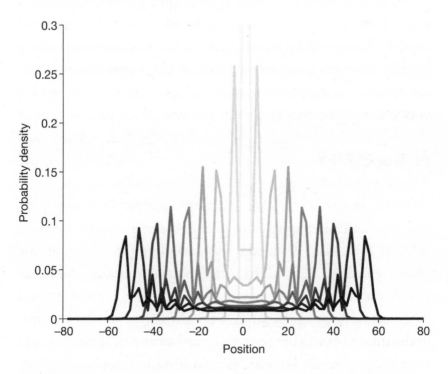

FIGURE 11.2 Top panel shows a schematic diagram of the quantum walk. The bottom panel shows a sequence of probability distributions for every tenth time step to a maximum of 80. The distribution now develops two peaks which speed away from one another.

extremes, and is relatively low in the middle. It isn't normal, it's paranormal. The jagged shape is typical of pure quantum probability distributions, and tends to smooth out during calculations when other factors such as a degree of decoherence are taken into account.

Finally, another difference between the classical and quantum models is that while the former grows with the square root of time, the latter expands linearly with time, so much faster, as shown in the bottom panel of Figure 11.2. The plot is reminiscent of those video clips where they demolish a skyscraper by detonating a charge at its base, and the materials cascade down in a spreading wave. The classical version from Figure 11.1 is graceful and controlled, but the quantum version represents a much more violent explosion, with two peaks that race away from each other like a shock wave. In fact the quantum walk is used in quantum computer algorithms for things like searching a database for exactly this reason of speed. But it also applies to the way that we think about markets.

AT THE MONEY

The quantum walk has received a lot of research attention in recent years, not just because of its use in quantum computing, but also because it appears to play a role in a number of physical and biological processes, such as energy transport during photosynthesis. It has also found use as a model of human cognition.

In quantum cognition, as seen already, a person's mental state is modelled as being in a superposition of different states – for example, the beliefs that a particular stock will go up or down by a certain amount in the next month. It therefore makes sense to ask how this superposition state will evolve in time. If we only consider discrete time steps, this amounts to applying a unitary transformation at each step. The result will be a version of the quantum walk.

Viewed as a simple model, not of how markets behave, but of how speculators think markets might behave in the future, the quantum walk model appears more realistic than the classical one. Instead of being clustered around zero, the probability distribution for price changes has two distinct peaks, which correspond to the possibility that prices will go up, and the possibility that they will go down. And instead of growing slowly with the square root of time, the volatility grows at a constant rate, corresponding to the belief that asset prices will rise or fall by a certain percentage each month or year.

Another feature of the quantum walk, as with all quantum models, is that it is sensitive to the effects of decoherence, which makes it behave in a more classical fashion. If we treat the purely quantum model as a simulation of subjective projections about the future, and the classical model as a simulation of how prices objectively tend to behave, then the level of decoherence can be treated as a tuneable parameter which allows us to capture the balance of subjective and objective effects. For example, an investor's interest in purchasing an option will be shaped by their beliefs about future price changes, but these beliefs will be tempered by objective factors, such as historical price data, or the accumulated wisdom of other investors. In particular, the seller may be more attuned to the objective odds, since they are in the position of selling what amounts to a kind of lottery ticket (see the discussion of preference reversal in Chapter 8).

Given the different behaviours of the classical and quantum models, it is unsurprising that they give rather different estimates for the price of an option. Option prices depend on a number of factors, including the current price of the stock, its volatility, the risk-free interest rate, the maturity time, and finally the strike price at which the option is exercised. For example, if the current price is $10, the strike price is $11, and the maturity time is one year, then the option is a contract that allows the owner to purchase the stock in a year's time at the strike price of $11. If a speculator is convinced that the price will rise to more than $11 over that time period, then purchasing an option is a good way to make that bet: it is much cheaper than buying the actual stock, and if they are wrong then all they have lost is the price of the option.

As an example, Figure 11.3 shows option price versus strike price for a particular option to buy a stock in six months' time, where the current value of the stock is 1. The solid line shows the quantum model, while the dashed line shows the classical

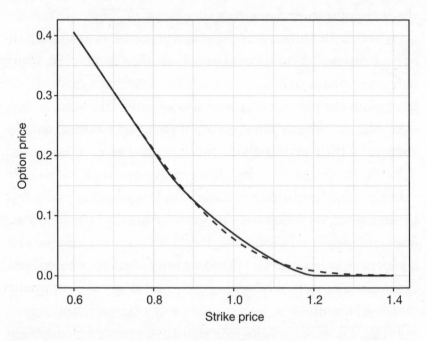

FIGURE 11.3 Plot of option price as a function of strike price for an initial stock price of 1, annualised volatility 20 per cent, risk-free interest rate 2 per cent, and maturity time six months.

case. The two models agree quite closely; however, an interesting feature is that the quantum model predicts a higher price for so-called at-the-money options, which have a strike price close to the current price, in the range 0.9 to 1.1.

In practice, prices tend to conform rather closely with the classical model, which is unsurprising given that for the half-century since large-scale option trading became a thing this has been accepted as the correct way to price options. If the quantum model is telling us something, it is that it makes sense to look not so much at prices, which are set by the vendors, but at the level of interest from individual investors, who are more likely to be influenced by subjective factors. If buyer and seller were both using the classical model, there would be no reason to prefer one strike price over another; however, if buyers are influenced more by subjective factors, then the volume should be higher for these at-the-money options.

A more detailed prediction can be made by applying the quantum model of supply and demand (Chapter 6), which specifies the propensity to trade as a function of price. A historical analysis of option prices shows exactly the same pattern as predicted by the model.[17] The volume is much higher for options with a strike price near the current price, even though it is the out-of-the-money options which should provide a more interesting proposition for traders who are looking for a quick profit, since they amount to a kind of leveraged bet on price movements. The Black–Scholes model may be quite good at predicting price, but the quantum walk model, when coupled with the quantum model of supply and demand, can predict volume as well.

The quantum model also makes intuitive sense. As an extreme example, suppose a person was considering an early investment in bitcoin back in 2016 when the price was around

$1,000. In their head, one scenario would be that the price would increase at a certain rate, say 20 per cent each year on average. That scenario would be balanced by the possibility that the price would collapse, or the holding might disappear altogether. (As in 2014, when hackers stole some 7 per cent of all bitcoins then in existence from a site called Mt Gox – so named because it was originally set up to trade cards for an online game called Magic: The Gathering. The name stands for Magic: The Gathering Online eXchange.) So instead of making finely graded bets about future price changes, they would want to reserve the ability in the future to be able to buy the coins at the same kind of $1,000 price, which is the same as an at-the-money option.

Behavioural economics, which typically equates subjectivity with error and objectivity with truth, would say that this is just another example of a cognitive glitch, as uninformed investors pile into the same trade. Again, though, if everyone were perfectly rational, and markets were efficient, then there would be little impetus to buy options in the first place, and volume would be zero.

Some banks seem to be making similar option-style bets on quantum computing. As RBS's head of innovation, John Stewart, said in 2020: 'Maybe a million-dollar investment in order to understand something that could jeopardise your multi-billion-dollar business is a great trade-off at this stage.'[18] As another example, the Toronto-based technology writer Alex Danco has compared startup scenes in different cities. According to Danco, venture capital 'is a financial invention that's been perfected to purchase call options on a different future, not in definably achieved milestones to date'.[19] The reason Silicon Valley succeeds is in part because its venture capitalists, many of whom made their money through their own startups, take a long approach and don't worry too much about things like meeting fixed milestones, whereas in more conventional business environments, the emphasis is on defending valuations and thereby 'collapsing them to their literal milestone value'.

In the quantum view, the subjective model involves projections of future growth which may or may not come true, but collapsing the model by constant measurement makes that growth impossible. The same could be said for any creative endeavour – Van Gogh famously sold only a handful of paintings during his life, so it was just as well he wasn't obsessed with meeting targets. It is the social equivalent of the phenomenon known as the quantum Zeno effect, where repeatedly observing a particle and thus collapsing its wave function can freeze it in place. Or the adage that a watched pot never boils.

OPTIONS AT THE SPEED OF LIGHT

Another advantage of the quantum walk model, of course, is that it is native to quantum computers, or for that matter any device which can perform a quantum walk. One can therefore expect to see the development of more sophisticated quantum algorithms as the use of quantum technology grows in finance. Indeed, a major focus of quantum computing, led by banks such as RBS, J.P. Morgan, and Goldman Sachs, along with specialised firms such as Multiverse Computing and QuantFi, is in the area of option pricing. So far, the emphasis has mostly been on using quantum computers to run classical algorithms such as Black–Scholes, but this is beginning to change as the advantages of quantum methods become apparent.

A report from the European Union's NExt ApplicationS of Quantum Computing (NEASQC) project on 'state-of-the-art' risk pricing models identified the complex cognitive interactions captured by the quantum walk model as 'possibly a crucial device' for modelling financial dynamics,[20] while the Oxford University spinout Quantum Dice decided to develop a commercial, fully integrated, on-chip device based on the approach, to be used for finance applications.[21] Instead of static qubits, the quantum entities are individual photons. These are produced from a source which is connected via a wave guide to an array of beam splitters, as shown in Figure 11.4. Each time a photon encounters a beam splitter, it has an equal chance of being transmitted or reflected. After performing the desired number of steps, the output is transported to a photon detector. Finally, the result is converted to a digital signal and interpreted using a classical processor such as a computer. The design, which also allows for a degree of decoherence to be added if desired, can be compared with Figure 11.2 above (or for that matter with the Pythagorean tetractys depicted in Figure 2.1). The price of options is therefore written in a beam of light.

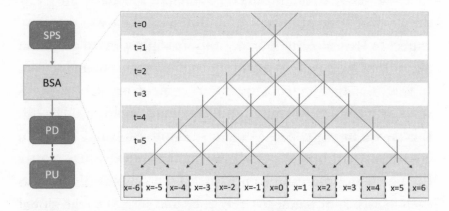

FIGURE 11.4 Schematic of a quantum walk device. On the left, optical transport is indicated with solid arrows, electron transport is indicated with a dashed arrow. SPS = single photon source, BSA = beam splitter array, PD = photon detector unit, PU = processing unit. (Source: Quantum Dice)

Full-blown quantum computers of sufficient power will take longer to develop, but banks are getting prepared. William Zeng, head of quantum research at Goldman Sachs, told a conference in December 2020 that quantum computing could have a 'revolutionary' impact on their operations.[22] As the *Economist* magazine remarked, a quantum finance algorithm 'could be deployed in days. And given the scale of the markets, even a tiny advantage could be worth a great deal of cash.'[23] According to Forbes, the 'largest near and far-term benefits' of quantum computing will be in financial services.[24] A report from Boston Consulting Group claims that 'the size of the prize is enormous – up to almost $70 billion in additional operating income for banks and other financial-services companies as the technology matures over the next several decades'.[25] McKinsey warns that businesses in 'first-wave sectors', such as finance, 'need to develop a quantum strategy quickly or they will be left behind by innovative companies'.[26] Hedge fund manager Ray Dalio predicts that quantum computing with AI will lead to 'the greatest shift in wealth and power that the world has ever seen'.[27]

Given that already most financial transactions are carried out not by people, but by machines running complex algorithms, this might again give the impression that mere mortals will have no chance competing against quantum brazen heads. But the quantum approach also reminds us of the irreducible complexity of things like value, risk, and power. The biggest implication of the quantum model, for the quadrillion or so dollars' worth of financial derivatives which sit atop the global financial system, is not that the calculations can be sped up: it is that, by ignoring these factors, they might be wrong. The next chapter explores how the same elements combine alchemically in the production of money.

CHAPTER 12

THE MONEY POWER

Money is gold, and nothing else.
J.P. MORGAN, TESTIMONY BEFORE THE BANK AND CURRENCY
COMMITTEE OF THE HOUSE OF REPRESENTATIVES, 1912

*Credit alone is money. Credit and not gold or
silver is the one property which all men seek.*
ALFRED MITCHELL-INNES, 'WHAT IS MONEY?', 1913

Real wealth is energy, *not gold.*
BUCKMINSTER FULLER, 1966[1]

Mainstream economics assumes that prices are set by impartial and objective market forces. A corollary of this assumption is that power, of the social or financial sort, is not important, which is why it has been widely neglected in orthodox theory. However, the quantum approach naturally draws attention to the role of power in the creation and control of money, in the distribution of wealth, and in financial transactions and negotiations. This chapter focuses on the wizardly power of money, and shows how it distorts our modern world, including even our perception of time.

Many magic tricks involve the magician turning one thing into another: a person into a tiger, a random card into one chosen by an audience member. One of Houdini's most famous tricks was called 'Metamorphosis', which he performed with his wife Bess. She was locked inside a large box, a curtain was held up for a few seconds, and when it was raised the magician and his assistant had magically switched places.

Perhaps the most famous transformation myth is that of the Lydian King Midas, whose touch turned anything to gold, even his own daughter. According to one version, Dionysus told him to wash in the river Pactolus to release the spell. He did so, and all the gold flowed into the river – providing the raw material for all those Lydian coins.

Money too has transformation hardcoded into its very essence. According to Hjalmar Schacht, who served as a central banker under the Weimar Republic in the 1920s, 'The magic of money lies in its protean nature, which enables it to be used at all times, in all directions and for all purposes. This constitutes its wizardry, its secret, its mystery, its magic.'[2]

The connection between magic and money, and in particular its transformative powers, was brilliantly revealed in the epic play *Faust* by the German poet Johann Wolfgang von Goethe, who himself served as finance minister in Weimar a century earlier. The story was based on an ancient legend about a magician who sells his soul to the devil in return for knowledge and power. Goethe started work on the first version of what is now known as Part I around 1772, but it was only published years later in 1790. Part II was the main project of Goethe's later years; it was completed in 1831, and published posthumously in 1832. What was it about this story that made it so interesting to one of the great thinkers of his, or any, time; so interesting, in fact, that it would hold his attention through six decades of his life?

Brief plot synopsis: in Part I, we meet Faust, who is a depressed scholar and alchemist. He has prepared a potion and is about to kill himself with it when a chorus of angels intervenes. He goes for a walk instead. A black dog follows him home, and when they get to his room the dog transforms into Mephistopheles (the Devil). Faust complains to Mephistopheles about his frustration with his work, life, quest for eternal knowledge, etc. Mephistopheles offers him a wager. He promises to personally serve Faust and give him a moment of transcendence which is so amazing that Faust will want to remain in that moment forever. If he succeeds, however, the downside is that Faust must be his servant for ever back in hell. Being a depressed cynic, Faust thinks that the Devil can never deliver and so accepts the wager. (Spoiler alert: this is a big mistake!)

Mephistopheles introduces Faust to the young, beautiful Gretchen, who is soon diverting Faust from his gloomy introspection. With the Devil coaching from the sidelines, Faust makes excellent progress towards his goal of transcendence. To make a (very) long story somewhat shorter, Gretchen absconds with Faust, becomes pregnant by him, her brother challenges Faust to a duel, Faust kills him, then Faust and Mephistopheles leave to kick back and discuss the state of the world with artists and philosophers. Later, he learns that Gretchen killed their infant daughter, and has been thrown in jail. Faust and Mephistopheles visit her in prison but she has gone mad and they have to flee. Thus endeth Part I.

In Season 2 – sorry, Part II – written while Goethe was finance minister, we are back with our heroes Faust and Mephistopheles – but now they are business partners. The action kicks off in the court of a cash-strapped emperor who is besieged by people to whom he owes money. Mephistopheles offers a solution; he claims that he has discovered the secret, long sought by alchemists, of how to produce gold from nothing. Faust shows up at a carnival ball dressed as Plutus, god of wealth. Together with Mephistopheles, he makes the emperor sign a piece of paper which reads: 'To whom it may concern, be by these presents known, this note is legal tender for one thousand crowns and is secured by the immense reserves of wealth safely stored underground in our Imperial States.'

When the emperor wakes up the next morning, he has forgotten all about it; but during the night the Devil has been cranking out thousands of copies in different denominations and distributing them to the masses (what Ben Bernanke later called 'helicopter money'). Soon the economy is humming again. Everyone has enough cash, debts can be settled, investments made, entrepreneurial spirits unleashed etc. The emperor is amazed by the change. 'And people value this the same as honest gold? The court and army take it as full pay? Much as I find it strange, I see I must accept it.' As their reward, he makes Faust and Mephistopheles masters of the treasury.

After appearing to fix in a single stroke the monetary problems of the empire (though this soon goes to hell in a spiral of hyperinflation – Goethe based his story in part on the downfall of John Law's System, described in Chapter 1), and some tomfoolery involving an alchemically created homunculus, Helen of Troy, a journey to the underworld, etc., our heroes turn their attention to real estate development. In the final act, Faust is now an old man who has joined the ranks of the ultra-wealthy by investing his share of the money in property. He lives in a large castle, built on land reclaimed from the sea through the judicious use of dykes and dams. All is good, except that there is this one couple who live in a ratty peasant cottage that spoils the view, ruins the tone of the neighbourhood, and negatively impacts property prices. Like the empty house up my street, I suppose.

Faust tells Mephistopheles to sort it out but of course he goes overboard and murders the couple. Faust is wracked with guilt and shame and drops dead. After some Bohemian Rhapsody-like debate over his soul, he is admitted into heaven, much to the frustration of Mephistopheles, who spits fire and morphs into a real estate agent.

Now, obviously we don't want to try to reduce Goethe's great work to some banal punchline, but it's pretty clear that he is comparing money to alchemy. As portrayed by Goethe, money is a way of transforming something that is economically useless – be it a foundering empire, a marshy piece of coastland, or a piece of paper – into something that is highly valuable.

On one level, money accomplishes this trick by borrowing from the future. The banknotes which Faust and Mephistopheles print for the emperor were a promise on 'reserves of wealth safely stored underground', i.e. on precious metal yet to be mined. And in a capitalist system, it is the promise of future earnings which drives the economy onwards. For example, when a company issues a stock or a bond, it is in effect offering a stake in future earnings.

On a more profound level, though, money aims for the same kind of transcendence that Faust was looking for. In Part I, Faust tries unsuccessfully to reach this state of transcendence with Gretchen; in Part II he comes closer with money. But how exactly does money accomplish these tricks? What is the source of its magic? Is it the work of the Devil – and does dabbling with it threaten eternal damnation? (Flash of light, puff of smoke etc.)

The answer to these questions is related to the notions of time and power – which, for money, are where the magic gets in.

WHERE'S THE MASS?

As discussed already, neoclassical theory simulates market forces through static curves of supply and demand whose intersection represents the optimal equilibrium price. While this mechanistic theory is often described as Newtonian, this isn't quite accurate because in Newtonian mechanics a force is something that acts on a mass to produce acceleration. It isn't possible to achieve equilibrium instantly, just as it is impossible to move a car from one spot to another in zero time.

By insisting that the system is always at equilibrium, neoclassical economics effectively eliminates the dimension of time from its equations. The only place where it enters is as a kind of scaling, so for example the supply of some good will be expressed in terms of units per month or year. Some models of the sort used by macroeconomists also simulate perturbations which relax to equilibrium over a characteristic time period, but these additions are epicycles rather than an intrinsic part of the approach. After all, equilibrium lasts forever, so is timeless. (The same is not true in heterodox economics, where non-equilibrium approaches based on things like systems dynamics are more common.)

In mathematical terms, one consequence of eliminating time from the analysis is that it doesn't make sense to talk about energy or power. For example, in Chapter 8 we spoke of the energy associated with an entropic force, but a first step was to determine the nature of the force, and a force acts in time. Power, meanwhile, is just the energy expended per unit time. The energy used by a lightbulb over a certain time period is calculated by multiplying the power by the total time; an oven that uses 3 kilowatts and is run for one hour will use an energy of 3 kilowatt-hours (or 11 megajoules in standard SI units).

In other words, just as money (as a thing in itself, rather than a metric) is excluded from neoclassical economics, so is the topic of power. This is true mathematically, but also in terms of economists' world view. After all, standard economic theory was inspired by the Pythagorean belief that everything can be reduced to number – or, as Paul Romer put it, 'that math could tell you the deep secrets of the universe' – so if it's not in the equations, it doesn't matter. For example, the law of supply and demand assumes a world where an infinite number of economic agents are in perfect competition with one another, as opposed to the real world where prices are usually set by the most powerful players. And as Norbert Häring and Niall Douglas note in their book *Economists and the Powerful*, imbalances due to things like influence, access to information, connections, gender, race, class, and so on are 'defined away by standard assumptions of most mainstream economic models'.[3]

According to the quantum social theorist Michael Murphy, in the Newtonian world view, 'such forces as racism, sexism, inequality, and sovereignty are all rendered *unimaginable* in a fundamental sense, despite their important structural effects' (his emphasis).[4] The economist Blair Fix did a word-frequency analysis of economics textbooks, and indeed found that 'What defines econospeak is that power is conspicuously absent', with the words 'sexism' and 'racism' missing entirely from the corpus.[5] On the other hand, according to one count, Mankiw's textbook alone mentions 'equilibrium' 669 times, which shows persistence if nothing else.[6]

In general, the issue of power is seen – to quote one economist – as 'airy-fairy' and 'an empty concept' because you can't put a hard number on it (which will be news to world leaders and the military).[7] By rendering power invisible, economists (again with some exceptions)[8] therefore encourage its misuse. Economist Michael Perelman explains the trick as follows: 'Economists consistently have upheld the power of elites. They have done this by ignoring or obscuring power, giving economics a veneer of science, in which the impact on people and the environment is hidden from public view ... Of course, this systematic exclusion is, in itself, an inexcusable exercise of power.'[9]

Perhaps the most obvious expression of money and power can be seen in the pattern of societal wealth distribution, which naturally has not been a popular topic in mainstream economics. One person to have a run at it was the American economist J.B. Clark, who wrote in the Preface to his 1899 book *The Distribution of Wealth*: 'It is the purpose of this work to show that the distribution of the income of society is controlled by a natural law, and that this law, if it worked without friction, would give to every agent of production the amount of wealth which that agent creates.' This was a useful result for capitalist owners at the time, given that they were under threat from communist-sympathising union leaders.

The 'natural law' boils down to a version of the law of supply and demand, applied to the labour market. In a free market, prices correspond to intrinsic value, which for a worker is the number on their pay cheque. Mainstream economists apparently saw the question of wealth distribution as thus closed, since it became, as with other things to do with money, something of a taboo topic. Lionel Robbins argued in the 1930s, for example, that because the subjective utility of one person cannot be measured versus that of another, the whole question of fair distribution is 'entirely foreign to the assumptions of scientific Economics'.[10] Or as Nobel laureate Robert Lucas put it in 2004, 'Of the tendencies that are harmful to sound economics, the most seductive, and in my opinion the most poisonous, is to focus on questions of distribution.'[11] When former UK central banker David Blanchflower was asked in a 2015 interview whether quantitative easing represented an unfair subsidy to banks, he replied, 'I'm passing on it. I mean, economists are not good at what's fair, right? ... Good try though [laughter].'[12]

Again, the silence on this question is a useful result for the wealthy, who have benefited enormously from redistribution of the upwardly directed sort. A 2020 study by RAND found that if economic proceeds had been shared as equally since 1975 as they were during the previous three decades, the median worker in the US would be earning about twice as much as they in fact are.[13] The real 'purpose of this work', to use Clark's phrase, was therefore not to tackle inequality, but to provide a cover story. Any society where the wealth is concentrated in the hands of a small elite needs a convincing explanation. In medieval times it was the divine right of kings; today it is neoclassical economics. This has become so obvious that in 2021 a senior Federal Reserve economist felt compelled to footnote a technical discussion paper with the remark: 'I leave aside the deeper concern that the primary role of mainstream economics in our society is to provide an apologetics for a criminally oppressive, unsustainable, and unjust social order.'[14]

As The New School's Darrick Hamilton argued in a lecture, 'What we need to do as economists is a better job at understanding the roles of power and capital in our political economy.'[15] Of course, this is not to say that economists have ignored the question of power altogether – only that, like money, it was stripped of any real weight. Introductory textbooks, for example, discuss 'market frictions' and 'anomalies' such as the appearance of monopolies. The discussion of power in Mankiw's textbook is limited to a paragraph on 'market power', which is defined as a 'possible cause of market failure' where 'a single person (or small group of people)' can 'unduly influence market prices'.[16] However, a far more common problem in the real economy is the appearance of oligopolies, which are defined as markets controlled by a small number of suppliers or consumers. Anyone who doubts the price-setting power of such arrangements should try taking out a mobile phone plan in Canada. The wireless industry is divided between the three big carriers – Rogers, Bell and Telus – who charge remarkably similar (and very expensive) prices.

Given that they collectively employ over 140,000 people, this is hardly a 'small group of people', unless you conflate people with firms.

Similarly, there aren't an infinite number of credit card companies engaged in a ruthless profit-destroying competition for survival ('Will that be Visa or Mastercard?'). And then there are the Amazons, Apples, Googles and Facebooks – or rather, there aren't, because there is only one of each. As the economist Paul Sweezy observed in 1939, 'it becomes very doubtful whether the traditional search for "the" equilibrium solution to a problem in oligopoly has very much meaning', given that the assumption of perfect competition is no longer relevant.[17]

As already mentioned, most of the value in major exchanges derives from intangible assets such as intellectual property, software, and so on. Its monetary value is protected by things like patent laws, which are a way of enforcing a temporary monopoly (Stewart Brand said that information wants to be free, but many people make a living by preventing that from happening). The problem with 'big data' is less with the data itself than with the fact that giant firms can distort regulatory frameworks and maintain oligopolistic control over it. Efficient market theory assumes that information is available to all, which is ironic given that these markets rely on barriers to the flow of information.

Neoclassical economists also pump the notion that, as Paul Samuelson put it, 'The consumer is sovereign'. But the reality is that prices are often set by the supplier, not the consumer, for the simple reason that the supplier is usually in a more powerful position – they have a greater mass in the transaction. In mainstream economics, inflation is purely due to an excess money supply. Money in this picture is just a metric, so changing the amount of money in circulation is like changing the measurement scale. But inflation is also caused by an imbalance between the power of producers and consumers, or between capital and labour.[18]

After the financial crisis, even orthodox economists realised that rampant inequality was becoming an issue. Thomas Piketty's book on the subject, *Capital in the Twenty-First Century*, became an unlikely international bestseller.[19] But inequality has only continued to grow. So again, can the quantum approach help?

UTILITY BILL

As Dylan Grice from the investment firm Calderwood Capital observed, 'People don't understand the logic of power, which has its own mathematics and its own dynamic.'[20] To analyse the role of power in the economy, the place to start is with its role in money creation. As discussed earlier, a debt-based money object such as a tally stick can be represented using a quantum circuit, which involves the creditor who issues the tally, and the debtor who must pay it off. The propensity of the debtor to default is initially close to 1, but must be reduced to near 0 if the tally stick is to serve as money. To accomplish this feat, the creditor must apply a force which counteracts the entropic force of the debtor. The result is an expression for the energy captured by the tally. A similar argument applies to a Faustian banknote, with the difference that the coercion in that case is supplied more by the emperor's promise of gold than the threat of force. (And in today's neofeudal system, the role of the sovereign is played by the bank.)

Of course, the tally will not remain a valid form of money indefinitely. So if we assume for simplicity that the tally is for a tax debt that must be paid within a year, then the energy required to enforce the contract can be expressed as a certain power multiplied by that time period. This energy represents the total effort expended by the sovereign to enforce the contract. Following quantum decision theory, we can think of this energy as having two components: a 'hard' objective component, which reflects say the strength of the army, or the value of the material; and a 'soft' subjective component, which is a measure of things like loyalty, obedience or goodwill.

The flip side of this is that money can be thought of as a form of power (Nietzsche described it as 'the crowbar of power').[21] It is no coincidence that the world's reserve currency is backed by the world's largest army. Spies also play a part: the United States Secret Service was originally formed in 1865 as part of the Department of Treasury, with the specific mandate of stopping counterfeiting. And while cliché has it that money runs on trust, it also runs on power. When Marco Polo compared the marvel of thirteenth-century Chinese paper money to 'the secret of alchemy in perfection', part of its success was due to the fact that counterfeiters were put to death. When Newton was Master of the Mint, penalties for counterfeiters included being hanged, drawn and quartered. We talk about 'the magic of money' but this part isn't very magical. It is like the trick where a magician saws their assistant in half, except *they actually saw the assistant in half*.

Economic activity has also long been associated with energy consumption of the direct physical sort, usually from burning something, be it wood (the discovery of fire kick-started the caveman economy), whale oil, coal, natural gas or crude oil. The Industrial Revolution was less about human industry than harnessing fossil fuels to do the work for us. The rapid industrialisation of countries like the United States in the early twentieth century was on the back of electricity networks. More recently, studies have shown that electricity consumption tracks economic growth, to the point where it can almost be used as a proxy for GDP. In some developing countries, GDP is impossible to measure directly, but can still be inferred from power use. Indeed, GDP seems a better metric of energy consumption than it is of economic health or human well-being. In much of the world we tend to take access to reliable and affordable energy for granted, but that may change as the use of fossil fuels faces limits.

One way to estimate the relationship between money and power is by viewing the global economy as a giant thermodynamic system, and analysing its total energy consumption over time. The physicist Timothy Garrett performed such an exercise and concluded that there has been a remarkably stable relationship between the two: 'Effectively, what sustains the purchasing power embodied in each one thousand dollar bill, and distinguishes it from a mere piece of paper, is a continuous 7.1 ± 0.1W of primary energy consumption.'[22] One way to see this is as an emergent property of the economic system. According to Garrett, global wealth typically increases at an inflation-adjusted rate of around 2 per cent per year. Since in a closed system this growth is driven by energy consumption, it can be viewed as the annual energy cost of maintaining the civilisational conditions that underpin the money supply.

KEEP THE LIGHT ON

This empirical, emergent relationship between money and energy can be tested in a number of ways. For example, maintaining an amount of US$10,000 should use up about the same amount of power as a 70-watt lightbulb. (The median net worth of people around the globe has been estimated to be about $4,210, which is a 30-watt bulb.)[23] Another way to compare money and power is to turn this around and ask how much power you could purchase by investing the money. If you invested the same amount at a return of 2 per cent (so, equal to the global growth rate), you would earn $200 per year; if you left a 70-watt lightbulb burning for a year, at a typical electricity cost of $0.15 per kilowatt-hour, it would cost about $92, which is lower but in a similar range given the uncertainties involved (electricity costs are often subsidised and vary depending on source and location; in Germany the average electricity cost at the time of writing is $0.37, while in China it is $0.09).[24] In terms of power, the interest on $10,000 therefore matches up with a fairly bright light.

Each year, a single dollar invested at 2 per cent should yield a proportionate power of 0.007 watts, which might make a little LED light glow faintly. If we divide the power by the rate of return, we get the energy of one dollar, which works out to about 28 kilowatt-hours. It takes about 1 kilowatt-hour to boil a kettle of water, so a dollar translates to about a month's worth of morning teas, which is about right.[25] A barrel of oil contains 1,700 kilowatt-hours, which prices a barrel of oil at about $60. Of course, these comparisons depend on things like exchange rates and energy costs, but again the answer is in the right kind of fuzzy range (at the time of writing this chapter, in mid-2021, the price for a barrel of West Texas Intermediate Crude happens to be about $60).

For comparison, our basic metabolic processes consume about 2 kilowatt-hours of energy each day, and a human labourer can perform about 0.6 kilowatt-hours in one workday, which translates to about 2 cents per day, or about $5 per year.[26] If that number seems ridiculously low, the median per-capita income of Ghana is reported to be $47.[27] (Such countries have plenty of debt, though – the investment firm Blackrock alone holds close to US$1 billion of debt across Ghana, Kenya,

Nigeria, Senegal and Zambia.[28]) It also explains why the modern economy doesn't depend much on direct physical labour: the relative feebleness of our bodies stands in stark contrast to our ability to commandeer large quantities of energy by doing things like filling our car up with gasoline, or buying a house on credit. In 1900, it took a US production worker about one hour of work to earn enough to buy 1 kilowatt-hour of energy; today it takes about fourteen seconds.[29]

The global average daily rate of energy consumption, on the other hand, is currently around 50,000 kilocalories, or 58 kilowatt-hours, which equates to about $2 per day, though this varies: in the United States, for example, consumption is four times higher.[30] For comparison, prehistoric hunter-gatherer societies ran on around 5 kilowatt-hours, while the Roman Empire at its peak tore through about 12 kilowatt-hours.[31]

Money may be a form of information, but as always, information and energy are connected: it costs energy to produce money, and money can be used to buy energy. Instead of a Faustian 'legal tender for one thousand crowns', a dollar represents a claim on 28 kilowatt-hours. The big idea of Modern Monetary Theory is that a sovereign state can never run out of money, so long as its debts are in its own currency, because it can always print more. But as Frederick Soddy wrote in 1922, 'The principles and ethics of human law and convention must not run counter to those of thermodynamics'.[32] While a country can't run out of its own money, it might run low on the ability to harness and exploit energy. And when a private bank creates a loan of a million dollars to buy a house, that money, which is apparently created out of nothing, corresponds to a very real claim on the planet's resources, as bullionists have long known.

The currency which has the most direct relationship with energy is bitcoin, because the value of a bitcoin is determined by 'miners' whose primary cost is electricity consumption. Miners therefore usually locate themselves in jurisdictions with cheap electricity rates. According to one analysis from 2020, a miner could break even if the energy price were a little less than $0.12 per kilowatt-hour.[33] Bitcoin is often considered to be an unenvironmental currency because of the huge amount of energy its network consumes (though some of that is renewable),[34] but at least it doesn't need a massive banking infrastructure, or an army.

To compare these rough estimates with the energy in a nuclear device, the Trinity blast was equivalent to about 22 kilotons of TNT or 25 million kilowatt-hours. In terms of money, this is nearly a million dollars. A modern device might be 100 times more powerful, so contain the energy of $100 million. There are roughly 10,000 nuclear weapons in the world, so the total energy is in the area of a trillion dollars. The largest bomb ever to have been tested was the Russian 'Tsar Bomba', whose detonation in 1961 released an energy of about 67 billion kilowatt-hours, which in terms of money is about $2.4 billion. It created a mushroom cloud with a base of about 40 km width. One of its designers was Andrei Sakharov, who soon afterwards turned his own energy towards the anti-nuclear movement and became a leading dissident.

The total value of residential property in Canada was estimated in 2015 at $4.8 trillion and has since grown to around $8.1 trillion (Canadian dollars). This equates to 110 billion barrels of oil, which is becoming comparable with the country's reserves (about 170 billion barrels including that from the oil sands). If we wanted to back each dollar of this geological-scale wealth with oil underground, Faustian-style, we would soon be running out of oil, which is impressive for a country with the world's third largest reserves after Venezuela and Saudi Arabia.

Finally, we might ask how these amounts of energy relate to the energy of the climate system. The mass of the atmosphere is estimated to be about 5 quadrillion metric tons.[35] The energy needed to increase the average temperature by a single degree works out in terms of money to $50 trillion. Global GDP is about $81 trillion, which hints at why we have a climate problem.

Of course, none of these rough calculations or warning signs matters in mainstream economics, because (along with money) they largely omit energy from their analysis. As ecological economist Nate Hagens notes (his emphasis), '*Economists view capital, labor and human creativity as primary and energy secondary or absent. The opposite is, in fact, true. We are energy blind.*'[36]

THE COLOUR OF MONEY

Money is the product of hard objective and soft subjective factors, which, as seen already, add together in complicated ways, so any comparison with a physical system will be approximate. For example, just because something uses energy doesn't mean it's valuable; and the volatility of oil prices shows the fickleness of the relationship between money and energy over short timescales (as Garrett argues, however, the relationship has been very stable over longer time periods). Crashing costs of renewable energy could also affect the balance. The economy is not a physical system, it is a mental construct on top of a physical system. However, it is exactly this uncertainty and incompatibility which makes the quantum framework appropriate; we only need to be careful about defining our terms and units.

In quantum physics, the energy of a quantum particle is given by a number, known as Planck's constant, multiplied by a frequency, which refers to the wave aspect of matter. For a photon, the frequency is just that of the light wave, which for visible light corresponds to colour. In quantum economics, the corresponding formula for the value of a money object such as a dollar bill can similarly be expressed as a financial version of Planck's constant, multiplied by a frequency.[37] (Because we are dealing with an economic system, values are defined in terms of currency units rather than physical units.) The frequency will then scale with the face value (here $1), and depends also on the interest rate, which plays a similar role to default risk in the example of the tally stick.

In physics, Planck's constant refers to a quantum of action, which has units of energy multiplied by time.[38] Planck originally chose the letter h as the symbol for his constant; however, the physicist Paul Dirac later replaced it (for reasons of mathematical convenience) with a modified version divided by 2π, which he denoted with the symbol $\hbar$ ('h-bar'). Alchemists would have recognised this as the alchemical symbol for Saturn, which was associated with lead. The aim of financial alchemy is, of course, to transform that lead into gold in the least amount of time.

As described in Chapter 8, the quantum threshold effect, which affects a variety of phenomena including the rate of mortgage default, is similar to the photoelectric effect in physics, where an electron is dislodged only when it is struck by a photon from a light source of sufficiently high frequency. In the economics version, what counts is the associated frequency of the money object, which depends on both the face value and a rate of interest which indirectly measures the soundness of the money supply. A common American expression is 'the colour of someone's money', which according to one online dictionary means 'proof that someone is going to pay you'.[39] Since the colour of light is a measure of its frequency, the quantum interpretation adds another layer of meaning to this expression – and to the Pythagorean connection between number and the frequency of a musical note.

Of course, we don't have a neat formula for a quantum of mental energy with which to calculate the threshold effect, because the amount of mental energy will vary with context and with the person. And the idea of associating money with frequency (even if it is in a sober physics journal)[40] sounds like a New Age scam – tune yourself in to the vibrational frequency of money and get rich! Or perhaps worse, it sounds like another attempt to appropriate the high prestige of physics, to apply a standard put-down.

However, the idea is again not to create a perfect map between physics and economics, because such a thing does not exist; and nor is it to suggest that money can be reduced to a direct measure of energy, any more than it can be reduced to a measure of labour or utility. Instead, the idea is to create a map between quantum mathematics and economics, independently of physics. Recall again that the main feature of quantum mathematics is that it is based on probabilistic propensity, as analysed using the 2-norm, and this leads naturally to a full panoply of quantum phenomena including superposition, interference and entanglement, which appear to be well suited to modelling things like the flow of information in the economy, and the measurement of value through financial transactions.

The quantum model therefore combines objective and subjective phenomena in equal measure. If we choose to express the analogue of energy in units of currency, or measure the energy of a money object in terms of a frequency, this doesn't mean that these quantities have the same physical meaning, because they have a subjective component – and we all know that our perception of time and energy does not conform perfectly with some objective yardstick. However, these terms do provide a new way of thinking about money and the economy.

In quantum physics, the frequency is related to the rapidity with which a system reacts to perturbations. The mental version could be viewed as a measure of attention or concentration, with dimension related to the experience of subjective time. We all know the psychological connection between large amounts of money and a feeling of time pressure. Benjamin Franklin is credited with the statement that 'time is money' but really it would be more accurate in a psychological sense to say that time is the inverse of money – which would explain why the world seems to be speeding up as it becomes more financialised.

FAST TIMES

To pursue this excursion into soft, subjective, and generally unsuitable-for-a-serious-science-book ideas a little further, one example of a subjective time compression effect is shown by historical attitudes towards architectural projects. Most modern firms or governments would be loath to commit to enormous projects which stretch over generations – even if they did promise an enormous pay-off in the long run. However, back in the time of medieval tally sticks, one of the largest expenses for the Church was the building of magnificently expensive cathedrals. Notre-Dame in Paris, for example, was paid for by a combination of grants from the Church, bequests from rich bishops and burgesses, and a head tax known as the *taille*. Many towns such as Amiens took out large loans to finance their buildings.

Cathedrals were the tourist attractions of the day, drawing in huge numbers of pilgrims, and even today they continue to boost their local economies. Construction often went on for centuries; in part this was because financing was sporadic, but it also tells us something about the attitude towards money and time in the Middle Ages. Usury was considered a sin, so in principle at least, there was less hurry to pay debts. The main argument against usury was that it was considered to be a form of the mortal sin of avarice; however, it was also considered to be a type of theft, namely of time. Usury made money out of the time it took to repay a loan, and time – including the time it took to build a cathedral – belonged only to God.

More generally, the Medieval period can be seen as being based on a version of a gift economy, which as Karl Polyani wrote 'was embedded in the labyrinth of social relations'.[41] The core principle of social relationships, as taught by both universities and the Church, was, as already mentioned, the idea of *caritas*, or charity. Much of the labour used to build cathedrals was by unpaid volunteers. As Thomas Aquinas wrote, 'Charity is the mother of all virtues, inasmuch as it informs all virtues.'

The ban on usury reflected a relatively static world view in which everything had its place in God's scheme – and time-scales were correspondingly long. Economic theories and ideas also seemed to be more related to the exchange of gifts, rather than the hard calculation of commercial value. St Francis even told his followers that 'we ought not to have more use and esteem of money and coin than of stones'.[42] We often envisage the lot of the Medieval peasant as one of unremitting hard labour, but as economist Juliet Schor notes, 'Before capitalism, most people did not work very long hours at all. The tempo of life was slow, even leisurely; the pace of work relaxed. Our ancestors may not have been rich, but they had an abundance of leisure.'[43]

The idea of a slow society that was based on *caritas*, and saw avarice as a deadly sin, is in stark contrast to our money-based peak-usury system, which replaces charity with the invisible hand, and ethics with the unbridled pursuit of wealth; and which appears to be doing so at an ever-faster rate. Perhaps the most obvious example of time compression is that which has occurred in recent decades in financial markets. According to the New York Stock Exchange, the average holding period for stocks declined steadily from 100 months in 1960 to around six months today.[44] Much trading activity is performed by high-frequency-trading (HFT) firms such as Citadel, which make thousands or millions of stock and option trades every day, often holding them for only a few seconds or less.[45]

In more ways than one, the financial clock is running at a faster and faster rate. It is perhaps unsurprising that a similar speed-up effect is seen with human behaviour, at least where the wealthy are concerned. In one experiment, a team led by the American psychologist Paul Piff monitored the behaviour of drivers at crossroads, and found that drivers of high-status cars are four times more likely to cut off other drivers, and three times more likely to not yield at pedestrian crossings.[46] According to UCLA neuroscientist Keely Muscatell, wealth inhibits the part of the brain associated with empathy (or *caritas*): 'As you move up the class ladder, you are more likely to violate the rules of the road, to lie, to cheat ... Straightforward economic analyses have trouble making sense of this pattern of results.'[47] A quantum perspective, which sees the connection between money and a kind of subjective frequency, would explain such phenomena by simply saying that money makes people impatient. That ticking sound you hear is the money bomb – and it seems to be speeding up. In the final chapter, we ask how we can disable this device before it does some real damage.

CHAPTER 13

BOMB SQUAD

On the other hand, the men of business, stooping as they walk, and pretending not even to see those whom they have already ruined, insert their sting – that is, their money – into some one else who is not on his guard against them, and recover the parent sum many times over multiplied into a family of children: and so they make drone and pauper to abound in the State.

PLATO, THE REPUBLIC

We need the growth.

BANK OF CANADA, 2021

Money is quantum, debt is fissile, and the world economy is sitting on a massive store of borrowed energy. This final chapter shows how money's bewitching properties have allowed the financial wizards at banks to accrue huge power over our lives; and argues that we need to retake control and dismantle the financial bomb which threatens society and the planet. The secret of money is also revealed.

During the Manhattan Project, one of the biggest challenges faced by scientists was not just how to generate a nuclear chain reaction, but how to slow it down enough to make a functioning device. The main advance was made by the Italian physicist Enrico Fermi, who had left fascist Italy before the war. According to Fermi, graphite was the ideal substance to soak up neutrons and therefore moderate the reaction rate. In collaboration with Leó Szilárd, who had first demonstrated the nuclear chain reaction in 1939, he set up the top-secret experiment known as Chicago Pile-1 to test the method.

The experiment was held in a rackets court under the University of Chicago's football stadium. The apparatus consisted of a large pile of uranium blocks weighing almost 500 tons, interspersed with graphite blocks to slow the reaction rate. Graphite control rods could also be inserted to act as a further brake. Through the alchemy of nuclear transmutation, a byproduct of the reactions would be a new element, named plutonium (after the then-planet Pluto), which was more amenable to fission than uranium.

The pile was activated on 2 December 1942 by removing the control rods. Detectors monitored its activity. As Fermi's wife Laura wrote: 'The counters stepped up; the pen started its upward rise. It showed no tendency to level off. A chain reaction was taking place in the pile. In the back of everyone's mind was one unavoidable question, "When do we become scared?"'[1]

After four and a half minutes, Fermi ordered that the control rods be reinserted to shut down the experiment. A little longer, and Chicago might have been the site of the world's first nuclear meltdown. As it was, Fermi and the other scientists and technicians present were exposed to dangerously high levels of radiation. Fermi later died of cancer at the young age of 53.

Of course, that was nothing compared to the radiation emitted by the actual weapons. In his obituary, the *New York Times* called Fermi the father of the atomic bomb.[2] But perhaps that role should be reserved for uranium's namesake, the sky god Uranus.

THE BREEDING REACTOR

According to Hesiod's *Theogony*, the original nuclear family was created when Uranus mated with Gaia, the Greek earth goddess, and produced numerous children. Unfortunately, he hated his children, and they hated him. One of them, Cronus, went so far as to castrate Uranus and throw the severed genitals into the sea. This left a white foam in the ocean, which grew into Aphrodite, the goddess of love. So the story ends well, anyway.

The mythographer Apollodorus described Uranus simply as 'the first who ruled the whole world'.[3] Now, of course, that role has been taken by money. So in order to protect Gaia, the planet Earth, from its ravagings, do we now need to metaphorically castrate money, throw the parts into the sea, and begin a new era of love? Or will it suffice to insert a few control rods?

The association of money with children and breeding, in a different sense, goes back to Plato – who wrote in *The Republic* that money's tendency to multiply into 'a family of children' could lead to social instability[4] – and Aristotle, who taught that monetary profit of any kind amounted to theft: 'The most hated sort, and with the greatest reason, is usury, which makes a gain out of money itself, and not from the natural object of it. For money was intended to be used in exchange, but not to increase at interest. And this term interest, which means the birth of money from money, is applied to the breeding of money because the offspring resembles the parent. Wherefore of all modes of getting wealth this is the most unnatural.'[5]

While these teachings were instrumental to the Church's ban against usury in the Middle Ages, such restrictions have long since worn off. Indeed, the financial framework for the modern economy is based entirely on the notion of usury. The money system is a kind of breeder reactor, whose main output is debt-based financial growth, but at the expense of dangerous levels of inequality, instability, and environmental damage. And when it runs out of control, it turns into a bomb.

As an example of such a device, we can return to the case of the Toronto housing market, which represents about a quarter of the country's total and has a total worth in the area of $2 trillion. In terms of stored energy, this is twice as big as the world's nuclear arsenal. Clearly, everyone is hoping it is under control.

So how can quantum economics help?

WHEN DO WE BECOME SCARED?

As mentioned at the start of the book, the world economy is faced with the pressing and interconnected problems of social inequality, financial instability, and the threat of impending environmental disaster. Something like a housing bubble might just seem to represent a pleasant lifting of prices, but in fact it contributes directly to all three of these problems.

Housing booms such as the one in Toronto and surrounding areas (many of which saw price appreciation of 30 per cent or more in 2020) contribute to inequality because the amount of property that people own tends to scale with their wealth, and people with low income don't qualify for mortgage loans. They also contribute to financial instability, because mortgages represent a highly leveraged bet on a financial asset. And finally, the housing boom contributes to environmental damage in a number of ways.

Data showed that around one in five Toronto homeowners owned two or more homes prior to the pandemic, and during it nearly 30 per cent of homes sold went to the same group.[6] Again, rapidly inflating prices have not deterred purchasers, who hoard housing as if it were made of gold. Some of these homes are let out but many are kept empty or used occasionally.[7] In a boom, when people move they often hold on to the original property, as a leveraged play on rising prices. Similar patterns are seen in other cities around the world, such as London, where in 2020 it was discovered that the president of the United Arab Emirates, Sheikh Khalifa bin Zayed Al Nahyan, owned some £5.5bn of real estate, not all of it fully occupied.[8] According to the UK Green Building Council, about 6 per cent of the UK's total carbon footprint is caused by new construction, while the built environment as a whole (including energy use for heating) contributes around 40 per cent. In order to meet Britain's obligations under the 2008 Paris agreement, the Council said this needs to decrease by about a factor of 4 by 2050.[9] But there is little financial incentive for energy-efficient design when the potential savings are miniscule compared to the cost of owning.

Canadian houses are instead getting larger, and have doubled in size since the 1970s. Instead of building timelessly glorious cathedrals, we build glorious homes, on a schedule. All of these houses require materials and energy to construct and maintain; they lead to low population densities, so contribute to sprawl and air pollution; they require energy for heating and cooling; and they absorb a lot of furniture and other objects. Many Torontonians, for example, have a home in the city and a 'cottage' (often the same size as their house) a few hours away next to a lake, plus maybe a condo to rent out. Each house has its own furniture, kitchen to stock, and so on; the cottage might come with boats or a snowmobile; and of course you need a large vehicle to shuttle back and forth between them – a recent study by the International Energy Agency (IEA) showed that Canadians drive the most polluting automobiles in the world, with the best-selling vehicle being a full-size Ford pickup truck.[10] This is a fun lifestyle, but it also seems an inappropriate response to the environmental crisis, in an era where human-made mass now exceeds all living biomass.[11] Gaia is not pleased.

Of course, this particular money bomb is just one of many such money-creation devices that have been installed around the globe. The largest is the one overseen by the US Federal Reserve, whose containment strategy seems to involve keeping interest rates as low as possible forever. This is less about banning interest on loans, as in the Middle Ages, than about putting usury on sale.

As Sheila Bair, who as Chair of the US Federal Deposit Insurance Corporation played a key role in the government's response to the 2008 financial crisis, wrote on Twitter in 2020: 'As with the related "side effects" of yawning wealth and income inequality, sustained low interest rates help the big get bigger, stifling innovation and productivity, while inflating the value of financial assets overwhelming owned by the rich. Yet, no one in either party talks about this. If there is bipartisan consensus on anything, it is to rely more, not less, on cheap debt to fuel economic growth. Ironically, I think the general public "gets it". But our political leadership seems unwilling to fundamentally rethink the role of monetary policy in our economy.'[12] Perhaps because there wasn't anything about financial bombs in their textbooks.

THREE STEPS

Many pages have been written about how to make the financial system more equitable, resilient, and environmentally friendly, by people who are more knowledgeable on the matter than myself (see my book *Quantum Economics* for a discussion of some of them). Paul Wilmott and I also had a stab at some suggestions for reforming (i.e. shrinking) the financial sector in our book *The Money Formula*. Note, though, that the title of this book is not 'How to Regulate a Financial Bomb'; and a growing number of people don't want to regulate or reform the system, they want to dismantle it.[13] I will therefore only describe a simple three-step approach, which does not require any advanced technical knowledge; and suggest some ways in which the quantum approach may prove useful.

Step 1

The first step is to detect the device in the first place. As discussed in Chapter 4, 'The Vanish Trick', financial bombs are protected by a magical invisibility cloak made of mainstream economics. In order to successfully locate the device, the area must first be cleared of this economics. It is important that the economics is actually removed – we are really past the 'rethinking' stage. The field does seem to be slowly imploding under the weight of its own contradictions, but that isn't quite the same thing and may even be dangerous.

Economists are likely to appear at this stage, and will come up with all sorts of excuses and smokescreens, like back in 2009 when Myron Scholes said that 'To say something has failed, you have to have something to replace it, and so far we don't have a new paradigm to replace efficient markets'.[14] (Which is a little odd, when you think about it – like saying a car's brakes haven't failed until they are replaced. Surely you can tell from the smoking wreckage?) But fortunately, fewer people are listening these days – and there *is* a new paradigm.

Once the device has been identified, carefully remove the economics packaging that protects the explosive contents, in order to inspect the device and examine the mechanism.

Exposing the device may, as in movies, trigger a sudden acceleration in its clock. But when you look more closely at the clock, which is what everyone has been worried about, you'll realise that it isn't actually attached to anything. The bomb already went off a while ago (see the exponential curve of Figure 1.1), its shock wave has quantum walked, and toxic radiation has spread throughout the land.

Step 2

Once the packaging has been gently peeled away, the second step is very simple. This is to sound the alarm, and back away. Once exposed, the device should eventually stop growing, or collapse entirely by itself. (If nothing seems to be happening, see below for some ways to hasten the process.) But your job is not to prevent some future crash – or 'legislate a precise correction that's both fair and controlled', as Canada's housing secretary optimistically put it at one point[15] – but to deal with the fallout. The inequality, the instability, and the environmental damage are not going to go away by themselves.

This brings us to the hard part, which is the final step.

Step 3

Do nothing.

The reason this is difficult is because policymakers will find it impossible to stand by and do nothing when the presumed source of infinite growth is no longer functioning as expected. In Toronto, for example, the real estate-financial complex dominates the economy, and a protracted housing recession would certainly be a challenge for the highly leveraged population. Some mortgages would go into default, some companies and individuals would declare bankruptcy, the money creation machine would go into reverse, and politicians would be looking for witches to burn. Everyone loves to mouth platitudes about 'housing that is affordable for everyone' and 'a sustainable economy' but getting there is going to require some painful political confrontation.

If doing nothing sounds impossible, just remember that governments carried out what one commentator called 'a controlled demolition of the world economy' that 'forced hundreds of millions into unemployment in a matter of weeks' in order to deal with the COVID-19 pandemic.[16] We also need to face the question posed by the Norwegian business author Anders Indset in his 2020 book *The Quantum Economy: Saving the Mensch with Humanistic Capitalism*: 'What systems and models should we keep? Which do we need to rebuild or get rid of entirely?'[17] In this case, the aim is not to help the damaged sectors recover, but encourage only the parts which are useful for achieving societal aims such as improving social balance, financial stability, and environmental health, which realistically is not much (again, it shouldn't take a major fraction of GDP to house people).

If things do get out of hand, then debts may need to be restructured or reduced (perhaps in exchange for an equity stake). One option, much-discussed in heterodox circles, would be to launch a debt jubilee by handing out funds that are earmarked for cancelling debts if a person has them.[18] While this might seem like giving debtors a free ride, and a source of moral hazard, jubilees are as old as money and are an ancient remedy for a recurring problem (though as already mentioned, debt levels have never been as high). Debt relief today is usually reserved for powerful banks and corporations following a crisis, but there is no reason the same idea couldn't be applied more generally. The real source of moral and ethical hazard is financial bombs. (People could instead take it upon themselves to stop repaying debt, in a direct-action do-it-yourself jubilee, but the outcome would be a little more chaotic.)

An alternative bomb-disarming technique would be for central banks to somehow engineer just the right amount of the right kind of inflation, and inflate the debt away.[19] But central banks have for years proved themselves unable to deliberately inflate anything except asset prices (the appropriate magic term is what behavioural economists call 'the illusion of control'). Furthermore, once inflation starts in the broader economy, it is very hard to rein in (a topic of concern in late 2021, as prices start to spike); and inflation is just another kind of redistribution, one which punishes savers and people on fixed wages. Perhaps instead they could try the idea of including house price growth in the inflation indices they target (currently it is excluded in many countries, including Canada),[20] which would draw attention to the fact that it is a form of inflation, and lead to fascinating debates over interest rates.

As for the climate aspect of the financial bomb: to keep the planet within a 1.5°C temperature rise, it has been estimated that global greenhouse gas emissions must be approximately halved by 2030, and reach net zero by around 2050. As the OECD notes, 'That is a transformative task of unprecedented proportions, made greater by the need to tackle simultaneously biodiversity loss, soil degradation, and pollution.'[21] If we shut down major parts of the economy, such as aviation, to flatten the infection curve for a virus, it surely makes sense to shrink parts of the economy that are highly energy-consuming, but also largely unproductive and parasitic, in order to flatten the curve for the climate. As Greta Thunberg said, 'The climate and ecological crisis cannot be solved within today's political and economic systems.'[22] And it certainly can't be solved when *the country's main business model* consists of building scores of over-priced monster homes and putting the owners on a treadmill to pay off the debt.

THE MAGICIANS WHO ENTANGLE HUMANITY

Of course, it isn't just homeowners in rich Western countries who struggle with debt. For example, there is the issue of sovereign debt for impoverished countries in places like Sub-Saharan Africa. In 2020, the head of the World Bank, David Malpass, decried the fact that 'there's not a sovereign bankruptcy process that allows for partial payment and reduction of claims ... In the worst cases, it's the modern equivalent of debtor's prison'.[23] Much of this debt is owed to rich corporations such as Goldman 'God's Work' Sachs, HSBC, and Blackrock, along with the China Development Bank; and those financial chains are just as real as the iron ones that were in vogue back in the day of the slave-trading South Sea Company. As former central banker William White points out, rather than agree to restructurings, creditors around the world 'extend and pretend that the debt is still viable. And it's all made superficially viable by easy monetary policy.' But ultimately, 'A lot of it has to be written off. Otherwise these countries are going to be forced to continue to try to pay, and they will do it at the expense of healthcare and so on. That's a recipe for human disaster.'[24]

Ultimately one suspects, as Frederick Soddy did in an earlier age, that our money system – based as it is on a public-private power-sharing relationship between sovereign states and private banks – is not fit for purpose in the 21st century. Soddy's own suggestion, in *The Role of Money*, was to stop paying tax – much of which goes towards paying off debt to the financial sector. 'It only remains for a sufficient number of substantial people to get together and refuse to pay their taxes on the ground that owing to the private issues of money on a colossal scale, a large fraction of the whole tax is bogus, to make a clean sweep of all the webs woven to entangle humanity by the magicians who have discovered how to get something out of nothing and, moreover, to make it bear perennial interest.'

This tax-revolt technique probably wouldn't work, in Canada at least, especially since capital gains on a principal residence are tax-free, so home ownership is officially the one thing in life that is left untaxed. (The banking-adjacent C.D. Howe Institute warned that 'taxing capital gains won't cool the housing market', but since when do we tax something to lower prices?)[25] However, at the time of writing, in 2021, Extinction Rebellion (XR) campaigners in the UK are planning to launch a one-year tax strike in which they withhold about 3.5 per cent from business or income tax, which they argue corresponds to the percentage the government spends on 'harming the planet'. As XR co-founder Gail Bradbrook said, our economic ideology is based on the ideas of 'scarcity, separation and powerlessness'.[26] It is time to 'challenge a system that has destruction baked in and incentivises harm ... It is no longer seen as radical and ridiculous to say the political economy needs to dramatically change. It has become a mainstream conversation.'[27] A first step is to 'shatter the illusion that this current system has our best interests at heart'.[28] The banks managed to evade any real culpability for the 2007/8 financial crisis, but the next crisis may not go as smoothly.

Writing in that well-known revolutionary rag the *Financial Times* in 2021, the market strategist Chris Watling called for a 'great reset' of the financial system, which would aim to make the economy 'less reliant on debt creation and more reliant on gains from productivity, global trade and innovation. In that environment, income inequality should recede as the gains from productivity growth become more widely shared.' The solution would involve both debt cancellation and agreement between countries on 'some form of anchor – whether it's tying each other's currencies together, tying them to a central electronic currency or maybe electronic special drawing rights, the international reserve asset created by the IMF'.[29]

As the monetary theorist Bernard Lietaer pointed out, 'every modern society – independently of its cultural or political background – has accepted the current money system as self-evident'.[30] But money is a technology, and like our economics it is overdue an upgrade. The split between what Soddy called real and virtual wealth will never be removed, because it reflects the two incompatible but intertwined aspects of money; but perhaps we can make the economy a little more real, and reduce its dependence on virtual debt. Again, it is hard to see such a reset happening at the moment – and some will see a crisis as an elitist ploy to pave the way for a 'New World Order', as H.G. Wells called it in his 1940 book of the same name, run by a socialist global government – but no monetary system lasts for ever, and experiments with central bank digital currencies are broadening the range of possibilities, with China leading the way. As Barry James of RemakingMoney.com notes, such currencies could potentially provide central banks with a range of new tools far more precise than existing methods such as quantitative easing, and help to 'disentangle money creation from commercial banks so that it can be owned by the people and run for their benefit'. However, they could also turn into a tool of control and surveillance (and not just in China), which is why there needs to be a 'thorough public debate about the design and all its implications'.[31]

THE QUANTUM LEAP

Now, it might seem to the reader who has struggled this far with the book, that the ideas sketched above do not rely directly on quantum economics, which after all is the school of magic being championed here, and that it isn't very helpful disarming a bomb if it just melts down anyway. But it isn't enough to dismantle financial devices, since that comes a little late; we need to dismantle the set of ideas and the power structure that led to their creation in the first place. Which is where quantum comes in. As always, financial and mental phenomena are linked; and while it is hard to pop a financial bubble directly, we can pop the mental bubble – the collective social wave function – which ultimately supports it.

The core narrative of mainstream economics is that people behave like classical atoms: hard, independent, stable, eternal. The economy can therefore be modelled as an equilibrium system. This narrative has been highly successful: as we have seen, it taps into ancient mythology, appeals to our desire for order, and distracts us from following the money. The result, however, has been an unfair and unsustainable economy dominated by an unstable financial sector. The main message of quantum economics is that people are entangled: with their own subjective feelings, with other people, with what they read in the news, and above all through the money system. The economy is a complex, dynamic, living system which can be modelled using a mix of techniques, so long as they respect the quantum, indeterministic, and entangling nature of both mind and money, and particularly the ability of the money system to scale up cognitive and financial entanglements to the societal level.

Mainstream economics has long averted its eyes from the delicate topic of money, while benefitting vicariously from its role as chief apologist for the financial sector. The quantum approach turns this approach on its head by putting money at the centre of the analysis. Prices are seen not as a measure of utility, but as the emergent result of financial transactions which depend on propensities to buy or sell. These propensities in turn are the product of a mix of objective and subjective factors, and are subject to interference and entanglement, which can lead to complex behaviour such as threshold effects. Money objects are unique in that they have a fixed defined price in their own currency units, yet their colour – i.e. what we can actually buy with them – depends on subjective trust in the money supply.

In this picture, things like housing booms are best seen as symptoms not of supply and demand, but of the dynamics of money. So as long as policymakers continue to be influenced by mainstream economists, who ultimately (if often unwittingly) represent the banks, they will do whatever they can to reflate bubbles, and create new financial bombs to replace the old ones. Quantum economics offers a new understanding of financial power, the two-sided nature of debt, the possibility of radical change, and the fissile nature of money, all of which we need if we are to build a more fair, stable, and sustainable economy.

On the first of these points, the quantum approach emphasises the role of power, both in the creation of money and in the economy as a whole. As seen in Chapter 1, the real estate-financial complex has a highly paid and well-motivated army of realtors, brokers, bankers, lawyers, economists, and so on to enforce its will – and they don't want to hear a twenty-point policy proposal on how they can make less money, or free clients from debt. But once we understand that, we can concentrate on what we *can* change, starting with our own attitude to money and debt.

One reason why our current system has persisted as long as it has is because we have blinded ourselves to the dangers of the radioactive substance at its core. Just as radium was once seen as harmless, and was even used as a health cure, so debt has been sold by economists, bankers, and others as either a neutral or a positive thing. 'Leverage is how true wealth is built,' as the realtor put it. 'You need to get your money working.' As the quantum analysis shows, however, debt money gets its value primarily through the power of coercion, so entanglement through debt is a kind of peonage. The slogan adapted from the *Communist Manifesto* used to be: 'Workers of the World, Unite. You have nothing to lose but your chains!' Today, the workers have turned into debt slaves, the chains are made of financial entanglements such as loans and mortgages, and their labour helps provide the fuel for the financial bomb. Instead of money working for them, the boss in that relationship is money.

More generally, quantum economics can also free our minds to imagine and invent a radically different kind of economy. Because neoclassical economics is based on the idea that the economy has a stable equilibrium, its methods only apply to small departures from that equilibrium. It assumes the old principle that *natura non facit saltum*: nature makes no sudden leaps. It therefore is not equipped to deal with major quantum jumps, of the sort that are necessary to deal with structural problems. Climate change, for example, won't be solved by incremental changes or subtle behavioural nudges, especially when we have received many non-subtle nudges from the climate system already, such as countries catching on fire. As sociologist Karen O'Brien argues, 'quantum social science metaphorically draws attention to the possibility for individuals to contribute to collective impact and a quantum leap to sustainability.'[32]

The usual way for investors such as pension funds to encourage companies to align with larger societal aims is through 'environmental, social and governance' or ESG investing, which ranks companies in terms of sustainability, diversity, and so on. In Canada, the real estate-financial complex would score quite high, and – at least in comparison with our pollution champions such as mining and oil – come across as paragons of corporate virtue. In 2021 the six largest banks even added ESG components to their chief executive officers' compensation frameworks. But viewed systemically, the industry as a whole is enormously damaging, in ways which don't even show up using traditional metrics. According to one report, since the Paris climate deal in 2015, the world's 60 largest banks, including the top Canadian banks, have provided \$3.8 trillion of financing for fossil fuel companies, which doesn't seem very ESG.[33] The climate activist group DeSmog claims that 82 per cent of the directors of Canadian banks have ties with high-carbon sectors, which might affect their motivations.[34] Rather than offer an ESG band-aid to the basic narrative – which equates price and value, conflates profit-seeking with rational behaviour, and confuses economic growth with progress – we need to replace it from the ground up, by acknowledging the entangled nature of society and the environment.

As emphasised by quantum decision theory, decisions to act – to take the quantum leap – arise as a mix of objective and subjective forces. Changing your mind, or that of someone else, is hard and usually happens because we reframe a problem in a way which triggers a different emotional response. In 1947, Einstein told the *Atlantic* magazine: 'The atomic scientists, I think, have become convinced that they cannot arouse the American people to the truths of the atomic era by logic alone. There must be added that deep power of emotion which is a basic ingredient of religion. It is to be hoped that not only the churches but the schools, the colleges, and the leading organs of opinion will acquit themselves well of their unique responsibility in this regard.'[35] The same sentiment applies to economics today, which has yet to come to grips with the truths of the financialised era in which we live.

In *Economyths*, I showed how ideas from areas such as complexity science and systems dynamics were working their way into economics; but progress over the last decade, since I wrote that book, has been slow. The environmental economist Duncan Austin could write in 2020 how economics has been 'in the grip of a reductionism that had slowly crept up from hard sciences to natural sciences to social sciences ... Today, natural sciences and many social sciences are retreating from the blinkered perspective of reductionism. Economics and finance remain the last bastions of reductionism but consequentially so, as these are the disciplines that continue to most shape our attitude to the world. We urgently need to unlearn 20th century economics and finance foundations.'[36] What better way to do that than to learn (or relearn) the quantum ideas which mathematicians and physicists developed a century ago, and which provide the necessary tools to understand the complex, entangled, living system known as the economy, but which have been left unused due to a mix of scientific taboos and financial incentives? As quantum social scientists are also finding, nothing will progress until we drop the view of ourselves and the world as a classical machine, and in economics this means replacing the classical atom at the theory's core with its mentally and financially entangled quantum counterpart. In science, quantum mechanics preceded and helped lay the ground for the complexity revolution; economics is going through the reverse process, as recognition of complexity at the system level makes us reexamine the foundations.

In summarising a 2021 talk by heterodox economist Michael Hudson, the economist Asad Zaman (who specialises in Islamic economics) could also have been summarising key arguments of this book when he wrote that 'Economic Theory is pure illusion; it is best understood as a projection of the power of top 0.01%. It is meant to deceive policy makers into worrying about the wrong issues, and conceal the REAL issues. If we want to understand why absolutely irrational economic policies, against self-interest of masses of public, are routinely implemented in democracies, we must understand political economy. Without understanding the power of the financial lobby, and their ability to use economic theory to further their interests, we cannot understand the world. To CHANGE policy, we must analyze power structures, gainers and losers, and create coalitions among losers, as well as knowledge, to counter financial power.'[37] But a first step to breaking the illusion, gaining that knowledge, and countering financial power is to understand the words in which those things are encoded; and the language of finance is quantum.

Finally, quantum economics can lead to a better understanding of money, in whatever form it takes, by exposing its tricks. In the early 1920s, in the midst of the quantum revolution which was revealing the magical quantum nature of reality, Harry Houdini set himself the task of debunking fraudulent clairvoyants and mediums who claimed to be in touch with the dead. He published his findings in a 1924 book called *A Magician Among the Spirits*. A century later, we need to do something similar in economics, and strip money of some of its power to amaze and deceive – not by ignoring it, or turning a blind eye to the paranormal happenings (the thumping in the floorboards, the books flying across the room, the flickering of the lights), but by looking at how it works. Which brings us to …

'THE SECRET'

Readers may worry that by hinting at 'the secret' of money in the book's introduction I was trying to imitate the success of the best-selling 2006 New-Age self-help book and movie of that name, according to which the best way to make money is to just visualise it, because the 'law of attraction' means that your thoughts become real. Doing so will apparently turn you into 'the most powerful magnet in the Universe!', which would be awkward during airport security scans. The reason why the wealthiest 1 per cent of the population is rich is because they understand this secret, and of course they want to keep it hidden from everyone else.

While *The Secret* enlisted a number of dubious 'quantum physicists' to add pseudo-scientific flesh to these claims, the quantum economics argument is a little different. The wealthy elites probably *want* you to believe that the trick of becoming rich is to think about attracting money. What better way to deflect you from thinking about structural causes of inequality?

So what is the real secret of money (and can we use it to get rich)? Of course, I am not in possession of any special occult knowledge, but we can at least compile some quantum clues from the story of money. In the past, economists argued that money was a measure of labour, or utility, or was just an inert metric. Bullionists, from the Latin *bullire*, 'to boil', think that the secret sauce is in a cauldron of molten metal, while chartalists, from *charta*, for a token or record, think that it is a record in a scribe's account. A litmus test for these theories is cybercurrencies such as bitcoin, which make no sense according to bullionism (it's not gold), chartalism (it's not government debt), or conventional economics (it isn't used much as a means of exchange or a unit of account), which is why mainstream economists from Alan Greenspan to Eugene Fama to Nouriel Roubini have long declared it valueless.

Other theories also exist: authors have described money as a memory substitute, a vector of human desire, a symbolic quantification of societal power, a kind of narrative device, and so on. While each of these theories captures an aspect of money, few of them emphasise (or sometimes even mention) its most obvious feature, which is its association with number. And as argued in this book, money objects are better seen as quantum entities with dual real/virtual properties, and prices as emergent features. Money does not measure anything directly, other than currency units, but it can be seen as a store of energy and information, which are related through the concept of entropy. So money is much more than a passive metric, as it is usually portrayed in economics textbooks.

Money itself gets its name from the fact that Roman coins were first minted in the temple of Juno Moneta. Juno was the goddess of marriage, and was associated with youth and vitality, but she was often portrayed as having a warlike aspect and was seen as a protector of the community. With money's marriage of the soft and the hard, its connection with energy and creativity, and its military credentials, the name seems to fit. But this still doesn't quite answer why money has taken on such importance in our lives.

As a final example of its strange powers, consider the 'gold farmers' of Venezuela. These are people, mostly young men, who play video games where they are rewarded with virtual gold, or game points, or character upgrades, or virtual land in a virtual city, that they can sell to other players for real money, by which they mean bitcoin. They prefer old games such as Tibia and RuneScape because they still have lots of players, and the internet connections in Venezuela are too slow and unreliable for more up-to-date ones. Such 'farmers' might only make a couple of dollars a day, but that makes them better off than most people who are paid in the devalued national currency. One of them, a young man in his early twenties who spent his workday killing virtual minotaurs, described his routine in a Bloomberg interview as 'Hunt, kill, click, repeat'.[38] Another said he plays seven days a week in order to support his wife and child: 'As man of the house I should be paying the bills.' His wife initially disapproved of his gaming, but said, 'I can't argue with what he's making.'

Again, this drives home the dual real/virtual nature of money, as emphasised by Frederick Soddy, and quantum economics. On the one hand it is virtual – killing minotaurs for points and investing it in 'virtual estate' has nothing to do with the real world – but on the other hand it does put food on the table.

However, it also draws attention to another aspect of money, and the ultimate source of power for financial bombs, which is that money taps into something very deep about the structure of the universe – namely that reality is a magic trick.

NEGATIVE MAGIC

Consider, for example, the similarities between reality and a video game. Virtual reality games are already getting to the point where people can be tricked into confusing what they see with reality. Imagine what the games will be like in a hundred years' time, when they might be running on quantum computers. According to the philosopher Nick Bostrom, they may in fact be so sophisticated that the little figures running around in them will actually be conscious. Since simulations are cheap and plentiful, 'we would be rational to think that we are likely among the simulated minds rather than among the original biological ones'.[39] In which case, those gold farmers are playing a game within a game.

This idea that nothing is real and it's all made up, known as the Simulation Hypothesis, is taken seriously by many clever people, including Elon Musk, who probably uses it to justify the

Tesla share price. So it's not something that *I* made up. Many mystical traditions such as Buddhism and Hinduism hold that the universe itself is an illusion, or *maya* to use the Sanskrit term. The word 'Buddha' means 'one who is awake' and refers to the idea that we 'wake up' when we come to this realisation.

Personally, I hold out hope that we are not just apps on some future teenager's phone, but the point is that, in principle at least, it *could* be a simulation. After all, we think that everything that we experience comes through our senses, but actually that isn't true – we get some prompts from the world around us, and then our brains fill in the rest by making predictions based on prior experience, and packaging impressions into consistent memories of what has just happened. For example, our eyes might be our lead asset when it comes to sensory perception, but they only see clearly a little spot which is about a thousandth of the entire visual field – the rest is very low resolution. They compensate, to a degree, by moving rapidly to scan the scene; but according to Stephen Macknik, a neuroscientist at SUNY Downstate Medical Center, 'Almost everything you see – 99 percent or more – is fabricated by your brain. It's an estimation of what's actually happening out there'.[40] The real and the virtual become confused.

As a result, the brain can be easily fooled, as can be seen from the cognitive glitches beloved of behavioural psychologists and magicians alike.[41] Most decisions are taken unconsciously, and our vaunted powers of rationality are used more to confabulate a consistent story about our experiences, and maintain a stable sense of self, than they are to make reasoned arguments. The brain doesn't just ignore, it actively represses information that doesn't gel with this account. Consciousness itself therefore involves producing an illusion; and if the world were a low-grade virtual reality game, we would accept it with unblinking faith. (Note that this is not the same as the reductionist idea explained by one biologist, that 'free will genes' cunningly create an illusion of consciousness equivalent to 'a belief in magic' in order to provide the 'evolutionary advantage of conferring the illusion of responsibility' – as if only genes are real.)[42]

Any game also needs a way to keep score; and the reason money is so effective in this role is because it taps into this illusion-creating mental machinery. Again, money's trick of collapsing subjective value down to a hard number isn't some new thing that we invented, but can be viewed as a prosthetic extension of the two-sided structure of the human brain, with its specialised hemispheres; and the same phenomenon is of course intrinsic to the dual wave/particle nature of reality, where measurements occur by collapsing a wave function down to a precise number (with money, the power battle is over whose numbers we're going to use). The fact that money objects blend in so well with our mental processes, and tap into this unconscious sense-making apparatus, means that they seem an innocuous and natural but also highly engaging and entrancing addition. And economics is the story we tell to make sense of it all and distract from any glitches in the stage machinery. ('Yes, the house price is $X million. It reflects supply and demand, population pressures, current market realities – unless you're from Ghana or outer space.')

The good news, though, is that we have control over the money illusion, because this is one we invented. So if we want to change our own behaviour, then the best way to do that is to change the rules of the game. A first step is to take a long, hard look at money – and realise that there isn't a secret that is only known to the ultra-wealthy, or that promises to make you rich if you discover it. It's actually pretty transparent.

Money is a powerful social technology, and as we have seen, it has displayed over the millennia the ability to perform impressive and bewitching tricks, including helping to kick-start a magical flowering of human activity and build civilisation. It is especially renowned for its ability to dazzle, distract, and exert hypnotic control over our minds, in ways that are always surprising and entertaining. The audience made up of future generations, or passing UFOs, will be amazed that it (with help from its famuli, those huddled confabulators of neoclassical economics) had us seriously believing that humans are rational and unentangled, markets are efficient, and usury is a wonderful thing; that measuring our success through energy burn, or its proxy, GDP, is an appropriate strategy as we spiral into environmental crisis; and above all, that it itself is nothing special, just a passive and inert medium of exchange.

But while this is a type of magic, it is a cheap copy of the real magic, which is that of the universe. (An author once said that 'adulthood means recognising that magic doesn't exist', but really it means that we stop recognising the magic of existence.)[43] Money is its opposite in that it distracts the audience by reducing everything to the uniform sameness of number. It replaces social bonds with the financial kind. It makes us dependent while giving the illusion of independence. It is a quantum technology that makes us think classically. And it penetrates everywhere. So money is a negative form of magic, not just in the sense of a taboo, but because – when used improperly – it hacks our minds, interferes with *caritas*, and removes the real magic from life, which is our sense of surprise and delight with the world. The fact that we think that maximising it or putting it to work will magically make our problems go away, is money's greatest trick of all.

ACKNOWLEDGEMENTS

For useful discussions and questions, wise insights and advice, and much-appreciated help along the way, thanks to: Paul Wilmott; Alexander Wendt and the other speakers and organisers at the Mershon Center's quantum social science bootcamp; Asghar Qadir; Monireh Houshmand; Jack Sarkissian; and Marko Mayr and Ramy Aboushelbaya from Quantum Dice.

For their painstaking attention to detail coupled with openness to new ideas, thanks to the team at Icon Books, particularly Robert Sharman, Duncan Heath, and Andrew Furlow.

And thanks as always to my family.

FURTHER READING

Quantum economics is a new field, so most of the research is in the form of technical papers (many are cited throughout the book), but there are a number of books on related areas including quantum social science, quantum cognition, and quantum finance.

Perhaps the first book on quantum social science was Danah Zohar's *The Quantum Self* (Flamingo, 1990). Drawing on research by people such as the physicist Roger Penrose, who argued that mental phenomena are based ultimately on quantum processes inside the brain, Zohar's book linked psychological and social behaviour to that of quantum matter. It was followed in 1993 by *The Quantum Society*, which Zohar co-wrote with Ian Marshall, and later by a series of books on how quantum principles can be applied to areas such as management.

A more academic but still accessible take on the subject of quantum social science is provided by Alexander Wendt's *Quantum Mind and Social Science: Unifying Physical and Social Ontology* (Cambridge University Press, 2015) which aims to build a quantum ontology for the social sciences. A compilation of essays edited by James Der Derian and Wendt will be published in 2022 by Oxford University Press with the provisional title *Quantum International Relations: A Human Science for World Politics*.

While these books draw an explicit link between quantum physics and human behaviour, many researchers in quantum cognition concentrate on the use of quantum mathematics to model cognitive phenomena such as interference between incompatible concepts. The related area of quantum finance applies techniques from quantum mechanics to analyse market behaviour. Most of the publications in these areas are quite technical and aimed at an academic audience. A good introduction to quantum cognition is *Quantum Models of Cognition and Decision* by Jerome Busemeyer and Peter Bruza (Cambridge University Press, 2014). A useful take on quantum finance, written by a physicist-turned-trader, is Jack Sarkissian's *Quantum Markets: Physical Theory of Market Microstructure* (Advanced Scientific Publishing, 2020).

The approach outlined in the present volume, and in my previous books *The Evolution of Money* (Columbia University Press, 2016, co-authored with Roman Chlupaty) and *Quantum Economics: The New Science of Money* (Icon Books, 2018), is inspired less by physics than by the apparent suitability of quantum mathematics for the study of monetary transactions. The mathematical details, along with connections to quantum computing, are presented in *Quantum Economics and Finance: An Applied Mathematics Introduction* (2nd edition, Panda Ohana, 2021). A series of video tutorials can be found here: https://www.youtube.com/QuantumEconomicsAndFinance

This book also draws on my research published in various journals, including *Physica A* (physics), *Security Dialogue* (international relations), *Economic Thought*, *Quantum Reports*, *Frontiers in Artificial Intelligence*, and *Wilmott* (quantitative finance). A full list of research papers, articles, and other resources is available at: http://www.postpythagorean.com/quantumresources.html

NOTES

Introduction

1 Image from Wikipedia: http://en.wikipedia.org/wiki/Trinity_%28 nuclear_test%29

2 Median salary in 2018 was $34,600. A household with two workers will of course make about twice this. Statistics Canada. Table 11-10-0239-01: Income of individuals by age group, sex and income source, Canada, provinces and selected census metropolitan areas.

3 Minimum wage in Ontario in 2020 is $14 per hour. The cost of the house therefore represents 160,000 hours. Assuming 36½ hours per week, and five weeks for holidays and statutory days off, it will take 93 years to pay off the house. Land transfer and realtor fees add a few more per cent.

4 Fix, B. (2020), 'As We Exhaust Our Oil, It Will Get Cheaper But Less Affordable'. https://economicsfromthetopdown.com/2020/12/03/ as-we-exhaust-our-oil-it-will-get-cheaper-but-less-affordable/

5 A standard DOT-111 railcar holds 717 barrels. https://en.wikipedia.org/ wiki/DOT-111_tank_car

6 The average price for a detached home in Toronto was about $1,360,000 at the time.

7 James Coursier, quoted in: Godwin, R. (15 November 2020), 'How much have you got? Breaking the taboos on money'. *Guardian*.

8 Speciale, A. and Seputyte, M. (11 May 2016), 'ECB Can Still Pull Rabbits Out of the Hat, Council Member Says'. Bloomberg.

9 National Public Radio (23 October 2015) *Planet Money*, Episode 659: 'How To Make $3 Trillion Disappear'.

10 Schacht, H. (1967). *The Magic of Money*. London: Oldbourne.

11 Scheffer, M., Van Bavel, B., Van de Leemput, I.A., Van Nes, E.H. (2017), 'Inequality in nature and society'. *Proceedings of the National Academy of Sciences* 114(50): 13154-13157.

12 This isn't unusual: in 2020, over half of Canada's major real estate markets inflated by more than the median family income. Punwasi, S. (17 February 2021), 'Canadian Bank: "Your House Makes More Than You Do," Draw Your Own Conclusion'. Better Dwelling. https:// betterdwelling.com/canadian-bank-your-house-makes-more-than-you- do-draw-your-own-conclusion/

13 Wheatley, J. (18 November 2020), 'Pandemic fuels global "debt tsunami"'. *Financial Times*. Canadian mortgage debt grew by 7.7 per cent in 2020 alone: see Erik Hertzberg (19 February 2021), 'Canadians pile into mortgage debt at fastest pace in a decade'. Bloomberg.

14 Minsky, H.P. (1972), 'Financial instability revisited: the economics of disaster', in *Reappraisal of the Federal Reserve Discount Mechanism* (Washington, DC: Board of Governors of the Federal Reserve System), pp. 95–136.

15 Wilmott, P., Orrell, D. (2017), *The Money Formula: Dodgy Finance, Pseudo Science, and How Mathematicians Took Over the Markets*. Chichester: Wiley.

16 The notional value of a derivative is based on the value of the underlying assets. See Wilmott, P., Orrell, D. (2017), *The Money Formula: Dodgy Finance, Pseudo Science, and How Mathematicians Took Over the Markets*. Chichester: Wiley.

17 Dittli, M. (16 November 2020), 'Central Banks Keep Shooting Themselves in the Foot'. https://themarket.ch/interview/william-white-central-banks-keep-shooting-themselves-in-the-foot-ld.3053

18 Strange, S. (1986), *Casino Capitalism*. Oxford: Basil Blackwell.

19 In 2021, Morgan Stanley CEO James Gorman accurately warned Reddit traders, who had bid up prices on unloved companies such as Gamestop in order to burn hedge funds who had bet on their demise, that they were 'in for a very rude awakening at some point here'. Not like Morgan Stanley, then, which was one of the biggest recipients of bailout funds in the aftermath of the 2007/8 financial crisis. Or Gorman himself, whose pay package in 2020 amounted to $33 million in a year when, according to Bank of America's chief investment strategist Michael Hartnett, 'policy stimulus in 2020/21 continues to flow directly to Wall St not Main St, inciting historic wealth inequality via asset bubbles'. Natarajan, S. (28 January 2021), 'Gorman Says Reddit Rally Traders Are Headed for "Rude Awakening"'. Bloomberg. Durden, T. (15 February 2021), 'BofA Hints That Weimar 2.0 Could Be Coming'. Zero Hedge. https://www.zerohedge.com/markets/bofa-hints-weimar-20-could-be-coming

20 Hagens, N.J. (2020), 'Economics for the future – Beyond the superorganism'. *Ecological Economics* 169: 106520.

21 McNutt, L. (14 April 2020), 'Why is Real Estate an Essential Service?'. RE/MAX. https://blog.remax.ca/why-is-real-estate-an-essential-service/

22 'Housing. It's a Human Right'. http://www.unhousingrapp.org/.

23 Evans, P. (10 September 2020), 'Canadians have deferred $1B a month worth of mortgage payments since pandemic began'. CBC News.

24 Samuelson, P.A. (1973), *Economics* (9th edn). New York: McGraw-Hill, p. 55.

25 https://twitter.com/paulkrugman/status/1180457374705999872

26 Letter to A.L. Bowley, 27 February 1906.

27 Coecke, R., De Felice, G., Meichanetzidis, K., Toumi, A. (2020), 'Foundations for Near-Term Quantum Natural Language Processing'. https://arxiv.org/pdf/2012.03755.pdf

28 Sheng, A. (July 2019), 'A New Bretton Woods Vision for a Global Green New Deal'. *Revitalizing the Spirit of Bretton Woods: 50 Perspectives on the Future of the Global Economic System.* Bretton Woods Committee, pp. 360–367.

29 The excerpt read:

'So: students. Decision time. You live at what many believe is a bifurcation point in human history. You've seen all the graphs with lines curving up like a ski jump. Human population. Gross domestic product. Species extinction. Carbon emissions. Inequality. Resource shortages. You know that something has to give. You've got an idea that the price isn't right. Maybe you're even suspicious that, if the world economy does turn out to be a Ponzi scheme, you or your children are a little bit late in the game.

'You therefore stand at a fork in the road. You can take the orthodox route – and risk ending up with a qualification as impressive as a degree in Marxist ideology right after the fall of the Berlin Wall. Or you can take a chance on regime shift, by speaking up, questioning your teachers, being open to disruptive ideas, and generally acting as an agent of change.

'You can insist that the economy is a complex, dynamic, networked system – and demand the tools to understand it.

'You can point out that the economy is unfair, unstable, and unsustainable – and demand the skills to heal it.

'You can tell the oracles that they have failed.

'You can go in and break the machine.

'And then you can do something new.'

Chapter 1: Transmutation

1 Sclove, R.E. (1989), 'From Alchemy to Atomic War: Frederick Soddy's "Technology Assessment" of Atomic Energy, 1900–1915'. *Science, Technology, & Human Values* 14(2), 163–194.

2 *Times Literary Supplement* (26 August 1926), p. 565.

3 Knight, F. (16 April 1927), 'Money'. *Saturday Review of Literature*, p. 732.

4 Russell, A.S. (30 November 1956), 'F. Soddy, Interpreter of Atomic Structure'. *Science* 30: 1069–70.

5 Krugman, Paul (10 February 2015), 'There's Something About Money (Implicitly Wonkish)'. *New York Times*. http://krugman.blogs.nytimes.com/2015/02/10/theres-something-about-money-implicitly-wonkish/

6 Soddy, F. (2003), *The Role of Money: What It Should Be, Contrasted with What It Has Become*. London: Routledge.

7 Fisher, I. (1911), *The Purchasing Power of Money*. New York: The Macmillan Co.

8 Constâncio, V. (11 May 2017), Speech at the second ECB Macroprudential Policy and Research Conference, Frankfurt am Main. Retrieved from European Central Bank: https://www.ecb.europa.eu/press/key/date/2017/html/ecb.sp170511.en.html

9 In 2018, the Rebuilding Macroeconomic Theory Project, for example, emphasised 'incorporating financial frictions rather than assuming that financial intermediation is costless'. Vines, D. and Wills, S. (2018), 'The rebuilding macroeconomic theory project: an analytical assessment'. *Oxford Review of Economic Policy* 34(1–2): 1–42 (p. 4).

10 Storm, S. (8 March 2021), 'The Standard Economic Paradigm is Based on Bad Modeling'. Institute for New Economic Thinking. https://www.ineteconomics.org/perspectives/blog/why-dsge-models-are-not-the-future-of-macroeconomics

11 Sclove, R.E. (1989), 'From Alchemy to Atomic War: Frederick Soddy's "Technology Assessment" of Atomic Energy, 1900–1915'. *Science, Technology, & Human Values* 14(2), 163–194.

12 In Kumar, M. (2008), *Quantum: Einstein, Bohr and the Great Debate About the Nature of Reality*. London: Icon Books, p. 75.

13 Wennerlind, C. (2011), *Casualties of Credit: The English Financial Revolution, 1620–1720*. Cambridge, MA: Harvard University Press.

14 Flynn, J.T. (1941), *Men of Wealth : The Story of Twelve Significant Fortunes from the Renaissance to the Present Day*. New York: Simon & Schuster.

15 Jevons, W.S. (1905), *The Principles of Economics: A Fragment of a Treatise on the Industrial Mechanism of Society; and Other Papers*. London: Macmillan & Co.

16 Nicolaisen, J. (25 April 2017), 'Jon Nicolaisen: What should the future form of our money be?' Retrieved from Bank of Norway: http://www.norges-bank.no/en/published/speeches/2017/2017-04-25-dnva/

17 McLeay, M., Radia, A., and Thomas, R. (14 March 2014), 'Money Creation in the Modern Economy'. *Quarterly Bulletin 2014 Q1* (Bank of England).

18 Deutsche Bundesbank (25 April 2017), 'How money is created'. https://www.bundesbank.de/en/tasks/topics/how-money-is-created-667392

19 Atkins, R. (29 May 2018), 'Radical reform: Switzerland to vote on banking overhaul', *Financial Times*.

20 Turner, A. (10 November 2014), 'Printing money to fund deficit is the fastest way to raise rates'. *Financial Times*.

21 https://twitter.com/t0nyyates/status/1318290412512153603

22 Anonymous (2019), 'Global house price index'. *Economist*. https://www.economist.com/graphic-detail/2019/06/27/global-house-price-index

23 Gross domestic product (GDP) at basic prices, by industry, annual average (×1,000,000), Statistics Canada, Table 36-10-0434-03, 2020.

24 Maloney, M., Somerville, T. and Unger, B. (2019), 'Combatting Money Laundering in BC Real Estate'. https://news.gov.bc.ca/files/Combatting_Money_Laundering_Report.pdf

25 Watling, C. (18 March 2021), 'Time for a great reset of the financial system'. *Financial Times*.

26 https://en.wikipedia.org/wiki/List_of_largest_public_companies_in_Canada_by_profit

27 Di Matteo, L. (2017), 'Supply Constraints and Ontario Housing Prices'. Worthwhile Canadian Initiative, 15 February 2017. https://worthwhile.typepad.com/worthwhile_canadian_initi/2017/02/suuply-contraints-and-ontario-housing-prices.html

28 Kirby, J. (31 March 2017), 'Stephen Poloz: "No one wins a trade war. Everybody loses"'. *Maclean's*.

29 https://twitter.com/owenbigland/status/1297912062463500288

30 Younglai, R. (20 February 2021), 'Defying gravity'. *Globe and Mail*. Residential investment grew by 22 per cent in 2020.

31 Porter, D. (22 January 2021), 'Unbreakable Canadian Housing?'. BMO Capital Markets Economics. https://economics.bmo.com/en/publications/detail/9b7433d3-ae19-4687-a26f-747e3093b35b/

32 Bradshaw, J. (24 April 2021), 'More research needed on factors driving high home prices, National Bank CEO says'. *Globe and Mail*.

33 To use a Juice Media expression. In contrast, a number of financial advisors have publicly warned of a housing bubble, notably Hilliard MacBeth, author of the book *When the Bubble Bursts: Surviving the Canadian Real Estate Crash*.

34 Carmichael, K. (3 November 2020), 'The Bank of Canada is supposed to be independent, but it might not hurt if it knew what Finance was up to'. *Financial Post.*

35 Zochodne, G. (24 February 2021), 'Bank CEOs see low rates, high savings driving steady demand in housing markets'. *Financial Post.*

36 Vandaelle, I. (19 March 2021), 'Canada's hot housing market a trade-off to stave off a "bad recession": Poloz'. BNN Bloomberg.

37 National Democratic Party (20 February 2019), 'Jagmeet Singh Wants to Keep the Dream of Home Ownership Alive'. https://www.ndp.ca/news/jagmeet-singh-wants-keep-dream-home-ownership-alive

38 Sibley, R. (9 April 2011), 'Chomsky talks fear in western society'. *Ottawa Citizen.*

39 TVO (8 April 2021), 'What Should the Government Do About Housing?'. https://www.tvo.org/video/what-should-the-government-do-about-housing

40 Desjardins, J. (19 July 2019), 'Mapped: The Countries With the Highest Housing Bubble Risks'. The Visual Capitalist. https://www.visualcapitalist.com/mapped-the-countries-with-the-highest-housing-bubble-risks/

41 Tanzi, A. (5 August 2021), 'U.S. Housing Boom Rescues More Than 1 Million "Underwater" Homes'. Bloomberg.

42 Bloomberg News (28 July 2021), 'In its latest crackdown, China intensifies focus on real estate'. Bloomberg.

43 Anonymous (16 January 2020), 'Home ownership is the West's biggest economic-policy mistake'. *Economist.*

44 'R&D-intensive industries – aircraft, computing and the like – will be disproportionately harmed when the financial sector grows quickly … a sector with high R&D intensity located in a country whose financial system is growing rapidly grows between 1.9 and 2.9% a year slower than a sector with low R&D intensity located in a country whose financial system is growing slowly.' Bank for International Settlements (2012) 82nd Annual Report, 1 April 2011– 31 March 2012. Basel.

Chapter 2: The penetration trick

1 Iamblichus (1918), *The Life of Pythagoras.* Translated by T. Taylor. Kila, MT: Kessinger.

2 Orrell, D. (2007), *Apollo's Arrow: The Science of Prediction and the Future of Everything.* Toronto: HarperCollins.

3 Koestler, A. (1959), *The Sleepwalkers: A history of man's changing vision of the Universe.* New York: Macmillan.

4 Fludd, R. (1626), *Philosophia sacra et vere christiana seu meteorologia cosmica*. Frankfurt: Francofurti prostat in officina Bryana.

5 Mayeda, A. (18 November 2016), 'The Rebel Economist Who Blew Up Macroeconomics'. Bloomberg.com.

6 Guthrie, W.K.C. (1962), *A History of Greek Philosophy, The earlier Presocratics and the Pythagoreans* (6 vols). Cambridge: Cambridge University Press, Vol. 1, p. 221.

7 Wertheim, M. (3 October 2006), 'Numbers Are Male, Said Pythagoras, and the Idea Persists'. *New York Times*.

8 Aristotle (1943), *Generation of Animals*. Translated by A.L. Peck. Cambridge, Mass.: Harvard University Press, p. 184.

9 Orrell, D. (2016), 'A quantum theory of money and value'. *Economic Thought* 5(2): 19–36.

10 Hossenfelder, S. (2016), 'I've read a lot of books recently'. Available at: http://backreaction.blogspot.com/2016/09/ive-read-lot-of-books-recently.html. For my review of Hossenfelder's book, see https://futureof everything.wordpress.com/2018/07/04/lost-in-math/

11 Harding, S.G. (1986), *The science question in feminism*. Ithaca: Cornell University Press, p. 31.

12 Keller, E.F. (1985), *Reflections on gender and science*. New Haven, CT: Yale University Press, p. 69.

13 Coburn, E. (2016), 'Economics as ideology: challenging expert political power'. Transnational Institute. Retrieved from: https://www.tni.org/en/publication/economics-as-ideology-challenging-expert-political-power

14 Dolar, V. (2021), 'The gender gap in economics is huge – it's even worse than tech'. *The Conversation*. https://theconversation.com/the-gender-gap-in-economics-is-huge-its-even-worse-than-tech-156275

15 Wen Jian (2020), 'A graphical view of gender imbalance in economics and why it matters'. https://www.linkedin.com/pulse/graphical-view-gender-imbalance-economics-why-matters-wen-jian/

16 Casselman, B. and Tankersley, J. (10 January 2019), 'Female Economists Push Their Field Toward a #MeToo Reckoning'. *New York Times*.

17 Akerlof, G.A. (2020), 'Sins of Omission and the Practice of Economics'. *Journal of Economic Literature*, 58(2): 405–18.

18 Midgley, M. (1985), *Evolution as a religion: Strange hopes and stranger fears*. London: Methuen, p. 98. This is a shortened version of her table.

19 Roszak, T. (1999), *The Gendered Atom: Reflections on the Sexual Psychology of Science*. Berkeley, CA: Conari, p. 39.

20 Quoted in Roszak, T. (1999), *The Gendered Atom: Reflections on the Sexual Psychology of Science*. Berkeley, CA: Conari, p. 88.

21 Nelson, J.A. 'The masculine mindset of economic analysis'. *The Chronicle of Higher Education* 42 (1996): B3.

22 Ferber, M.A. and Nelson, J.A. (eds) (1993), *Beyond Economic Man: Feminist theory and economics*. Chicago: University of Chicago Press, pp. 75–6. See also: McCloskey, D. (2000), 'Crossing Economics'. *International Journal of Transgenderism* 4(3).

23 Zohar, D. (1990), *The Quantum Self*. London: Flamingo, pp. 133–4.

24 Barad, K. (2007), *Meeting the Universe Halfway: Quantum Physics and the Entanglement of Matter and Meaning*. Durham, NC: Duke University Press.

25 Watson, J.B. (1913), 'Psychology as the Behaviorist Views it'. *Psychological Review* 20: 158–77, p. 177.

26 Midgley, M. (1985), *Evolution as a religion: Strange hopes and stranger fears*. London: Methuen.

27 Wendt, A. (2015), *Quantum Mind and Social Science: Unifying Physical and Social Ontology*. Cambridge: Cambridge University Press, p. 19.

28 Marçal, K. (2021), *Mother of Invention: How Good Ideas Get Ignored in an Economy Built for Men*. Toronto: Doubleday Canada.

29 Ghosh, J. (24 November 2020), 'Discrimination and bias in economics, and emerging responses'. *Real-World Economics Review* blog. https://rwer.wordpress.com/2020/11/24/discrimination-and-bias-in-economics-and-emerging-responses/

Chapter 3: To be, and not to be

1 Levin, N. (ed.) (2018), *Ancient Philosophy Reader*. N.G.E. Far Press.

2 Greenberger, D.M. and Zeilinger, A. (1995), *Fundamental problems in quantum theory: A conference held in honor of professor John A. Wheeler*. New York, NY: The New York Academy of Sciences, 1995.

3 Heisenberg, W. (1959), *Physics and Philosophy*. London: George Allen.

4 Aaronson, S. (2013), *Quantum Computing Since Democritus*. Cambridge: Cambridge University Press.

5 Other properties such as linearity can also be deduced. Aaronson, S. (2013), *Quantum Computing Since Democritus*. Cambridge: Cambridge University Press.

6 Trimmer, J.D. (1980), 'The Present Situation in Quantum Mechanics: A Translation of Schrödinger's "Cat Paradox" Paper'. *Proceedings of the American Philosophical Society* 124(5): 323–38.

7 Meyer, D.A. (1999), 'Quantum strategies'. *Physical Review Letters* 82: 1052–1055.

8 IBM (n.d.), 'Quantum Computing for Financial Services'. https://www. ibm.com/quantum-computing/technology/quantum-in-finance/

Chapter 4: The vanish trick

1 Wendt, A. (2006), 'Social Theory as Cartesian Science: An Auto-Critique from a Quantum Perspective'. In *Constructivism and International Relations: Alexander Wendt and his Critics*, by Stefano Guzzini and Anna Leander. London: Routledge, pp. 181–219.

2 'Q and A: Alexander Wendt on "Quantum Mind and Social Science"'. https://kb.osu.edu/bitstream/handle/1811/88121/Mershon_News_2015-11-16.pdf

3 For an assortment of such comments, see Orrell, D. (2021), *Quantum Economics and Finance: An Applied Mathematics Introduction* (2nd edn). New York: Panda Ohana.

4 TEDxColumbus (9 September 2019), 'An Interview With Speaker Alexander Wendt. https://www.tedxcolumbus.com/2019/09/09/an-interview-with-speaker-alexander-wendt/

5 Wendt, A. and Duvall, R. (2008), 'Sovereignty and the UFO'. *Political Theory* 36(4): 607–633.

6 Illing, S. (2020), 'It's time to take UFOs seriously. Seriously'. Vox. Retrieved from: https://www.vox.com/policy-and-politics/2020/5/8/21244090/pentagon-ufo-report-navy-alexander-wendt

7 See: Intelligence Authorization Act For Fiscal Year 2021. https://www.intelligence.senate.gov/publications/intelligence-authorization-act-fiscal-year-2021

8 Cillizza, C. (19 May 2021), 'Barack Obama just said something *very* interesting about UFOs'. CNN. https://www.cnn.com/2021/05/19/politics/barack-obama-ufos/index.html

9 Barnes, J.E. and Cooper, H. (3 June 2021), 'U.S. Finds No Evidence of Alien Technology in Flying Objects, but Can't Rule It Out, Either'. *New York Times*.

10 https://www.alexanderwendt.org/

11 Huxley, A. (1929), 'Wordsworth in the tropics'. In *Do what you will: Essays*. London: Chatto & Windus.

12 Wittgenstein, L. (1980), *Culture and value*. Edited by G.H. von Wright and H. Nyman. Chicago: University of Chicago Press.

13 Weiner, C. (20 April 1969), *Interview with Sir James Chadwick*. Cambridge.

14 Werner, R.A. (2016), 'A lost century in economics: Three theories of banking and the conclusive evidence'. *International Review of Financial Analysis*, 46: 361–79.

15 Häring, N. (2013), 'The veil of deception over money'. *Real-World Economics Review* 63, 2–18.

16 Lietaer, B.A. (2009), 'The New Paradigm of Money: Monetary blind spots and structural solutions'. Covering the Crisis Conference, Brussels, 9–10 November 2009.

17 See masterclass.com/classes/paul-krugman-teaches-economics-and-society/chapters/what-is-economics

18 Hudson, M. (2018), 'How Bronze Age Rulers Simply Canceled Debts'. *Evonomics*. https://evonomics.com/how-bronze-age-rulers-simply-canceled-debts/

19 Strange, S. (1970), 'International Relations and International Economics: A Case of Mutual Neglect'. *International Affairs* 46(2).

20 Strange, S. (1989), 'I Never Meant to Be an Academic'. Joseph Kruzel and James N. Rosenau (editors), *Journeys Through World Politics: Autobiographical Reflections of Thirty-four Academic Travellers*. Lexington: Lexington Books, pp. 429–36.

21 Orrell, D. (2020), 'The value of value: A quantum approach to economics, security and international relations'. *Security Dialogue* 51(5): 482–498. The paper also appears as a chapter in: Der Derian, J., Wendt, A. (2022), *Quantum International Relations: A Human Science for World Politics*. New York: Oxford University Press.

22 Nitzan, J. and Bichler, S. (2009), *Capital as Power. A Study of Order and Creorder*. New York: Routledge.

23 Carroll, S. (2016), *The Big Picture: On the Origins of Life, Meaning, and the Universe Itself*. New York: Dutton, p. 160.

24 In Kumar, M. (2008), *Quantum: Einstein, Bohr and the Great Debate About the Nature of Reality*. London: Icon Books, p. 125.

25 Letter from Einstein to D. Lipkin, 5 July 1952, Einstein Archives. In: Fine, A. (1996), *The Shaky Game*. Chicago: University of Chicago Press, p. 1.

26 Hossenfelder, S. (2018), *Lost in Math: How Beauty Leads Physics Astray*. New York: Basic Books, p. 124.

27 Acacio de Barros, J. and Oas, G. (2015), 'Quantum Cognition, Neural Oscillators, and Negative Probabilities'. In: Haven, E. and Khrennikov, A. (eds), *The Palgrave Handbook of Quantum Models in Social Science*. London: Palgrave Macmillan, pp. 195–228.

28 Everett, H. (1957), 'Relative state formulation of quantum mechanics'. *Rev. Mod. Phys.* 29: 454–462.

29 'Quantum computing 101'. Institute for Quantum Computing, University of Waterloo. Retrieved from: https://uwaterloo.ca/institute-for-quantum-computing/quantum-computing-101 (accessed 1 May 2021).

30 Sutherland, R. (2018), *Alchemy: The Dark Art and Curious Science of Creating Magic in Brands, Business, and Life*. New York: William Morrow, p. xi.

31 Žižek, S. (2002), *Did Somebody Say Totalitarianism?: Five Interventions in the (mis)use of a Notion*. New York: Verso, p. 216.

32 Kevles, D.J. (1995), 'Good-bye to the SSC: On the life and death of the Superconducting Super Collider'. *Engineering and science* 58(2): 16.

33 As the Republican Senator Dave Durenberger put it, 'if this project would lead to an enhancement of our national security, then I would be willing to continue funding the project. But … we face no such threat.' Quoted in Kevles, 1995.

34 Available at https://paulromer.net/trouble-with-macroeconomics-update/WP-Trouble.pdf.

35 Wilmott, P., Orrell, D. (2017), *The Money Formula: Dodgy Finance, Pseudo Science, and How Mathematicians Took Over the Markets*. Chichester: Wiley.

36 The physicist Lee Smolin wrote that 'The dark-matter hypothesis is preferred mostly because the only other possibility – that we are wrong about Newton's laws, and by extension general relativity – is too scary to contemplate.' Still, it seems easier than believing that 96 per cent of the universe has escaped detection. Smolin, L. (2006), *The Trouble with Physics: The Rise of String Theory, the Fall of a Science, and What Comes Next*. New York: Houghton Mifflin, p. 15. For a perspective from a physicist, see: McGaugh, S. (2021), 'Despondency'. Available from: https://tritonstation.com/2021/06/08/despondency/. Physicist Mike McCulloch says his opposition to dark matter has seen him 'banned from speaking at several campuses': https://twitter.com/memcculloch/status/1436286221580390406

37 *Physica A* editors include H. Eugene Stanley, one of the founders of the interdisciplinary field known as econophysics.

38 Fullbrook, E. (August 2002), 'A Brief History of the Post-Autistic Economics Movement'. Paecon.net. http://www.autisme-economie.org/article155.html

39 Keen, S. (2019), 'Economics: What to Do About an Unreformable Discipline?' *Islamic Economics* 32(2): 109–117.

40 Sahm, C. (29 July 2020), 'Economics is a disgrace'. http://macromom blog.com/2020/07/29/economics-is-a-disgrace/ See also: Parramore, L. (9 September 2020), 'What Happens When a Noted Female Economist Fights Toxic Culture in the Field?'. https://www.ineteconomics.org/ perspectives/blog/what-happens-when-a-noted-female-economist-fights-toxic-culture-in-the-field

41 Hidalgo, C.A. (24 February 2021), https://twitter.com/cesifoti/status/ 1364699994012459009

42 Manson, A., McCallum, P., and Haiven, L. (2015), *Report of the Ad Hoc Investigatory Committee Into the Department of Economics at the University of Manitoba*. Manitoba: Canadian Association of University Teachers.

43 Cohen, M. (2018), 'Post-crash economics: have we learnt nothing?' *Nature* 561, 151.

44 White, W. (11 February 2014), 'Central Banking ... Not a Science'. Retrieved from YouTube: https://www.youtube.com/watch?v= tCx-lKdRrPs

45 I even attended one; see: Orrell, D. (6 August 2018), 'A tale of two workshops'. *World Finance*.

46 Dutt, D. (23 October 2020), 'It's time to unlock the gates of the economics profession'. openDemocracy https://www.opendemocracy.net/ en/oureconomy/its-time-unlock-gates-economics-profession/

47 For a discussion, see: Wilmott, P., Orrell, D. (2017), *The Money Formula: Dodgy Finance, Pseudo Science, and How Mathematicians Took Over the Markets*. Chichester: Wiley.

48 Arlidge, J. (8 November 2009), 'I'm doing "God's work". Meet Mr Goldman Sachs'. *Sunday Times*.

49 Durden, T. (1 January 2021), 'Here Are All The Banks That Paid Janet Yellen $7.3 Million In Speaking Fees In The Past 2 Years'. Zero Hedge. https://www.zerohedge.com/markets/here-are-all-banks-paid-janet-yellen-73-million-speaking-fees-past-2-years

50 Mirowski, P. (1989), *More Heat than Light: Economics as Social Physics, Physics as Nature's Economics*. Cambridge: Cambridge University Press, pp. 391–92.

51 https://kzclip.com/video/dGDbpg1nG8Y/allen-savory-what-is-science. html

52 Fullbrook, E. (2012), 'To observe or not to observe: Complementary pluralism in physics and economics'. *Real-World Economics Review* 62: 20–28.

53 For a discussion of pluralism in quantum international relations, see: Murphy, M.P.A. (2021), *Quantum Social Theory for Critical International Relations Theorists: Quantizing Critique.* Cham: Palgrave Macmillan.

54 I am reliably informed that some of the material from my book *Quantum Economics and Finance* is on the menu at Moscow's State University of Management, for example.

55 See https://u.osu.edu/quantumbootcamp/

56 Anders Indset refers to Alexander Wendt as a 'quantum social scientist' in his 2020 book *The Quantum Economy – Saving the Mensch with Humanistic Capitalism.* For 'quantum economist' see: Sheng, A. (27 May 2019), 'Condivergence: The duality of life'. *The Edge Malaysia.*

57 Žižek, S. (2012), *Less Than Nothing: Hegel and the Shadow of Dialectical Materialism.* New York: Verso, p. 918.

58 Holton, G. (1970), 'The roots of complementarity'. *Daedalus* 99, 1015–55.

Chapter 5: Atomic money

1 From *Rewiring the Corporate Brain*, copyright © 1997 by Danah Zohar, Koehler Publishers, Inc., San Francisco, CA. All rights reserved. www.bkconnection.com

2 Farrell, T.F. (1945), 'Trinity test, July 16, 1945. Eyewitness Brigadier General Thomas F. Farrell'. *NuclearFiles.org.* http://www.nuclear files.org/menu/key-issues/nuclear-weapons/history/pre-cold-war/ manhattan-project/trinity/eyewitness-thomas-farrell_1945-07-16.htm (accessed 31 December 2011).

3 Laurence, W. (26 September 1945), 'Drama of the atomic bomb found climax in July 16 test'. *New York Times.*

4 In Davis, N.P. (1968), *Lawrence and Oppenheimer.* New York: Simon & Schuster, p. 309.

5 Quoted in Sime, R.L. (1996), *Lise Meitner: A life in physics.* Berkeley, CA: University of California Press, p. 244.

6 Rhodes, R. (1986), *The Making of the Atomic Bomb.* New York: Simon & Schuster, p. 292.

7 Einstein, A. (1960), Letter to President Franklin D. Roosevelt, 2 Aug 1939, delivered 11 Oct 1939. In Nathan, O. and Norden, H. (eds), *Einstein on Peace.* New York: Simon & Schuster, pp. 294–295.

8 Folger, T. (2001), 'Quantum Shmantum'. *Discover* 22(9).

9 Ragan, C.T. and Lipsey, R.G. (2011), *Economics* (13th edn). Toronto: Pearson Education Canada, p. 121.

10 Graeber, D. (2011), *Debt: The First 5000 Years*. Brooklyn, NY: Melville House.

11 Crawford, M.H. (1970), 'Money and exchange in the Roman world'. *Journal of Roman Studies*, 60, 40–48.

12 Schumpeter, J. (1954), *History of Economic Analysis*. London: Allen & Unwin, p. 53.

13 Samuelson, P.A. and Nordhaus, W.D. (2001), *Economics*. 17th edn. Boston, MA: McGraw-Hill, p. 511.

14 Hirsch, T. (2013), *The Future of Money, TEDx Edmonton*. https://www.youtube.com/watch?v=K0n3BGId9nU

15 Orrell, D. and Chlupatý, R. (2016), *The Evolution of Money*. New York: Columbia University Press.

16 https://www.parliament.uk/about/living-heritage/building/palace/architecture/palacestructure/great-fire/

17 Edgeworth, F.Y. (1881), *Mathematical psychics: An essay on the application of mathematics to the moral sciences*. London: C.K. Paul.

18 Verlinde, E. (2011), 'On the Origin of Gravity and the Laws of Newton'. *Journal of High Energy Physics* 2011(4): 29.

19 Freund, P.G.O. (2010), 'Emergent Gauge Fields'. arXiv:1008.4147.

Chapter 6: Not A Cross But A Wave

1 Alexander Carlyle, quoted in: Ozler, S. (2012), 'Adam Smith and Dependency'. *Psychoanalytic Review* 99(3): 333–358.

2 Hamilton, Sir William (1858), *The Collected Works of Dugald Stewart, Esq. F.R.SS*. London: Thomas Constable and Company.

3 Smith, A. (1776), *An Inquiry into the Nature and Causes of the Wealth of Nations*. London: W. Strahan & T. Cadell.

4 Sedláček, T. (2011), *Economics of Good and Evil: The Quest for Economic Meaning from Gilgamesh to Wall Street*. New York: Oxford University Press.

5 Mankiw, N.G. (2018), *Principles of Economics* (8th edn). Boston, MA: Cengage Learning.

6 Von Mises, L. (1949), *Human Action. A Treatise on Economics*. Yale University.

7 Dubner, S.J. (7 September 2016), 'Why Uber Is an Economist's Dream'. Retrieved from: Freakonomics.com: http://freakonomics.com/podcast/uber-economists-dream/

8 Bichler, S. and Nitzan, J. (2021), 'The 1-2-3 Toolbox of Mainstream Economics: Promising Everything, Delivering Nothing'. http://bnarchives. yorku.ca/678/4/20210300_bn_the_1_2_3_toolbox_wpcasp_web.htm

9 Sleeman, A.G. (2017), 'What Economics Majors and Economists Should Know About the Supply and Demand Model; Part 5: Is the Supply and Demand Model Empirically Useful?'

10 Krugman, P. (28 August 2012), 'Neo Fights (Slightly Wonkish and Vague)'. *New York Times*. https://krugman.blogs.nytimes.com/2012/08/28/neo-fights-slightly-wonkish-and-vague/

11 Keynes, J.M. (1936), *The General Theory of Employment, Interest and Money*. New York: Harcourt, Brace.

12 For a video introduction, see: Wilcox, R., 'Conjoint Analysis: Propensity Modeling'. Coursera video. https://www.coursera.org/lecture/uva-darden-bcg-pricing-strategy-customer-value/conjoint-analysis-propensity-modeling-JZjcJ

13 Kondratenko, A.V. (2015), *Probabilistic Economic Theory*. Novosibirsk: Nauka.

14 Orrell, D. and Bolouri, H. (2004), 'Control of internal and external noise in genetic regulatory networks'. *Journal of Theoretical Biology* 230(3): 301–12; Ramsey, S.A., Smith, J.J., Orrell, D., Marelli, M., Petersen, T.W., de Atauri, P., Bolouri, H. and Aitchison, J.D. (2006), 'Dual feedback loops in the GAL regulon suppress cellular heterogeneity in yeast'. *Nature Genetics* 38(9): 1082.

15 Orrell, D. (2021), *Quantum Economics and Finance: An Applied Mathematics Introduction* (2nd edn). New York: Panda Ohana.

16 Aaronson, S. (2013), *Quantum Computing Since Democritus*. Cambridge: Cambridge University Press.

17 As in the so-called vacuum energy of quantum field theory.

18 Orrell, D. (2020), 'A quantum model of supply and demand'. *Physica A* 539: 122928.

19 Source: lobsterdata.com.

20 The period of the swing is seen to be proportional to the square root of length divided by Newton's gravitational constant.

21 The spacing between the two curves equals their standard deviation divided by the square root of 2. See: Orrell, D. (2021), 'A quantum oscillator model of stock markets'. Available at SSRN: https://ssrn.com/abstract=3941518

22 Orrell, D. (2021), *Quantum Economics and Finance: An Applied Mathematics Introduction* (2nd edn). New York: Panda Ohana.

23 Einstein, A. (1905), 'Über einen die Erzeugung und Verwandlung des Lichtes betreffenden heuristischen Gesichtspunkt' (On a Heuristic Viewpoint Concerning the Production and Transformation of Light). *Annalen Der Physik* 17(6): 132–148.

24 Ahn, K., Choi, M.Y., Dai, B., Sohn, S. and Yang, B. (2017), 'Modeling stock return distributions with a quantum harmonic oscillator'. *EPL* 120(3): 38003. A full analysis, though, requires taking order book effects into account, see Sarkassian, J. (2020), *Quantum Markets: Physical Theory of Market Microstructure*. Honolulu, HI: Advanced Scientific Publishing.

25 Sarkissian, J. (2020), 'Quantum coupled-wave theory of price formation in financial markets: Price measurement, dynamics and ergodicity'. *Physica A: Statistical Mechanics and its Applications*, 554, 124300.

26 Byrum, J. (2021), 'Quantum Computing In Finance – Where We Stand And Where We Could Go'. *Science 2.0.* https://www.science20 .com/joseph_byrum/quantum_computing_in_finance_where_we_ stand_and_where_we_could_go-254398

27 Ali, A. (12 November 2020), 'The Soaring Value of Intangible Assets in the S&P 500'. *Visual Capitalist.* https://www.visualcapitalist.com/ the-soaring-value-of-intangible-assets-in-the-sp-500/

28 Radford, P. (2021), 'What do Durer and Soros have in common?' *Real-World Economics Review* blog. https://rwer.wordpress.com/2021/02/13/ what-do-durer-and-soros-have-in-common/

29 Cochrane, D.T. (2015), 'What's Love Got to Do with It? Diamonds and the Accumulation of De Beers, 1935–55'. Unpublished PhD dissertation. Program in Social and Political Thought. York University.

30 For a non-quantum version of this argument, see: Galbraith, J.K. (7 December 2020), 'Reconsideration of Fiscal Policy: A Comment'. Institute for New Economic Thinking. https://www.ineteconomics.org/ perspectives/blog/reconsideration-of-fiscal-policy-a-comment

31 Quoted in Salam, A. (1990), *Unification of Fundamental Forces*. Cambridge: Cambridge University Press, pp. 98–101.

32 Durden, T. (18 November 2020), '"Surreal Debt Tsunami": IIF Shocked To Forecast Global Debt Hitting $360 Trillion In Ten Years'. Zero Hedge.

Chapter 7: The utility switch

1 McGilchrist, I. (2009), *The Master and his Emissary*. London: Yale University Press, p. 233.

2 McGilchrist, I. (2009), *The Master and his Emissary*. London: Yale University Press, p. 209.

3 McGilchrist, I. (2009), *The Master and his Emissary*. London: Yale University Press, p. 503.

4 Evans, J. (2003), 'Dual-processing accounts of reasoning, judgment, and social cognition'. *Trends in Cognitive Sciences* 7(10): 454–459.

5 McGilchrist, I. (2009), *The Master and his Emissary*. London: Yale University Press, p. 120.

6 Bentham, J. (1907), *An Introduction to the Principles of Morals and Legislation*. Oxford: Clarendon Press.

7 Jevons, W.S. (1905), *The Principles of Economics: A Fragment of a Treatise on the Industrial Mechanism of Society; and Other Papers*. London: Macmillan & Co.

8 Edgeworth, F.Y. (1881), *Mathematical psychics: An essay on the application of mathematics to the moral sciences*. London: C.K. Paul, pp. 59, 15. https://archive.org/details/mathematicalpsy01goog/page/n69

9 Jevons, W.S. (1886), *Letters & Journal of W. Stanley Jevons*. London: Macmillan.

10 Jevons, W.S. (1909), 'The Solar Period and the Price of Corn' (1875), in H.S. Foxwell (ed.), *Investigations in Currency and Finance*. London: Macmillan, 194–205.

11 Robinson, J. (1962), *Economic Philosophy*. Harmondsworth, Middlesex: Penguin Books.

12 Lissner, W. (10 March 1946), 'Mathematical Theory of Poker Is Applied to Business Problems'. *New York Times*.

13 'The best books on Game Theory, recommended by Ariel Rubinstein'. https://fivebooks.com/best-books/ariel-rubinstein-on-game-theory/

14 Veblen, T. (1898), 'Why is economics not an evolutionary science?' *Quarterly Journal of Economics* 12(4): 373–397.

15 Robbins, L. (1932), *An Essay on the Nature and Significance of Economic Science*. London: Macmillan.

16 Arrow, K.J. and Debreu, G. (1954), 'Existence of a Competitive Equilibrium for a Competitive Economy'. *Econometrica* 22: 65–90.

17 Mason, J.W. (29 November 2018), 'Pulling Rabbits Out of Hats'. Jacobin. https://jacobinmag.com/2018/11/pulling-rabbits-out-of-hats

18 Edmonds, B. (25 February 2021), https://twitter.com/BruceEdmonds/status/1364892387101859840

19 Manson, A., McCallum, P., and Haiven, L. (2015), *Report of the Ad Hoc Investigatory Committee Into the Department of Economics at the University of Manitoba*. Manitoba: Canadian Association of University Teachers.

20 Krugman, P. (2018), 'Good enough for government work? Macroeconomics since the crisis'. *Oxford Review of Economic Policy* 34(1–2): 156–168.

21 Kahneman, D. and Tversky, A. (1976), 'Prospect Theory: An Analysis of Decision under Risk'. Office of Naval Research. https://apps.dtic.mil/dtic/tr/fulltext/u2/a045771.pdf

22 Thaler, R.H. (2016), *Misbehaving: The Making of Behavioral Economics*. New York: W.W. Norton & Company.

23 Cochrane, J. (22 May 2015), '*Homo economicus* or *homo paleas?*' Retrieved from The Grumpy Economist: http://johnhcochrane.blogspot.ca/2015/05/homo-economicus-or-homo-paleas.html

24 Moore, J.D. (10 October 2015), 'A Bowl of Cashews with Professor Richard H. Thaler'. *Chicago Booth Magazine*.

25 Fox, M. (10 February 2021), 'Elon Musk says in a tweet that he bought dogecoin for his son, sparking a 16% surge in the "meme" token'. *Reuters*.

26 Angner, E. (2019), 'We're all behavioral economists now'. *Journal of Economic Methodology* 26:3, 195–207.

27 Wilson, D.S. (2013), 'A good social Darwinism'. Aeon. https://aeon.co/essays/social-darwinism-is-back-but-this-time-it-s-a-good-thing

28 Orrell, D. (2021), *Behavioural Economics: Psychology, Neuroscience, and the Human Side of Economics*. London: Icon Books.

29 Vines, D. and Wills, S. (5 January 2018), 'The rebuilding macroeconomic theory project: an analytical assessment'. *Oxford Review of Economic Policy* 34(1–2): 1–42.

30 Hubbard, W.H.J. (2017), 'Quantum Economics, Newtonian Economics, and Law'. *Michigan State Law Review* 425 (2018).

31 Cochrane, J. (22 May 2015), '*Homo economicus* or *homo paleas?*' Retrieved from The Grumpy Economist: http://johnhcochrane.blogspot.ca/2015/05/homo-economicus-or-homo-paleas.html

32 Krugman, P. (2018), 'Good enough for government work? Macroeconomics since the crisis'. *Oxford Review of Economic Policy* 34(1–2): 156–168.

33 Morrissey, M. (3 March 2016), 'The State of American Retirement'. Economic Policy Institute. https://www.epi.org/publication/retirement-in-america/

Chapter 8: Of mind and money

1 Young, T. (1807), *On the nature of light and colours*. Vol. 1 in *A Course of Lectures on Natural Philosophy and the Mechanical Arts*. London: Joseph Johnson.

2 Taylor, G.I. (1909), 'Interference fringes with feeble light'. *Proc. Cam. Phil. Soc.* 15: 114.

3 Feynman, R. (1964), *The Feynman Lectures on Physics.* Vol. 1. Reading, MA: Addison Wesley.

4 Lin, Y. (1937), *The Importance of Living.* New York: John Day.

5 Tversky, A. and Shafir, E. (1992), 'The disjunction effect in choice under uncertainty'. *Psychological Science* 3: 305–309.

6 Yukalov, V.I. and Sornette, D. (2018), 'Quantitative Predictions in Quantum Decision Theory'. *IEEE Transactions on Systems, Man & Cybernetics: Systems* 48(3): 366–381.

7 Wang, Z., Solloway, T., Shiffrin, R.S., and Busemeyer, J.R. (2014), 'Context effects produced by question orders reveal quantum nature of human judgments'. *Proceedings of the National Academy of Sciences* 111(26): 9431–6.

8 Stigler, G.J. and Becker, G.S. (1977), 'De Gustibus Non Est Disputandum'. *American Economic Review* 67(2): 76–90.

9 This version based on Kahneman, D. (2011), *Thinking, Fast and Slow.* New York: Farrar, Straus and Giroux, p. 355.

10 Grether, D.M. and Plott, C.R. (1979), 'Economic Theory of Choice and the Preference Reversal Phenomenon'. *The American Economic Review* 69(4): 623–638.

11 Kahneman (2011), p. 356.

12 Tversky, A., Slovic, P. and Kahneman, D. (1990), 'The Causes of Preference Reversal'. *The American Economic Review* 80(1): 204–217.

13 Tversky, A. and Thaler, R.H. (1990), 'Anomalies: preference reversals'. *Journal of Economic Perspectives* 4: 201–11.

14 Kahneman, D., Knetsch, J.L. and Thaler, R. (1990), 'Experimental Tests of the Endowment Effect and the Coase Theorem'. *Journal of Political Economy* 98: 1325–1348.

15 Guiso, L., Sapienza, P., and Zingales, L. (2013), 'The determinants of attitudes toward strategic default on mortgages'. *The Journal of Finance* 68(4): 1473–1515.

16 White, B.T. (2010), 'Underwater and Not Walking Away: Shame, Fear, and the Social Management of the Housing Crisis'. *Wake Forest Law Review* 45: 971–1023.

17 Bhutta, N., Dokko, J. and Shan, H. (2010), 'The Depth of Negative Equity and Mortgage Default Decisions'. *Federal Reserve Board*, FEDS Working Paper No. 2010-35: 21.

18 White (2010).

19 Moerman, D.E. (2002), *Meaning, Medicine, and the 'Placebo Effect'*. Cambridge: Cambridge University Press.

20 Goodhart, C., Romanidis, N., Tsomocos, D., and Shubik, M. (2016), 'Macro-Modelling, Default and Money'. LSE, FMG Discussion Paper DP755.

Chapter 9: Entangled choices

1 O'Brien, K. (2021), You Matter More Than You Think: Quantum Social Change for a Thriving World. Oslo: cCHANGE Press.

2 Original letter from Isaac Newton to Richard Bentley. http://www.newtonproject.ox.ac.uk/view/texts/normalized/THEM00258

3 Janiak, A. (2008), *Newton as Philosopher*. Cambridge: Cambridge University Press.

4 Harrison, P. (1995), 'Newtonian Science, Miracles, and the Laws of Nature'. *Journal of the History of Ideas* 56(4): 531–553.

5 Flood, A. (2 June 2020), 'Isaac Newton proposed curing plague with toad vomit, unseen papers show'. *Guardian*.

6 Keynes, J.M. (1946), 'Newton, the Man'. https://mathshistory.st-andrews.ac.uk/Extras/Keynes_Newton/

7 Einstein, A., edited by Dukas, H. and Hoffmann, B. (1979), *Albert Einstein, The Human Side: Glimpses from His Archives*. Princeton, NJ: Princeton University Press.

8 Tversky, A. and Shafir, E. (1992), 'The disjunction effect in choice under uncertainty'. *Psychological Science* 3: 305–309. See also: Wendt, A. (2015), *Quantum Mind and Social Science: Unifying Physical and Social Ontology*. Cambridge: Cambridge University Press, p. 172.

9 Der Derian, J. (1998), 'Review: The Scriptures of Security'. *Mershon International Studies Review* 42(1): 117–122.

10 See https://robertnorthcott.weebly.com/papers.html. See also Northcott, R. and Alexandrova, A. (2015), 'Prisoner's Dilemma doesn't explain much'. In: Martin Peterson (ed.) *The Prisoner's Dilemma* (Cambridge 2015), pp. 64–84.

11 https://mostlyeconomics.wordpress.com/2012/06/08/why-study-game-theory-when-it-has-limited-practical-applications-in-real-life/. See also: https://larspsyll.wordpress.com/2017/08/28/on-the-limits-of-game-theory/. Bernard Guerrien (2018), 'On the current state of game theory'. *Real-World Economics Review* 83: 35–44.

12 Camerer, C. (2003), *Behavioral Game Theory*. Princeton, NJ: Princeton University Press.

13 As one physicist warned me, 'Maybe one or two "crackpot" people claim otherwise, but they are not to be trusted.' Quoted in: Orrell, D. (2021), *Quantum Economics and Finance: An Applied Mathematics Introduction* (2nd edn). New York: Panda Ohana.

14 Wendt, A. (2015), *Quantum Mind and Social Science: Unifying Physical and Social Ontology*. Cambridge: Cambridge University Press, p. 3.

15 Lambert, N., Chen, Y.-N., Cheng, Y.-C., Li, C.-M., Chen, G.-Y., and Nori, F. (2013), 'Quantum biology'. *Nature Physics*, 9(1): 10–18.

16 Adams, B. and Petruccione, F. (January 2021), 'The light of the mind'. *Physics World*.

17 Laughlin, R.B. (2005), *A different universe: Reinventing physics from the bottom down*. New York: Basic Books.

18 This is the interpretation used in quantum decision theory. See: Yukalov, V.I. and Sornette, D. (2018), 'Quantitative Predictions in Quantum Decision Theory'. *IEEE Transactions on Systems, Man & Cybernetics: Systems* 48(3): 366–381.

19 Orrell, D. (2021), *Quantum Economics and Finance: An Applied Mathematics Introduction* (2nd edn). New York: Panda Ohana; Orrell, D. and Houshmand, M. (2021), 'Quantum propensity in economics', *Frontiers in Artificial Intelligence* (in press).

20 Khan, F.S., Solmeyer, N., Balu, R. and Humble, T.S. (2018), 'Quantum games: a review of the history, current state, and interpretation'. *Quantum Information Processing* 17(11): 309.

21 Güth, W., Schmittberger, R. and Schwarze, B. (1982), 'An experimental analysis of ultimatum bargaining'. *Journal of Economic Behavior and Organization* 3(4): 367.

22 Hardin, G. (1968), 'The Tragedy of the Commons'. *Science*, 162(3859): 1243–8.

23 Charness, G., Karni, E. and Levin, D. (2010), 'On the conjunction fallacy in probability judgement: new experimental evidence regarding Linda'. *Games and Economic Behavior* 68: 551–556.

24 Guiso, L., Sapienza, P., and Zingales, L. (2013), 'The determinants of attitudes toward strategic default on mortgages'. *The Journal of Finance* 68(4): 1473–1515, p. 1514.

25 Midgley, M. 'Rings and Books', unpublished script, available at www. womeninparenthesis.co.uk/wp-content/uploads/2016/05/rings-and-books.pdf

26 Pope Francis (2020), *Let Us Dream: The Path to a Better Future*. New York: Simon & Schuster, 2020.

27 The right hemisphere 'sees each thing in its context'. McGilchrist, I. (2009), *The Master and his Emissary*. London: Yale University Press, p. 49.

28 McGilchrist, I. (2009), *The Master and his Emissary*. London: Yale University Press, p. 65.

29 Brain image source : https://en.wikipedia.org/wiki/Lateralization_of_brain_function#/media/File:Cerebral_lobes.png

Chapter 10: Brazen head

1 From *The Feynman Lectures on Physics, Vol. II* by Richard P. Feynman, copyright © 1964. Reprinted by permission of Basic Books, an imprint of Hachette Book Group, Inc.

2 Quoted in: Orrell, D. (2021), *Quantum Economics and Finance: An Applied Mathematics Introduction* (2nd edn). New York: Panda Ohana.

3 Keynes, J.M. (1936), *The General Theory of Employment, Interest and Money*. New York: Harcourt, Brace.

4 Wood, G. (2002), *Living Dolls: A magical history of the quest for mechanical life*. London: Faber and Faber.

5 Poe, E.A. (1836), 'Maelzel's Chess Player'.

6 Cochrane, J. (2011), 'How Did Paul Krugman Get it So Wrong?' *IEA Economic Affairs* (June): 36–40.

7 Solow, R.M. (1957), 'Technical Change and the Aggregate Production'. *The Review of Economics and Statistics* 39(3): 312–320.

8 Romer, P.M. (1990), 'Endogenous Technological Change'. *The Journal of Political Economy* 98(5): S71–S102.

9 Attanasio, O., Bandiera, O., Blundell, R., Machin, S., Griffith, R. and Rasul, I. (20 December 2017), 'Dismal ignorance of the "dismal science" – a response to Larry Elliot'. *Prospect*.

10 Stahel, A.W. (2020), 'Is economics a science?' *Real-World Economics Review* 94: 61–82.

11 Quoted in: Bernstein, P.L. (1998), *Against the Gods: The Remarkable Story of Risk*. Toronto: John Wiley, p. 203.

12 Storm, S. (8 March 2021), 'The Standard Economic Paradigm is Based on Bad Modeling'. Institute for New Economic Thinking. https://www.ineteconomics.org/perspectives/blog/why-dsge-models-are-not-the-future-of-macroeconomics

13 Keen, S. (13 November 2020), 'Introduction to The New Economics: A Manifesto'. https://www.patreon.com/posts/introduction-to-43848097

14 See, for example, https://www.vanityfair.com/news/2016/11/giving-thanks-hedge-fund-managers-are-still-super-rich-edition

15 Clarke, A.C. (August 1958), 'The Ultimate Machine'. *Harper's*.

16 Kelly, K. (1 July 1994), 'Cracking Wall Street'. *Wired*.

17 Mistry, H.B. and Orrell, D. (2020), 'Small Models for Big Data'. *Clinical Pharmacology & Therapeutics* 107: 710–711.

18 Keen, S. (2019), 'The Cost of Climate Change'. *Evonomics*. Retrieved from: https://evonomics.com/steve-keen-nordhaus-climate-change-economics/

19 Norgaard, R.B. (2021), 'Post-economics: Reconnecting reality and morality to escape the Econocene'. *Real-World Economics Review* 96: 49–66.

20 Mixon, S. (2009), 'Option markets and implied volatility: past versus present'. *Journal of Financial Economics* 94, 171–191. Moore, L., Juh, S. (2006), 'Derivative Pricing 60 Years before Black–Scholes: Evidence from the Johannesburg Stock Exchange'. *The Journal of Finance* LXI (6), 3069–3098.

21 MacKenzie, D., Millo, Y. (2003), 'Constructing a market, performing theory: The historical sociology of a financial derivatives exchange'. *American Journal of Sociology* 109, 107–145.

22 Soros, G. and Schmitz, G.P. (24 April 2014), 'The Future of Europe: An Interview with George Soros'. *New York Review of Books*. Retrieved from: https://www.nybooks.com/articles/2014/04/24/future-europe-interview-george-soros/

23 Roche, D. (2021), 'Quantum economics chapter 2: the truth to tell'. Independent Strategy.

24 Danchin, A. (2002), *The Delphic Boat: What Genomes Tell Us*. Cambridge, MA: Harvard University Press.

25 See https://www.physiomics.co.uk/services/virtual-tumour-technology/

26 For a discussion of quantum agent-based models, see: Orrell, D. (2021), *Quantum Economics and Finance: An Applied Mathematics Introduction* (2nd edn). New York: Panda Ohana.

27 Kondratyev, A. (2020), 'Non-Differentiable Learning of Quantum Circuit Born Machine with Genetic Algorithm'. Available at: https://ssrn.com/abstract=3569226

28 Penrose, R. (1989), *The Emperor's New Mind: Concerning Computers, Minds and The Laws of Physics*. Oxford: Oxford University Press.

29 Der Derian, J., Wendt, A. (2020), '"Quantizing international relations": The case for quantum approaches to international theory and security practice'. *Security Dialogue* 51(5): 399–413.

Chapter 11: A quantum walk down Wall Street

1 Jensen, M. (1978), 'Some Anomalous Evidence Regarding Market Efficiency'. *Journal of Financial Economics* 6: 95–102.

2 Fama, E.F. (1991), 'Efficient capital markets II'. *The Journal of Finance*, 46(5): 1575–1617. Cochrane, J.H. (2011), 'Presidential address: Discount rates'. *The Journal of Finance*, 66(4): 1047–1108.

3 Bessa, O. (8 November 2015), 'Nobel Prize Winner Eugene Fama on Bitcoin'. Retrieved from CoinTelegraph: http://cointelegraph.com/news/115593/nobel-prize-winner-eugene-fama-on-bitcoin

4 Einstein, A. (1905), 'Über einen die Erzeugung und Verwandlung des Lichtes betreffenden heuristischen Gesichtspunkt' (On a Heuristic Viewpoint Concerning the Production and Transformation of Light). *Annalen Der Physik* 17(6): 132–148.

5 Metropolis, N. and Ulam, S. (1949), 'The Monte Carlo method'. *Journal of the American Statistical Association* 44: 335–341.

6 Clark, M. (director) (1999), *The Midas Formula* (motion picture).

7 Mackenzie, D. (2006), *An Engine, Not a Camera: How Financial Models Shape Markets*. Cambridge, MA: MIT Press, p. 158.

8 Clark, M. (director) (1999), *The Midas Formula* (motion picture).

9 Patterson, S. (2009), *The Quants: How a New Breed of Math Whizzes Conquered Wall Street and Nearly Destroyed It*. New York: Crown, p. 194.

10 Brown, A. (2012), *Red-Blooded Risk: the secret history of Wall Street*. Hoboken, NJ: Wiley.

11 Kocherlakota, N. (22 September 2016), 'Professors Aren't Feeling the Economy's Pain'. Bloomberg.com.

12 Earle, J., Moran, C., and Ward-Perkins, Z. (2016), *The Econocracy: The Perils of Leaving Economics to the Experts*. Manchester: Manchester University Press.

13 Barnichon, R., Matthes, C., and Ziegenbein, A. (August 2018), 'The Financial Crisis at 10: Will We Ever Recover?'. *FRBSF Economic Letter*.

14 US Department of Justice (5 February 2013), *Acting Associate Attorney General Tony West Speaks at the Press Conference Announcing Lawsuit Against S&P, Washington, DC*.

15 Graeber, D. (2018), *Bullshit Jobs: A Theory*. New York: Simon & Schuster.

16 Triana, P. (2009), *Lecturing Birds on Flying: Can Mathematical Theories Destroy the Financial Markets?* New York: Wiley, p. 163.

17 Orrell, D. (2021), 'A quantum walk model of financial options'. *Wilmott* 2021(112): 62–69.

18 Fortson, D. (5 July 2020), 'How RBS made a quantum leap into the future'. *The Sunday Times*.

19 Danco, A. (2021), 'Why the Canadian Tech Scene Doesn't Work'. https://alexdanco.com/2021/01/11/why-the-canadian-tech-scene-doesnt-work/

20 Nogueiras, M., et al. (2021), 'Review of state-of-the-art for Pricing and Computation of VaR'. NEASQC. https://www.neasqc.eu/wp-content/uploads/2021/06/NEASQC_D5.1_Review-of-state-of-the-art-for-Pricing-and-Computation-of-VaR_R2.0_Final.pdf

21 See guest chapter by Ramy Aboushelbaya and Marko Mayr in: Orrell, D. (2021), *Quantum Economics and Finance: An Applied Mathematics Introduction* (2nd edn). New York: Panda Ohana.

22 Anonymous (2020), 'Wall Street's latest shiny new thing: quantum computing'. *Economist*.

23 Anonymous (26 September 2020), 'Commercialising quantum computers'. *Economist*.

24 Ibaraki, S. (29 January 2021), 'What You Need for Your Quantum Computing Pilots In 2021'. *Forbes*.

25 Bobier, J.-F., Binefa, J.-M., Langione, M., and Kumar, A. (2020), 'It's Time for Financial Institutions to Place Their Quantum Bets'. Boston Consulting Group. https://www.bcg.com/publications/2020/how-financial-institutions-can-utilize-quantum-computing

26 Ménard, A., Ostojic, I., Patel, M., and Volz, D. (6 February 2020), 'A Game Plan for Quantum Computing'. McKinsey & Company. https://www.mckinsey.com/business-functions/mckinsey-digital/our-insights/a-game-plan-for-quantum-computing

27 Dalio, R. (2021), *Principles for Dealing with the Changing World Order: Why Nations Succeed and Fail*. New York: Simon & Schuster.

Chapter 12: The money power

1 Tomkins, C. (1 January 1966), 'In the Outlaw Area'. *The New Yorker*.

2 Schacht, H. (1967), *The Magic of Money*. London: Oldbourne.

3 Häring, N. and Douglas, N. (2012), *Economists and the Powerful*. London: Anthem Press, p. x.

4 Murphy, M.P.A. (2021), *Quantum Social Theory for Critical International Relations Theorists: Quantizing Critique*. Cham: Palgrave Macmillan, p. 91.

5 Fix, B. (30 October 2020), 'Deconstructing Econospeak'. https://economicsfromthetopdown.com/2020/10/30/deconstructing-econospeak/

6 Bichler, S. and Nitzan, J. (2021), 'The 1-2-3 Toolbox of Mainstream Economics: Promising Everything, Delivering Nothing'. http://bnarchives.yorku.ca/678/4/20210300_bn_the_1_2_3_toolbox_wpcasp_web.htm

7 Even in conferences where the topic is rebuilding economics. https://twitter.com/natjdyer/status/1318923770866900992. This was a comment on the Third Annual Conference: Understanding Social Macroeconomics: Session 2: Evolutionary Economics. 21 October 2020.

8 See for example Bichler, S. and Nitzan, J. (2020), 'The Capital As Power Approach: An Invited-then-Rejected Interview'. Available from: http://bnarchives.yorku.ca/640/4/20200600_bn_the_casp_approach_invited_then_rejected_interview_web.htm

9 Perelman, M. (2015), 'How economics bolstered power by obscuring it'. In *State of Power: Annual Report 2015* (Amsterdam: The Transnational Institute), p. 97.

10 Robbins, L. (1932), *An Essay on the Nature and Significance of Economic Science*. London: Macmillan, p. 125.

11 Lucas, R.E. (1 May 2004), 'The Industrial Revolution: Past and Future – 2003 Annual Report Essay'. Federal Reserve Bank of Minneapolis.

12 National Public Radio (23 October 2015), 'Planet Money, Episode 659: How To Make $3 Trillion Disappear'.

13 Price, C.C., Edwards, K.A. (2020), 'Trends in Income From 1975 to 2018'. Santa Monica, CA: RAND Corporation. https://www.rand.org/pubs/working_papers/WRA516-1.html. See also: Hanauer, N., Rolf, D.M. (14 September 2020), 'The Top 1% of Americans Have Taken $50 Trillion From the Bottom 90%—And That's Made the U.S. Less Secure'. *Time*.

14 Rudd, J.B. (2021), 'Why Do We Think That Inflation Expectations Matter for Inflation? (And Should We?)'. Finance and Economics Discussion Series 2021-062. Washington: Board of Governors of the Federal Reserve System.

15 Hamilton, D. (2021), Fordham Distinguished Lecture in Economics.

16 Mankiw, N.G. (2018), *Principles of Economics* (8th edn). Boston, MA: Cengage Learning.

17 Sweezy, R.P.M. (1939), 'Demand Under Conditions of Oligopoly'. *Journal of Political Economy* 47(4): 568–573.

18 Nitzan, J. (2020), 'Neoclassical Political Economy: Skating on Thin Ice'. https://www.youtube.com/watch?v=LsUS3ynhAKY

19 Piketty, T. (2014), *Capital in the Twenty-First Century*. Cambridge, MA: Belknap Press.

20 'What Would A World Without Central Banks Look Like? | Dylan Grice'. https://www.youtube.com/watch?v=2QtmEKvucFg&ab_channel=Wealthion

21 Nietzsche, F. (2008), *Thus Spoke Zarathustra: A Book for Everyone and Nobody*. Oxford: Oxford University Press, p. 44.

22 Garrett, T. (2014), 'Long-run evolution of the global economy Part I: Physical basis'. *Earth's Future* 2: 127–151.

23 According to the 2018 Global Wealth Report from Credit Suisse Research Institute. https://www.credit-suisse.com/media/assets/corporate/docs/publications/research-institute/global-wealth-report-2018-en.pdf

24 Data from https://www.statista.com/statistics/263492/electricity-prices-in-selected-countries/

25 According to Npower, 'The average kettle holds 1.5 pints and uses about one unit of electricity to boil 12 pints of water (or 8 × 1.5 pint-full kettles) – so that's around 2.5p every time you boil a full kettle'. Since 1.5 pints is 0.71 litres, this works out to about 3.52p per litre. https://www.express.co.uk/life-style/life/877169/electric-energy-bill-electricity-kettle-running-cost

26 IIER (2011), 'Green Growth – an Oxymoron?'. IIER. http://www.iier.ch/content/green-growth-oxymoron

27 World Population Review. https://worldpopulationreview.com/country-rankings/median-income-by-country

28 Dearden, N. (14 October 2020), 'It's Official, The Global Economy Is a "Debtor's Prison"'. *New Internationalist*. https://newint.org/features/2020/10/14/official-global-economy-debtors-prison

29 Fix, B. (2020), 'Can the World Get Along Without Natural Resources?' Retrieved from: http://bnarchives.yorku.ca/644/2/20200700_fix_can_the_world_get_along_without_natural_resources_wpcasp.pdf

30 British Petroleum (2020), *BP Statistical Review of World Energy*. London: British Petroleum, p. 8. See also: Kolasi, E. (1 February 2021), 'The Ecological State'. *Monthly Review*.

31 Cook, E. (1971), 'The Flow of Energy in an Industrial Society'. *Scientific American* 225(3): 134–47. Malanim, P. (2011), 'Energy Consumption and Energy Crisis in the Roman World'. *Environmental History Conference* 4.

32 Soddy, F. (1922), *Cartesian Economics: The Bearing of Physical Science upon State Stewardship*. London: Hendersons.

33 Kraken Intelligence (September 2020), 'Kraken's The Great Debate: Bitcoin & Intrinsic Value'.

34 Gladstein, A. (2021), 'Can Governments Stop Bitcoin?'. *Quillette*. https://quillette.com/2021/02/21/can-governments-stop-bitcoin/. Other cryptocurrencies, including BitcoinSV, use less energy.

35 Trenberth, K.E., Smith, L. (2005), 'The Mass of the Atmosphere: A Constraint on Global Analyses'. *J. Climate* 18(6): 864–875.

36 Hagens, N.J. (2020), 'Economics for the future – Beyond the superorganism'. *Ecological Economics* 169: 106520.

37 Orrell, D. (2021), 'The Color of Money: Threshold Effects in Quantum Economics'. *Quantum Reports* 3(2): 325–332.

38 The motion of a particle can be expressed using the principle of least action, which asserts that the particle chooses a path which minimises the time-average kinetic energy, minus the time-average potential energy. For example, if you drive a car from point A to point B, your kinetic energy at any time is one half of the car's mass, multiplied by the speed squared. On a perfectly flat road, the potential energy would be the energy stored in the fuel. If fuel consumption varies, like kinetic energy, with the speed squared, then it is easily seen that the optimal path which minimises the action is a straight line at constant speed. Neoclassical economists emphasised monetary budgets in their models, which is like focusing only on energy expenditure, but action involves time as well, as captured by Planck's constant.

39 'The color of someone's money – definitions and synonyms'. Available online: https://www.macmillandictionary.com/dictionary/american/the-color-of-someone-s-money (accessed on 6 August 2020).

40 Orrell, D. (2021), 'The Color of Money: Threshold Effects in Quantum Economics'. *Quantum Reports* 3(2): 325–332.

41 Quoted in Le Goff, J. (2012), *Money and the Middle Ages*. Oxford: Polity, p. 128.

42 Francis of Assisi (1906), *The Writings of St Francis of Assisi*. Translated by Paschal Robinson. Philadelphia: Dolphin.

43 Schor, J.B. (2000), *The Overworked American: The Unexpected Decline of Leisure*. New York, Basic Books.

44 Harding, S. (2011), 'Stock market becomes short attention span theater of trading'. *Forbes*. https://www.forbes.com/sites/greatspeculations/2011/01/21/stock-market-becomes-short-attention-span-theater-of-trading/

45 According to the consultancy firm Tabb Group, HFT accounts for 'as much as 73 percent of US daily equity volume, up from 30 percent in 2005'. Bailey, T. (3 July 2015), 'Flash and burn: high frequency traders menace financial markets'. *World Finance*.

46 See Miller, L. (1 July 2012), 'The Money-Empathy Gap'. *New York*.

47 Quoted in Lewis, M. (12 November 2014), 'Extreme Wealth Is Bad for Everyone – Especially the Wealthy'. *New Republic*.

Chapter 13: Bomb squad

1 Fermi, L. (1954), 'Success'. In: Martin Gardner, ed. (1984) *The Sacred Beetle and Other Great Essays in Science*. Oxford: Oxford University Press.

2 Anonymous (23 November 1954), 'Enrico Fermi dead at 53; Architect of atomic bomb'. *The New York Times*.

3 Apollodorus (1921), *Apollodorus, The Library*, with an English Translation by Sir James George Frazer, F.B.A., F.R.S. in 2 Volumes. Cambridge, MA: Harvard University Press.

4 De Bruin, B., Herzog, L., O'Neill, M., and Sandberg, J. (2020), 'Philosophy of Money and Finance'. *The Stanford Encyclopedia of Philosophy* (Winter 2020 Edition), Edward N. Zalta (ed.). https://plato. stanford.edu/archives/win2020/entries/money-finance

5 Aristotle, *Politics*. http://classics.mit.edu/Aristotle/politics.1.one.html

6 Gold, K. (28 April 2021), 'In Vancouver and Toronto, as many as 1 in 5 homeowners own more than one property'. *The Globe and Mail*.

7 Bekkering, E., Deschamps-Laporte, J.-P. and Smaile, M. (27 September 2019), 'Residential property ownership: Real estate holdings by multiple-property owners'. https://www150.statcan.gc.ca/n1/pub/46-28-0001/ 2019001/article/00001-eng.htm

8 Davies, H. (18 October 2020), 'Revealed: Sheikh Khalifa's £5bn London property empire'. *Guardian*.

9 UK Green Building Council (2021), 'Climate change'. https://www.ukgbc. org/climate-change/

10 IEA (2019), *Fuel Economy in Major Car Markets*, IEA, Paris https:// www.iea.org/reports/fuel-economy-in-major-car-markets

11 Elhacham, E., Ben-Uri, L., Grozovski, J., et al. (2020), 'Global human-made mass exceeds all living biomass'. *Nature*.

12 Bair, S. (@SheilaBair2013) (23 August 2020). https://twitter.com/ SheilaBair2013/status/1297560979065184259

13 As Aaron White wrote, 'A new generation of people has blossomed from the ashes, intent not on reforming the system, but dismantling it'. White, A. (29 October 2020), 'This election can't contain the rage of young Americans'. openDemocracy. Available from: https://www. opendemocracy.net/en/oureconomy/this-election-cant-contain-the-rage-of-young-americans/

14 Anonymous (16 July 2009), 'Efficiency and beyond'. *Economist*.

15 https://twitter.com/TOAdamVaughan/status/1385077892900704258

16 Collum, D. (2020), '2020 Year in Review. Peak Prosperity'. https://www.peakprosperity.com/dave-collum-2020-year-in-review-part-1/

17 Indset, A. (2020), *The Q-Economy: Saving the Mensch with Humanistic Capitalism*. Berlin: Econ.

18 Vague, R. (2020), 'It's Time for a Debt "Jubilee"'. https://www.ineteconomics.org/perspectives/blog/its-time-for-a-debt-jubilee. Hudson, M. (2020), 'Jubilee Perspectives with Steve Keen'. https://michael-hudson.com/2020/12/jubillee-perspectives-with-steve-keen/

19 The Bank of England's chief economist Andy Haldane calls inflation 'the tiger whose tail central banks control'. Haldane, A. (26 February 2021), 'Inflation: A Tiger by the Tail?' Speech available at: https://www.bankofengland.co.uk/speech/2021/february/andy-haldane-recorded-mini-speech-on-inflation-outlook

20 There was a Canadian petition along these lines in 2021: https://petitions.ourcommons.ca/en/Petition/Details?Petition=e-3327

21 OECD (2020), *Beyond Growth: Towards a New Economic Approach*, in New Approaches to Economic Challenges series. Paris: OECD Publishing.

22 Rowlatt, J. (20 June 2020), 'Greta Thunberg: Climate change "as urgent" as coronavirus'. BBC. https://www.bbc.com/news/science-environment-53100800

23 Dearden, N. (14 October 2020), 'It's Official, The Global Economy Is a "Debtor's Prison"'. *New Internationalist*. https://newint.org/features/2020/10/14/official-global-economy-debtors-prison

24 Dittli, M. (16 November 2020), 'Central Banks Keep Shooting Themselves in the Foot'. https://themarket.ch/interview/william-white-central-banks-keep-shooting-themselves-in-the-foot-ld.3053

25 Kronick, J. and Laurin, A. (3 April 2021), 'Why taxing capital gains won't cool the housing market'. *The Globe and Mail*.

26 Bradbrook, G. (2019), 'Gail Bradbrook – A Personal Story of Psychedelics, Ceremony and My Journey in Extinction Rebellion'. https://www.youtube.com/watch?v=_92ZqEmeOFs&ab_channel=ExtinctionRebellion

27 Taylor, M. (5 April 2021), 'Extinction Rebellion to step up campaign against banking system'. *Guardian*.

28 Bradbrook, G. (2021), 'Better Broken Windows than Broken Promises'. https://www.youtube.com/watch?v=zRgDFtk18H0&t=6s&ab_channel=ExtinctionRebellion

29 Watling, C. (18 March 2021), 'Time for a great reset of the financial system'. *Financial Times*.

30 Lietaer, B. (2000), 'The Mystery of Money, Beyond Greed and Scarcity'. http://docs.banks-need-boundaries.net/en/Lietaer_Mystery_of_Money.pdf

31 James, B. (2021), 'Lose change'. https://www.themintmagazine.com/lose-change See also: Transparency Task Force (2021), 'The battle for the control of the digital pound; and why it really matters'. https://www.youtube.com/watch?v=vJHhmdmq5Xg&ab_channel=TTFTV

32 O'Brien, K. (2016), 'Climate change and social transformations: Is it time for a quantum leap?'. *WIREs Climate Change* 7(5): 618–626.

33 Orland, K. (18 March 2021), 'Canadian banks tie CEO pay to ESG, setting them apart from the crowd'. Bloomberg News. Rainforest Action Network (2021), 'Banking on climate chaos'. https://www.ran.org/bankingonclimatechaos2021/#score-card-panel

34 Holden, E. and Atkin, E. (7 April 2021), 'Banks pledge to fight climate crisis – but their boards have deep links with fossil fuels'. *Guardian.* Cooke, P., Sherrington, R. and Hopeon, M. (2021), 'Revealed: The Climate-Conflicted Directors Leading the World's Top Banks'. https://www.desmogblog.com/2021/04/06/revealed-climate-conflicted-directors-leading-the-worlds-top-banks/

35 Einstein, A. (November 1947), 'Atomic War or Peace'. *Atlantic.*

36 Austin, D. (14 September 2020), 'Milton Friedman's hazardous feedback loop'. *Responsible Investor.* https://www.responsible-investor.com/articles/duncan-austin-milton-friedman-s-destabilising-feedback-loop

37 Asad Zaman (2021), 'What they don't teach in economics textbooks'. WEA Pedagogy Blog. https://weapedagogy.wordpress.com/2021/07/28/what-they-dont-teach-in-economics-textbooks/

38 Rosati, A. (5 December 2017), 'Desperate Venezuelans Turn to Video Games to Survive'. Bloomberg.

39 Bostrom, N. (2003), 'Are You Living in a Computer Simulation?' *Philosophical Quarterly* 53(211): 243–255.

40 Hurt, A. (5 April 2021), 'What Magic Can Teach Us About the Human Mind'. *Discover.*

41 Macknik, S. and Martinez-Conde, S. (2011), *Sleights of Mind: What the Neuroscience of Magic Reveals about Our Everyday Deceptions.* London: Profile.

42 Zyga, L. (3 March 2010), 'Free will is an illusion, biologist says'. *Phys.org.* https://phys.org/news/2010-03-free-illusion-biologist.html

43 https://www.theguardian.com/books/2020/oct/24/how-do-we-become-a-serious-people-again-dave-eggers-annie-proulx-and-more-on-the-2020-election

INDEX

References to figures are indicated in *italics*. References to endnotes consist of the page number followed by the letter 'n' followed by the number of the note with the page number from the main text in brackets, e.g. 319n32 (39).

ABOUT THE AUTHOR

DAVID ORRELL is an applied mathematician and writer of books on science and economics. His books include *Economyths: 11 Ways Economics Gets It Wrong* and *Quantum Economics: The New Science of Money*, plus *Behavioural Economics* in the Hot Science series. He lives in Toronto.